Decisions and Images
The Supreme Court and the Press

Richard Davis
Brigham Young University

PRENTICE HALL, *Englewood Cliffs, New Jersey 07632*

Library of Congress Cataloging-in-Publication Data
Davis, Richard

 Decisions and images : the Supreme Court and the press / Richard
Davis.
 p. cm.
 Includes bibliographical references and index.
 ISBN 0-13-034505-9 (paper)
 1. United States. Supreme Court. 2. Journalism, Legal--United
States. I. Title.
KF8742.D38 1994
347.73"26--dc20
[347.30735]   93-11073
           CIP

Editor in Chief: Charlyce Jones Owen
Editorial/production supervision,
 interior design and electronic page makeup: Elizabeth Best
Copy Editor: Stephen C. Hopkins
Cover Design: Richard Dombrowski
Production Coordinator: Mary Ann Gloriande
Editorial Assistant: Nicole Signoretti

 ©1994, by Prentice-Hall, Inc.
A Paramount Communications Company
Englewood Cliffs, New Jersey 07632

Printed in the United States of America
10 9 8 7 6 5 4 3 2 1

ISBN 0-13-034505-9

Prentice-Hall International (UK) Limited, *London*
Prentice-Hall of Australia Pty. Limited, *Sydney*
Prentice-Hall Canada Inc., *Toronto*
Prentice-Hall Hispanoamericana, S.A., *Mexico*
Prentice-Hall of India Private Limited, *New Delhi*
Prentice-Hall of Japan, Inc., *Tokyo*
Simon & Schuster Asia Pte. Ltd., *Singapore*
Editora Prentice-Hall do Brasil, Ltda., *Rio de Janeiro*

To Robert and Jeanette Davis

Contents

Foreword, ix

Preface, xi

Chapter One—The Court and the Public, 1

Institutional Objectives, 1

Imagemaking, 3

The Image of Unanimity, 4
The Image of Independence, 6
The Image of Distance, 6
The Image of Immunity, 7

Communicating for Deference, 8

Constraints on Manipulation, 8
The Salience of Communication, 10
The Nature of the Message, 12

The Press as Linking Mechanism, 16

The Press as Gauge, 17
The Press as Deference Reinforcer, 19
A Poor Connection, 20

Press versus Court Imperatives,   21

Managing the Message,   23

Chapter Two—Institutionalizing Press Relations,   29

Tarnishing the Image,   31
Accommodating the Press,   35
Surveying Press Coverage,   38
Shaping the Image,   40
Summary,   44

Chapter Three—Speaking for the Court,   45

The Ritual,   45

The Mechanical Channel,   47

The No Information Office,   48
Documentary Source,   48
Reporting Justices' Activities,   50

The Screen,   50

The Protector of the Image,   53

The Outsider as Public Information Officer,   54

Press Policy Advisor,   56
Dispenser of Process Guidance,   58
Friend of the Press Corps,   60

Conclusion,   61

Chapter Four—On the Court Beat,   63

The Press Corps,   63

The Elite,   64
The Specialist,   65

The Pressroom,   69

The Routine,   70

Choosing What to Cover,   70
What Is Newsworthy,   72
Preparing Stories,   73
Covering Oral Arguments,   75

Writing the Decision Story,   77

> The Time Factor,   81
> Reading and Culling,   82
> Following the Formula,   83
> Remembering the Audience,   83
> Interpreting the Opinion,   84
> Using Sources,   85
> Information Sharing,   86
> The Role of the Elite,   92
> The Influence of the Wires,   92
> Working with Editors and Producers,   94

Conclusion,   99

Chapter Five—The Invisible Dance,   102

Reporters' Objectives,   103

Justices' Objectives,   104

Choosing the Tactics,   110

The Invisible Dance,   113

> Channeling Attention to Opinions,   114
> Selective Public Interaction with the Press,   118
> Offering Backgrounders,   119
> Closing Off Other Access Points,   122
> Emphasizing Minor Points,   125

Leading the Dance,   126

Conclusion,   130

Chapter Six—The Supreme Court as News,   132

> Following the Rhythm,   133
> Minimizing the Justices as Personalities,   134

The Interaction in One Story,   135

> Covering an Oral Argument,   137
> The Stories,   140
> Use of Sources,   142
> Technicality versus Human Interest,   142
> Homogeneity or Variety,   143

Conclusion,   144

Chapter Seven—Shroud or Soundbyte: The Court in the Media Age,   145

Changing Attitudes Toward the Court,   148

Accommodations-Present and Future,   148

Project Hermes, 149
Cameras in the Courtroom,   149
Other Reforms,   155

Abandoning the Robes,   156

The Permanency of Change,   157

The Nomination Process,   157
The Legitimacy of Mass Role,   158

The Court in the Media Age,   159

A Note on Methodology,   160

Observation,   161
Interviewing,   161
Survey,   161
Historical Research,   161
Content Analysis,   161

Appendix A,   163

Appendix B,   167

Appendix C,   175

Index,   185

Foreword

News reporters are often thought to be a cynical lot. Indeed, some believe it is an inevitable consequence of journalistic experience. (We do see many things go wrong, and make a living telling about it.) I generally shared this view prior to joining ABC News in 1977. I had already been in journalism for more than 15 years and the words of one of my earliest editors continued to ring in my ears: "The first thing you must always assume is that anyone in public life is lying."

At the Supreme Court, the first thing I learned was that the Justices who occupy this special bench—public officials too—are principally interested in honesty and fairly deciding cases. I had a privileged vantage point in the press gallery just twenty feet from where the justices sit.

Throughout U.S. history the Court has been almost as sharply criticized as any other institution of government. The major criticism of the last twenty years is that the Court tends to act as a super-legislature, seeking to make law rather than interpret it.

Irrespective of where one stands on this particular complaint, most of the journalists assigned to the Supreme Court on a regular basis believe that each Justice works diligently to be true to his or her own convictions. No deliberative body in government is less subject to political or other "undue" influence. No government agency has ever explained its decisions with the high level of care and scholarship as the Supreme Court. The Court "works," and works well, quite possibly is the best kept secret in American law and journalism.

Visitors to the Supreme Court still ask "Where does the jury sit?" "How come there's no witness stand?" Many of our citizens cannot appreciate the work of the Supreme Court because they have no idea what it is the Supreme Court does. Court rulings are routinely criticized by those who disagree with the result, without regard to whether the decision is consistent with the constitution the Justices are sworn to uphold.

To be sure, the popular media are due substantial amount of the blame for this popular ignorance, But as Professor Davis' exhaustive and entertaining study illustrates, a much larger degree of blame rests with the Court itself.

The proliferation of cable television and the availability of C-SPAN in most homes technically enables the country at large to have essentially the same close seats that we in the news media have long enjoyed. Alas, the Justices continue to prohibit televised coverage of their proceedings fearing 1) that hearings will be edited to give an inaccurate portrayal of what transpires in Court and 2) that televised coverage may undermine the "mystique" of the High Court. Lost is the idea that Americans could get an invaluable, unfiltered view of how, and how well, the Court works (a view one might think they were "entitled" to receive.) Gavel to gavel coverage would be available routinely on cable television from time to time even on commercial networks for major cases.

The issue of cameras in the courts is mistakenly viewed as an issue of "press access." Yet it is so much greater than that. Televised coverage of the Court's proceedings advances the public interest, the interests of the legal profession, and certainly of the Court itself. In time, this fact will surely be accepted by the Court. In the meantime, the American people will have to content themselves with the Court as seen through the eyes of the news media. I believe, and sense that Professor Davis shares the view, that the reporters covering the Court do a good job. What you get, however, is just not the same as being there.

Professor Davis has meticulously researched this examination of the interrelationship between the Court and the media. There is simply no other work like it. He explains with great care and precision life in the Supreme Court pressroom and the difficulty all journalists experience in presenting Supreme Court opinions to the public in a concise, comprehensible form. The work of the Supreme Court press corps, much like the work of the Supreme Court itself, is often misunderstood.

Decisions and Images goes some distance to correct the misperceptions. This book should occupy a special place in the libraries of those who care about the workings of the nation's highest tribunal, including the nine caretakers themselves.

Tim O'Brien
ABC News
Washington, D.C.

Preface

In American politics today the primary linking mechanism between political institutions and the public is the press. The Supreme Court usually has been excluded from a discussion of political institutions and their relationship with the press.

The relationship between the press and the Court has been the subject of a small number of empirical studies in the past. These studies primarily have focused on the amount and nature of news coverage of the Court.[1] All have concluded that news coverage of the Court is superficial and spotty. Moreover, inaccuracy of news stories announcing landmark decisions has contributed to critiques of press content concerning the Court.[2] Misinterpretation has been attributed to press deadlines and frequent errors in the encoding role of the press and the function of translation of legal language into lay language.[3]

---

[1] David Ericson, "Newspaper Coverage of the Supreme Court," *Journalism Quarterly* 54 (Autumn 1977): 605–607; Michael Solimine, "Newsmagazine Coverage of the Supreme Court," *Journalism Quarterly* 57 (Winter 1980): 661–663; Ethan Katsh, "The Supreme Court Beat: How Television Covers the U.S. Supreme Court," *Judicature* 67 (June–July 1983): 6–12; Richard Davis, "Lifting the Shroud: News Media Portrayal of the U.S. Supreme Court," *Communications and the Law* 9 (October 1987): 43–58; Jerome O' Callaghan and James O. Dukes, "Media Coverage of the Supreme Court's Caseload," *Journalism Quarterly* 69 (Spring 1992): 195–203; and Dorothy A. Bowles and Rebekah V. Bromley, "Newsmagazine Coverage of the Supreme Court During the Reagan Administration," *Journalism Quarterly* 69 (Winter 1992): 948–959.

[2] Chester A. Newland, "Press Coverage of the United States Supreme Court." *Western Political Quarterly* 19 (March 1964): 15–36; David L. Grey, *The Supreme Court and the News Media* (Evanston, Ill.: Northwestern University Press, 1968); Everette Dennis, "Another Look at Press Coverage of the Supreme Court," *Villanova Law Review* 20 (1974): 765–799.

[3] See William R. Dahms, "Press Coverage of the Supreme Court: A Troubling Question," *Intellect*, February 1978, pp. 299–301.

Less is known about the work of the journalists who cover the Court. Past studies of the press corps during the Warren years described a small press corps (five full-time reporters) untrained in legal issues, constrained from news analysis by the pressures of deadline and brevity, and overruled by editors who lacked the reporters' understanding of the Court. Moreover, they lacked the interaction with policymakers, even infrequently, common to their colleagues at the White House, Congress, or the executive agencies.[4] A more recent study found an enlarged and more professional press corps.[5] Missing from the extant literature is the process shaping the news product. That process includes several groups of players: reporters, editors, interest groups, and the justices.

One explanation for the paucity of research is the assumption the Supreme Court has no constituency similar to those of the members of Congress or the president. The Court's constituency, it is argued, is the legal profession. The logical extension of that argument is that the justices would be just as happy if the press would not cover the Court, since the Court's constituency, the legal profession, would still receive communication from the Court through its own formal channels.

The primary thesis of this book is that the Court, like other political institutions, pursues specific objectives in its relationship with the press. Contrary to the conventional wisdom, the Court is not sui generis as a political institution. It seeks manipulation of the press relationship with it to promote institutional power generally and its influence on specific policy issues.

The Court's power is preserved by public opinion and therefore the Court's primary objective vis-à-vis the public is to maintain public deference and secure widespread compliance with policy decisions. The press' role is to assist in the cultivation of a public image of the Court designed to enhance that deference and subsequent compliance. Also like other political institutions, however, the Court, as a body of individuals at times working at cross-purposes, does not always pursue unified objectives. The Supreme Court has been characterized as "nine little law firms," and the individual justice's approach to the press is distinctive and at times in contrast with the institution's objectives.

A second thesis proposes that each individual justice possesses objectives in press relations separate from those of the institution and that those are pursued through a variety of interactions with the press.

This book addresses the relationship between the Court and the press by describing the Court's strategies for press coverage and the tactics employed to achieve those strategies. The work of the players—the Public Information Office, the journalistic corps on the Court beat, and the justices themselves—is described. Chapter One outlines the Court's relationship with one of its constituencies—the public—and examines the institution's objectives in its public relations. The role of

---

[4]Chester A. Newland, "Press Coverage of the United States Supreme Court." *Western Political Quarterly* 19 (March 1964): 15–36; David L. Grey, *The Supreme Court and the News Media* (Evanston, Ill.:Northwestern University Press, 1968).

[5]Mitchell J. Tropin, "What, Exactly, Is the Court Saying," *The Barrister* (Winter 1984): 14.

the press as intermediary—feedback source for public opinion and Court messenger to the larger political environment—is described.

The second chapter narrates the origins and evolution of this relationship arguing that the Court has maintained a relationship with the press since its inception, but that coexistence has been affected by factors such as the Court's progression as an institution of power and the increased autonomy of the press.

Chapter Three describes the Court's officially acknowledged public relations effort. The role of the official public relations arm of the Court—the Public Information Office—in promoting the Court's agenda in press relations is explained.

In Chapter Four, the focus shifts to the reporters who are assigned to the Court beat. The chapter is a group study of the journalists who cover the Court. Their norms and routines, their relationships with sources and editors and each other, and the current issues of professionalism with which they wrestle are discussed.

The relationship between reporters and justices and the effects on news coverage are explored in Chapter Five. The first section of the chapter explores the objectives—both institutional and individual—of the justices in their interaction with reporters. The second section describes the dance between justices and reporters as the justices seek achievement of those objectives in the formation of news about the Court and as journalists respond to those efforts.

The concluding chapter addresses the changes in the press, interest groups, and public attitudes toward the Court and the Court's response to those changes. The Court's ability to adjust to changing perceptions of the Court, technological advances, and calls for more openness while preserving the institution's traditional aloofness is examined.

This book has been in the making for nearly four years. The idea was germinated even earlier. Many people have helped to bring this book into print.

Toni House, the Court's public information officer, allowed me to act as a "fly on the wall" in the pressroom and the Public Information Office as well as interview her on several occasions. She also received most of the chapters and commented extensively on them. Her comments resulted in the avoidance of numerous errors of fact. In fairness to her it must be stated that she disagrees with the premise of this book. Hence, her helpfulness and candor have been all the more appreciated.

The reporters who gave me insights into their work through opportunities to follow them or interview them have made this book possible. These include, in alphabetical order, Frank Aukofer, Rita Braver, Richard Carelli, Dawn Weyrich Ceol, Tony Collings, Jerome Cramer, Lyle Denniston, Glen Elsasser, Linda Greenhouse, Tony Mauro, Tim O'Brien, Henry Reske, Miranda Spivack, Stuart Taylor, Jim Vicini, and Stephen Wermiel. Also, other journalists on the Court beat participated through completion of a survey instrument. Others who allowed me to interview them included Stephen Bokat, Rene Craven, Bruce Fein, and Barrett McGurn. Unless footnoted, all direct quotations in the text are from interviews with the author. The staffs of the Library of Congress Manuscript Division and the

Manuscript Division at the Sterling Library at Yale University were helpful in locating documents.

Several people read drafts of chapters. Journalists who offered their time and provided useful commentary included Richard Carelli, Lyle Denniston, Tony Mauro, and Tim O'Brien, who also generously provided a foreword. Saul Brenner, University of North Carolina–Charlotte, Tim Cook, Williams College, and Timothy Prinz, University of Virginia, served as reviewers. Tim Cook gave important suggestions in periodic discussions throughout the project. However, none of these reviewers are responsible for any errors remaining. I alone take responsibility for the content.

I also wish to thank the editorial staff at Prentice Hall including Charlyce Jones Owens, Nicole Signoretti, and Elizabeth Best.

The College of Family, Home, and Social Sciences provided financial support for this research. Colleagues in the Political Science Department at BYU have given me a warm supportive environment for research and scholarly exchange.

Finally, I thank my wife, Molina, and our children for supporting me in completing this work and for tolerating my absences from home while conducting research.

Chapter One

The Court
and the Public

In his Federalist essay number 78, Alexander Hamilton argued that the Constitution would position the Court as "the least dangerous" because it would be "least in a capacity to annoy or injure" the rights provided in the Constitution. Hamilton based his evaluation on the Court's lack of power of the sword (execution of the law) or of command over the purse (policymaking through the budget). Therefore, Hamilton concluded, "It may truly be said to have neither Force nor Will, but merely judgment."

As such the Court is an institution that must cultivate its own power base. Thus the Court's power emanates not from the rule of law; rather "the only power the Court can assert is the power of public opinion."[1]

INSTITUTIONAL OBJECTIVES

To all appearances the Supreme Court building is the home of a great legal institution. Above the entrance the inscription reads: Equal Justice Under the Law. Within the Court chamber, visitors see a large ornately decorated room dominated by the raised bench where the justices are in a state of repose during the public sessions. Busts of past lawgivers—Mohammed, Charlemagne, Napoleon, John Marshall—line the wall.

But, the Court is more than a legal institution; it is also a political one. It was given birth by a political document. Its members are recruited through a political

[1]Philip B. Kurland, "'The Cult of the Robe' and the Jaworski Case," *Washington Post*, June 23, 1974, C2.

process and many have been drawn directly from the legislative or executive branches. And, through its judicial review function, the Court exerts a policy-making power in the political system.

Another yardstick of its political nature is the Court's involvement in issues once confined to the arena of political institutions.[2] The issue of whether the Court should be an activist body signals the shifting mores concerning the Court's policy-making role. Although recent appointees to the Court have advocated restraint and several cases suggest that direction, the Court will not suddenly become nonpolitical.

Even as a political institution, the Court has been considered an institution apart—a qualitatively different species from the Congress and the president. In some respects, the Court is distinctive. The Court's policy-making process is fundamentally nonrepresentative. The justices do not solicit public input nor do they usually recognize its role in their deliberative processes.

But in another sense, the similarities are more stark. Like other political institutions, public opinion of the Court is highly dependent on the events of the day. In his study of public opinion toward the Court, Gregory Caldiera found that "the dynamics of aggregate support for the Court bear a remarkable resemblance to those for Congress and the presidency" in that public evaluations of the Court respond to political events such as the salience of the Court, a major political crisis (e.g., Watergate), and presidential popularity.[3]

Larry Berkson has identified two constituencies of the Court: a highly attentive constituency that includes the legal profession as well as law enforcement officers and the legislative branch, but also a less attentive constituency within the general public.[4] The linkage between that second constituency has been largely unexplored, perhaps because of its presumed unimportance.

Yet that second constituency is, at heart, the base of power for the United States Supreme Court. The legal trappings mask the reality of an institution that thrives on public support and withers when bereft of it.

Only through the broadly consensual support of people, who are not part of the legal community and do not follow Court opinions avidly, does the Court work its will in the American political system. By paying deference to the Supreme Court, this constituency allows the Court to preserve its power. It complies with the Court's decisions. And it supports the Court in fending off challenges from other political institutions. Ironically, the Court only on rare occasions publicly acknowledges the role of this constituency in maintaining its power.

Not unlike other political institutions, the Supreme Court possesses inherent objectives in its relations with the general public. These objectives are to maintain

[2]For a discussion of the judiciary's increased role in social policy, see Donald L. Horowitz, *The Courts and Social Policy* (Washington, D.C.: Brookings, 1977).

[3]Gregory A. Caldiera, "Neither the Purse Nor the Sword: Dynamics of Public Confidence in the U.S. Supreme Court," *American Political Science Review* 80 (December 1986): 1224.

[4]Larry Berkson, *The Supreme Court and Its Publics* (Lexington, Mass.: Lexington Books, 1978).

public confidence and secure public compliance with Court decisions. According to Alexander Bickel, the "task of the Court is to seek and to foster assent, and compliance through assent."[5] These objectives are interlinked; failure of one produces the failure of the other.

The Court is hardly unaware of the base of its power. In the majority opinion in *Planned Parenthood v. Casey*, the Court stated:

> [T]he Court cannot buy support for its decisions by spending money and, except to a minor degree, it cannot independently coerce obedience to its decrees. The Court's power lies, rather, in its legitimacy, a product of substance and perception that shows itself in the people's acceptance of the Judiciary as fit to determine what the Nation's law means and to declare what it demands.[6]

The Court's legitimacy, it acknowledges, is a product of "substance and perception." The perceptions of the Court are the product of images of the Court in the minds of the nation's citizens.

IMAGEMAKING

The Court's objectives of deference and compliance will not be achieved regardless of the Court's actions. The Court must act to encourage positive affections toward the Court on the part of the public. Affections toward the Court are based on public perceptions about the Court. These, in turn, are produced, at least partly, through communications with the public by the Court.

The Court must pursue a policy of image-making directed at public perceptions in order to secure its objectives of public deference and compliance. If the Court fails to do so, others will shape the Court's image for it. That effort may or may not aid the Court's objectives.

For example, when the case of *United States v. Nixon* reached the Court in the summer of 1974, the Court did not appear to be expediting the decision-making process in order to resolve a national crisis. Senator Mike Mansfield, majority leader, issued a press release implicitly chastising the Court for its lack of haste in addressing the case. Warren Burger responded in a letter to Mansfield revealing the justices' (or at least Burger's) worry over the effect of Mansfield's press release on public perception of the Court: "Members of the Court were somewhat concerned by your letter and the accompanying press release, given the fact that your views are widely read and respected throughout the country as they are with us."[7] In a manner no different from other political bodies, the Court must be its primary advocate with the general public.

---

[5]Alexander Bickel, *The Least Dangerous Branch*, 2d ed. (New Haven, Conn.: Yale University Press, 1986), p. 251.

[6]*Planned Parenthood of Southeastern Pennsylvania v. Casey*, 120 L.Ed.2d 674 at 708.

[7]Letter from Warren Burger to Senator Mike Mansfield, June 7, 1974, William O. Douglas Papers, Box 1660, Library of Congress, Washington, D.C.

The Court must address at least two facets of the public's perceptions of the Court. These are its legitimacy and expertise.

Deference is linked to a social consensus regarding the Court's legitimacy and expertise.[8] The Court's power stems from the legitimacy granted it by the public. That legitimacy is communicated to other governmental actors—the presidency, the Congress, the states—and influences their approach to the Court.

It is also a product of the perception of expertise. The justices acquire the mantle of legal wisdom that separates them from others. It is partially derived from the Court's continuity—the link to the past. That continuity suggests a bank of wisdom among the justices. Alexander Bickel argued that the apparent sagacity of those with long tenure on the Court enhances the sense of mystique. "Senior members of the Court are witnesses to the reality and validity of our present...because in their persons they assure us of its link to the past...."[9]

A salient aspect of this expertise is the Court's unique linkage to the Constitution. This linkage has been cultivated by the Court itself. Through this association the Court has been seen to "possess a special competence" in understanding the document.[10]

The perception of expertise on the Court by others not on the Court is just that: *perception*. The vagaries of the confirmation process insure that the Court does not become a meritocracy. Failure of the Court to attain such a status is due not only to the appointment process, but also to the vagueness of the term "judicial merit."[11] But it is the Court's exposed status to the political process that impels the justices to shore up the image of special wisdom on constitutional matters.

Shorn of legitimacy and expertise, the Court becomes vulnerable to attack and domination from others. At crucial times in the Court's history, such as during the 1930s debate over the constitutionality of the New Deal, its vulnerability has been exploited by presidents and Congress.

The Court is not helpless in response to the potentiality of such attacks. The Court can and does pursue a policy of image-making to maintain the legitimacy and the perception of expertise. It attempts to preserve legitimacy and expertise through cultivating images of unanimity and independence.

The Image of Unanimity

When the Court has sought to exercise leadership in policy, it jeopardizes its legitimacy. If the Court is split over highly visible national issues, the aura of expertise is endangered and threatens the Court's continued role. In 1954 and

[8]See Richard M. Johnson, *The Dynamics of Compliance*, (Evanston, Ill.: Northwestern University Press, 1967).

[9]Bickel, op. cit.

[10]John Brigham, *The Cult of the Court* (Philadelphia: Temple University Press, 1987), p. 7.

[11]David O'Brien, *Storm Center: The Supreme Court in American Politics* (New York: W. W. Norton, 1986), pp. 44–45.

again in 1974, two crucial cases—*Brown v. Board of Education* and *United States v. Nixon*—challenged the Court's ability to exercise its leadership role.

In the *Brown* case, the justices realized their essay to assert a leadership role would be successful only if they stood united and if the image of expertise was not tarnished by divisions within the Court.[12] Their leadership role was directly challenged by the president in the case of *United States v. Nixon* when he implied that he would comply only in the case of a unanimous decision of the Court. The justices were cognizant of the diminution of authority the Court would experience if the president successfully resisted their decision. In a period when the number of concurring and dissenting opinions was rising, the eight participating justices forged a compromise in order to produce a single unanimous opinion.[13] Potter Stewart, who had intended to file a separate opinion, changed his mind admitting that "it seems essential to me that there be full intramural communication in the interest of a cooperative effort."[14]

The sit-in cases in the early 1960s presented another need for a consensual approach to blunt negative reaction from anti-desegregation groups. Earl Warren wrote to another justice that "I share the views of the Conference that it is highly desirable that we do present as united a front as possible, leaving some facets of the problem to be dealt with next term."[15]

Even in cases not involving controversial social policy or separation of powers, the justices prefer a broad consensus and they are often willing to compromise to achieve it, both in the writing of opinions and in the acceptance of others' writing. This willingness to achieve consensus is suggested in William O. Douglas's remark to a colleague that "I had trouble enough with Gideon, although Hugo [Black] steered close enough to the line to make it possible for me to go along."[16]

The justices' success at achieving the image of unanimity has been greatly diminished since the days Chief Justice John Marshall persuaded the Court to stop issuing seriatim opinions and limit dissent to internal debate. However, in more recent times the Court has been most successful in achieving unanimity when its institutional power is in jeopardy, such as the case of *United States v. Nixon*. Conversely, the justices' inability to resolve potent social policy issues in areas such as abortion, capital punishment, and affirmative action may be linked to their failure in achieving the image of unanimity that would undermine the legitimacy of proponents of opposing policy positions.

[12]For evidence of the justices' concern for unanimity, see Justice Douglas's conference notes, April 16, 1954, William O. Douglas Papers, Box 1149, Library of Congress, Washington, D.C.

[13]For statistics on trends in opinion writing during this period, see David O'Brien, *Storm Center: The Supreme Court in American Politics* (New York: W. W. Norton, 1986), pp. 262–275.

[14]Memorandum to Justices Douglas, Brennan, Blackmun, and Powell, July 22, 1974, William O. Douglas Papers, Box 1659, Library of Congress, Washington, D.C.

[15]Memo to William Brennan, May 18, 1963, Earl Warren Papers, Box 604, Library of Congress, Washington, D.C.

[16]Letter to William Brennan, June 3, 1964, William O. Douglas Papers, Box 1299, Library of Congress, Washington, D.C.

The Image of Independence

The Court strives to assert its independence as a policy-making body. As the last of the three branches to acquire an acknowledged role in public policy, and the one most susceptible to attack by the others, the Court is cognizant of the need to establish its independence. But to some extent the reality of independence stems from its perception. Other political institutions are less likely to challenge an institution that is generally perceived as independent and as one that ought to maintain its independence. The perception of independence is acquired through the image of distance and that of immunity.

The Image of Distance

A key ingredient to perceptions of independence is the image of distance—distance from other political institutions, public opinion, the press, interest groups, and the political process generally. The image of distance promotes the notion that the Court is separated from the ongoing political process and the forces that determine the outcomes of the process.

This image of distance is reinforced not only by a separate building, but also by a monastic lifestyle that even leads some of the justices to avoid Washington social encounters. "Members of the Court are really quite remote from Washington," according to Lyle Denniston, *Baltimore Sun* reporter. "Some of that is by choice. To some degree the justices cultivate this notion of being removed."

Historically, such aloofness has been less than constant. Justices have been involved in partisan politics, political appointments, congressional lobbying, and presidential decision making. Several, such as John McLean, Salmon P. Chase, Charles Evans Hughes, and William O. Douglas have made overt bids for the presidency or vice-presidency. While others, such as Earl Warren and Harold Burton were continually mentioned as a candidate for one of these positions.[17] Others such as William Howard Taft, Felix Frankfurter, and Fred Vinson have acted as advisors to presidents and closet lobbyists in Congress on matters related to judicial appointments and policy.[18] Still others, such as Abe Fortas, have advised on matters well beyond the scope of judiciary.[19]

But gradually throughout this century such activity has been discouraged. The most recent flagrant violation of this norm, the presidential advisor role of Abe Fortas, led to criticism of the Court and contributed to Fortas's failure to win confirmation as chief justice in 1968.

---

[17]Mary Frances Berry, *Stability, Security, and Continuity: Mr. Justice Burton and Decision-Making in the Supreme Court 1945–1958* (Westport, Conn.: Greenwood Press 1978), p. 89.

[18]William J. Cibes, Jr. "Extra-Judicial Activities of Justices of the United States Supreme Court." Unpublished Ph.D. dissertation, Princeton University, 1975; and Bruce A. Murphy, *The Brandeis/Frankfurter Connection* (New York: Oxford, 1982).

[19]Bruce A. Murphy, *Fortas* (New York: William Morrow, 1988), and Laura Kalman, *Abe Fortas* (New Haven, Conn.: Yale University Press, 1990).

The Image of Immunity

Another cardinal element of the effort to portray the Court as independent is the cultivation of the perception that the Court is immune to political pressure. The extent to which the Court is vulnerable to lobbying from other political actors must be publicly minimized. Justice Frankfurter, in his dissent in *Baker v. Carr* (1962), wrote: "The Court's authority—possessed of neither the purse nor the sword—ultimately rests on sustained public confidence in its moral sanction. Such feeling must be nourished by the Court's complete detachment, in fact and in appearance, from political entanglements..."[20]

In reality, the Court *is* detached from the lobbying efforts common to the legislative and executive branches. Interest group representatives do not ply the chambers of the justices as they do the halls of Congress. Interest groups do submit written briefs to the Court and public demonstrations in front of the Supreme Court building have become a common tactic of some interest groups.

Pressure also comes from the general public through letters. Up to a year after the *Roe v. Wade* decision, Justice William O. Douglas remarked to two of his colleagues that he was getting about fifty letters a day on the subject.[21]

But the pressure the Court feels may be in the nature of anticipation of certain consequences. For example, the justices may anticipate that the president may not comply or that widespread civil disobedience will occur if a case is decided in a certain way. Or the Court may be criticized for not acting quickly enough to resolve an issue.

The image of the Court bowing to political pressure is inimical to the interests of the justices. In its handling of *United States v. Nixon* (1974), the Court was torn between its penchant for maintaining the lengthy deliberative process and the potential for public criticism if the Court declined to expedite the decision making process to resolve a national crisis. Chief Justice Warren Burger, in writing his colleagues about the Court's dilemma, reflected the Court's agony over the necessity of publicly acquiescing to political pressure when he stated "we should not permit ourselves to be pressured or rushed by news media or anyone else, nevertheless the case is one of obvious importance."[22]

Political considerations in some cases are so obvious the justices cannot help but acknowledge them. Failure to do so runs the risk of inciting public criticism of the Court's actions. One decision that vexed Justice Lewis Powell was the court-martial of Lt. William Calley in 1974. As the head of that judicial circuit, Powell was faced with the decision of whether or not to grant a stay of the lower court's decision until the full Court could hear the case. He was urged by one of his clerks

[20]*Baker v. Carr*, 369 U.S. 186 (1962).

[21]Memo to William Brennan and Harry Blackmun, January 22, 1974, William O. Douglas Papers, Box 1622, Library of Congress, Washington, D.C..

[22]Statement by Chief Justice, May 25, 1974, William O. Douglas Papers, Box 1660, Library of Congress, Washington, D.C.

to deny the stay on legal grounds. But Powell wrote his colleagues that he could go either way, but he did not want to be overturned by the full Court because, wrote Powell, the case is "one of national import."[23] The case was not important due to groundbreaking legal doctrine, but due to its high visibility in the press.

COMMUNICATING FOR DEFERENCE

Realization of the Court's objectives is tied to a strategy of fostering an image of the Court. Imagemaking requires control over the communication process with the explicit purpose of manipulating information. Ethan Katsh has argued that rather than existing as some foreign process, the whole legal system rests on such a strategy. "Manipulation of information underlies the way legal institutions work, how legal doctrines are applied, and how social and moral values are translated into legal values. Law is a response to information received *from* the public. Law is also information that is communicated *to* the public."[24] The Court is an active agent in devising and pursuing a strategy that alters public perceptions in the direction of public deference and compliance.

Constraints on Manipulation

However, the Court unlike other institutions, cannot engage in the same public relations tactics as the Congress or the White House. Reticence to pursue these objectives in a similar fashion as other institutions is the product of distinctive characteristics of the Court and public expectations placed on the Court.

One of these characteristics is the Court's place within the judicial system, which possesses certain norms not shared by other institutions. These norms govern judicial behavior at all levels, not just at the Supreme Court.

One aspect of these judicial norms incorporates extrajudicial activity, including relations with the press. The justices follow a code of judicial ethics concerning their extrajudicial activities that admonishes them not to engage in behavior that would "cast reasonable doubt on the judge's capacity to act impartially as a judge" or to "demean the judicial office."[25] Although the justices adhere to this code voluntarily, as the occupants of the pinnacle of the judicial profession, they become the most visible national examples of judicial behavior and thus are disinclined to cast disrepute on the judicial system.

The Court's efforts to promote distance from other political actors, including the press, are undermined by overt communication strategies. A flurry of press

---

[23]Memorandum to Conference, June 22, 1974, William O. Douglas Papers, Box 1622, Library of Congress, Washington, D.C.

[24]Ethan Katsh, *Electronic Media and the Transformation of Law* (New York: Oxford University Press, 1989), p. 6.

[25]American Bar Association Standing Committee on Ethics and Professional Responsibility, "Model Code of Judicial Conduct," 1990.

releases, news conferences, or interviews to shape an image of distance would be counterproductive to the Court's desired image.

The most salient contraint is that between the nature of the image the Court seeks to portray as indifferent to public opinion, and the "special pleader" nature of tactics such as news conferences, photo opportunities, and news releases, and so on, generally employed by other institutions to affect public opinion. Although the Court is and must remain subject to public will in order to achieve deference and compliance, it cannot convey the impression that it is responsive to public opinion since such a perception would undermine its image of independence. This is the crux of the paradox in imagemaking—to engage in imagemaking while denying its existence to maintain the image.

The paradox is not one wholly of the Court's making, but rests in the public's role assignment for the Court. As Robert Dahl notes, the Court's role as a political institution is a unique one since "Americans are not quite willing to accept the fact that it *is* a political institution and not quite capable of denying it; so that frequently we take both positions at once." [26]

Perpetuation of this image requires the Court to eschew publicly efforts to explain and defend itself since such activity would suggest concern for public and press evaluations. In declining participation in a *Life* magazine article on the Court, Chief Justice Warren articulated the Court's attitude toward publicly utilizing the press for the Court's own purposes.

> The Court has always been opposed to participating in the writing of anything which portrays it and its work. They prefer to have whatever is written about the Court to be done entirely independent of it.
>
> I know that this practice has resulted in much misinformation about the Court which could be easily explained, but I have always joined with the majority of the Court in taking those chances rather than to have it appear that we are writing either in defense of ourselves or of the institution. [27]

It is not that the Court does not participate in the creation of its own image, but that it seeks to do so without the risk of public exposure. In 1962, Warren helped in the production of a CBS documentary "Storm Over the Supreme Court." Then, he petitioned Fred Friendly, CBS News executive producer, "not to have any public recognition" of the Court's assistance. [28]

The task for the Court is not as easy as for the Congress or the presidency. In its efforts to convey a certain image, the Court is constrained by its own distinctiveness and the nature of the image it seeks to convey.

[26]Robert A. Dahl,"Decision-Making in a Democracy: The Supreme Court as a National Policy-Maker," *Journal of Public Law* 6 (Fall 1957): 279.

[27]Letter to John D. Voelker, December 11, 1965, Earl Warren Papers, Box 666, Library of Congress, Washington, D.C.

[28]Letter, March 3, 1963, Earl Warren Papers, Box 666, Library of Congress, Washington, D.C.

The Salience of Communication

However, the Court cannot merely avoid communication with the public because general deference may not be sustained by neglect. Also, the Court will not achieve compliance in the absence of communication.

The Court's ability to perform a policy-making role in American politics rests on transforming deference toward the Court into widespread compliance with its decisions. Such compliance is at least partly a function of communication of the Court's decision. Not only does this mean public awareness of a decision, but also the absence of misinformation that may reduce deference or inhibit compliance.

The power of the Court to legitimate policy options, since it is directed at changes in public attitudes, hinges on communication of Court decisions. Walter F. Murphy and Joseph Tanenhaus have posited that the Court's role in legitimating change is conditioned on three factors: (1)the decisions of the Court must be visible; (2)the Court must be perceived as responsible for resolving constitutional conflicts; and (3)the Court must be highly regarded.[29] All relate to public opinion toward or public attention to the Court.

The justices themselves have acknowledged the importance of accurate communication with the general public and the link between such communication and public compliance with Court decisions. Earl Warren once wrote: "The importance of a proper understanding of the Court's work can hardly be overemphasized. The decisions of the Court, spanning as they do almost the entire spectrum of our national life, cannot realize true fulfillment unless substantially accurate accounts of the holdings are disseminated."[30]

However, the messages of the Court may not be getting through.[31] Broad sections of the public are woefully ignorant about the Court. According to a 1990 *National Law Journal*/Lexis survey, most people could not name any of the sitting justices. For those who could, name recognition was below 10 percent of the public for all of the justices, except Sandra Day O'Connor.[32] Only 9 percent of those surveyed in a *Washington Post* survey knew William Rehnquist was the chief justice.[33] Even recent nominees during the confirmation process do not possess high name recognition. Clarence Thomas became well known nationally during his confirmation hearings, but six weeks after David Souter's nomination, two-thirds of the public said they had not heard enough about him to form an opinion about him.[34]

---

[29]Walter F. Murphy and Joseph Tanenhaus, "Public Opinion and the United States Supreme Court," *Law and Society Review* 2 (February 1968): 357–382.

[30]Statement on Special Committee of Supreme Court Decisions, September 12, 1966, Earl Warren Papers, Box 665, Library of Congress, Washington, D.C.

[31]For a study with an opposing conclusion, see Berkson, *The Supreme Court and Its Publics*, pp. 16–21.

[32]Marcia Coyle, "How Americans View High Court," *The National Law Journal* (February 26, 1990): 1.

[33]See *Washington Post* Survey, June 18, 1989, Question ID: USWASHP.89825E R05.

[34]CBS News Poll, September 3, 1990.

The low level of cognitions about the individual justices can be seen through another measure. A 1991 survey found that only 42 percent of respondents agreed that the Court is made up mostly of conservative justices.[35]

But the greater problem for the Court is not identification of the justices by name or ideology, but miscommunication or even lack of information about the Court's decisions. This problem is real for the Court. Miscommunication has been documented in several cases. Following the *Engel v. Vitale* (school prayer) case in 1962, press reporting devoted greater attention to interest group reaction to the case, which generally exaggerated the decision's effects, than to the decision itself. In a rare move, the news reporting subsequently was criticized by one of the justices.[36] The controversy surrounding the case of *Gannett v. DePasquale* (1979) occurred partly due to misunderstanding. The Court's ruling that the public, including the press, had no constitutional right to attend pretrial hearings was interpreted by many reporters and editors as extending to criminal trials as well.[37] Lack of public knowledge of Court decisions is common. According to a 1990 survey, only half the public knew the Court had ruled that anti-flag burning legislation was unconstitutional. Nearly one-third thought it had ruled in the opposite direction.[38]

Even those groups most affected are often uninformed about a ruling.[39] In the mid-1970s, a survey of Florida public school teachers found only 17 percent were aware of the *Engel v. Vitale* decision, one of the more publicized of the Court's decisions.[40]

Major decisions of the Court receiving saturation press coverage, such as those on abortion, do penetrate mass awareness and shape attitudes. But these decisions are rare. Even these decisions often fail to affect attitudes because individuals do not receive enough information about them. According to one CBS/*New York Times* survey, two months after the *Webster* decision, three-fourths of the public said they had not heard enough about the decision to form an opinion.[41]

This lack of public knowledge leads to misunderstanding about policy the Court has declared or even about the role of the Court itself. For many Americans, the Court's role appears to be a blur. In one survey, less than half of the respondents mentioned the power of judicial review when asked what the Supreme Court is supposed to do.[42] If less than half of the public understand the Court's power of judicial review, then one of Murphy and Tanenhaus's conditions—perception of responsibility as constitutional arbiter—is unfulfilled.

[35]*Times Mirror* Center for The People & The Press Survey, July 18, 1991.

[36]Chester A. Newland, "Press Coverage of the United States Supreme Court." *Western Political Quarterly* 17 (March 1964): 15–36.

[37]David Shaw, *Press Watch* (New York: MacMillan, 1984), pp. 122–123.

[38]*Times Mirror* Center for The People & The Press Survey, July 12, 1990.

[39]Berkson, *The Supreme Court and Its Publics*, pp. 79–88.

[40]Lawrence Baum, *The Supreme Court*, 2d ed. (Washington, D.C.: CQ Press, 1985), p. 206.

[41]Everett Carll Ladd, *The Ladd Report #8* (New York: W. W. Norton, 1990), p. 12

[42]Walter F. Murphy and Joseph Tanenhaus, "Public Opinion and the United States Supreme Court," op. cit.

What many Americans know about the Court often is erroneous. Large segments of the general public possess inaccurate cognitions about the power of the Court. For example, more than three-fourths of the respondents in one survey believed every decision made by a state court can be reviewed and reversed by the U.S. Supreme Court. [43] Nearly half believed a Court decision could not be overruled. [44] Gregory Caldiera concluded that "Citizens, as individuals, evince little or no knowledge of or concern for the Court; to the extent that they express sensible opinions, they base judgements on the vaguest and crudest of ideological frameworks." [45]

The general public's lack of knowledge or faulty information, coupled with general disinterest, only reinforces the significance of the information about the Court that does penetrate the public's consciousness. Moreover, Caldiera found that the basis for the public's judgments about the Court is not general texts, but more transitory forces:

> Public evaluations of the Court do not float freely, in a seemingly aimless fashion, unconnected to the perturbations of the political and legal processes. Rather, in evaluating the justices, the public appears to respond to events on the political landscape and to actions taken by the Supreme Court. If, for example, the Court adopts a position against a law-making majority, the public accordingly exacts a cost in confidence... [46]

The Court's objective for strategic communication efforts is to maintain, or perhaps regain, the mystique surrounding the Court that contributed to public deference toward the Court's decision making. It is to perpetuate the image of the Court as a nonpolitical, independent institution that is a legitimate authority figure and endowed with a special expertise. In short, imagemaking supports the notion that the Court is worthy of the public's deference and therefore its compliance with Court decisions.

Therefore the Court's imagemaking efforts are not appendages to the Court's work. Rather, they are critical components of the Court's continued power in the American political system.

The Nature of the Message

By conveying certain messages to the public, the Court fosters public deference. And the messages communicated are not just verbal.

One such message concerns the majesty and dignity of the Court. This message is conveyed through the nature of the physical setting, the usage of ritual, and the style of communication.

---

[43] The Hearst Corporation, *The American Public, The Media, & The Judicial System*, A Hearst Report, 1983.

[44] The Hearst Corporation, *The American Public's Knowledge of the U.S. Constitution*, A Hearst Report, 1987.

[45] Gregory Caldiera, "Neither the Purse Nor the Sword: Dynamics of Public Confidence in the U.S. Supreme Court," *American Political Science Review* 80 (December 1986): 1223.

[46] Ibid.

The physical appearance of the Court's environs bespeak tradition and deference. The Court's "marble palace," patterned after the Temple of Diana at Ephesus, is an imposing structure to the casual tourist. It has been termed "a shrine" that acts as a "testament to the law as a symbol for the nation."[47] However, a less awed approach is evident in Justice Harlan Stone's alleged remark that "Whenever I look at that building I feel that the justices should ride to work on elephants."[48]

The courtroom in which the justices sit in public session reinforces legitimacy and expertise. The high wooden curved bench locates the justices well above all others in the room. Richard Johnson aptly describes the subliminal effects of the room: "This room, with its Ionic columns,...impressively high ceilings, and [marble] friezes depicting lawgivers of history and legend, exemplifies stability."[49]

The rituals of the Court act to perpetuate the mystique of the Court. Judicial attire, the formality of the public sessions (including appropriate honorifics), the location of the bench—all contribute to the maintenance of a mystical nature of the Court.

The formality of the ceremony of the Court embodies tradition. The inveterate nature of the Court is promoted in the traditional chant at the commencement of public sessions: "Oyez! Oyez! Oyez! All persons having business before the Honorable, the Supreme Court of the United States, are admonished to draw near and give their attention, for the Court is now sitting. God save the United States and this Honorable Court!"

The mode of dress—robes for the justices, formal coats for government attorneys—is distinctive and archaic in a society given to increasingly informal attire.

The language of the Court is another element of the message. The justices are addressed formally. Chief Justice Rehnquist has been known to correct counsel who err in addressing the justices. Decisions are "handed down."

Although the ceremony is actually viewed by a small fraction of Americans, the physical elements of the Court's message are conveyed through word-of-mouth and journalistic descriptions.

Another message is the Court's aloofness from the common and ordinary. The "cult of the judge" has been cultivated. Judges in American society have acquired a role as high priests of the legal system with powers beyond the common person. These powers rest on the judge's learning and his or her independence from other political forces.[50]

[47]John Brigham, *The Cult of the Court* (Philadelphia: Temple University Press, 1987), pp. 111–112.

[48]Drew Pearson and Robert S. Allen, *The Nine Old Men* (Garden City, N.Y.: Doubleday, Doran, 1936), p.9

[49]Johnson, *The Dynamics of Compliance*, p. 35.

[50]Brigham, *The Cult of the Court*, pp. 65–74.

The justices have promoted aloofness to avoid the trivialization of their work by its association with the justices' more human traits. Most of the justices attempt to withhold from the public the salient aspects in their deliberative process as well as their personal attitudes and relationships.

The justices rarely discuss the influence of their own backgrounds and worldview in the decision-making process. Justice Douglas once confessed in an interview that "...we all have subconscious parts, we're not entirely rational in our decisions [and] our likes and dislikes."[51] But such candor is unusual.

However, sometimes these efforts fail. Justice Frankfurter was disliked by some of his colleagues on the Court, and those justices expressed themselves to reporters.[52] Bob Woodward and Scott Armstrong's *The Brethren* revealed conflicts among the justices usually left concealed.

The justices' origins also suggest the distance of an intellectual, if not a social, aristocracy. While presidents and members of Congress are expected to retain a common person identification, however false in reality, justices are expected to enjoy a social and educational status foreign to the average citizen. The justices are supposed to be the products of the best law schools and the social aristocracy of the nation. And, for the most part, they are.[53]

The force of this tradition was evidenced in the nomination of G. Harrold Carswell to a Supreme Court vacancy. Carswell possessed slender legal qualifications and received no more than lukewarm approval from the legal community. Nebraska Senator Roman Hruska made the curious remark in support of Carswell that although Carswell may be mediocre, "there are a lot of mediocre judges and people and lawyers. They are entitled to a little representation, aren't they."[54] However, his comment was met with such ridicule that it hastened Carswell's eventual failure to be confirmed. Mediocrity and ordinariness are not expected as the norm for justices of the Supreme Court.

Another element of the message of separation is the perception of an "over-the-shoulder" nature of the public's role in the communication process. The Court does not appear to be speaking directly to those who are most affected by the decision. Although most decisions of the Court impinge on individuals and groups far beyond the legal community, the opinions are discernible almost exclusively by that community (and at times not even to them).

[51]Transcript, Knight-Ridder interview, October 29, 1973, William O. Douglas Papers, Box 621, Library of Congress, Washington, D.C.

[52]For examples of internal conflict involving Frankfurter, see Letter from William O. Douglas to Hugo Black, September 8, 1941; undated memorandum from Douglas to Black; and Letter from Harlan Stone to Hugo Black, September 7, 1945, William O. Douglas Papers, Box 308, Library of Congress. For a sample of press coverage of the justices' personal disputes, see Jay G. Hayden, "Supreme Court Feud," *Detroit News*, February 3, 1944; and Drew Pearson and Robert S. Allen, "Justice Frankfurter: A Powerful Prompter in U.S. War Policies," *Philadelphia Record*, June 1, 1942.

[53]See John R. Schmidhauser, *Judges and Justices: The Federal Appellate Judiciary* (Boston: Little, Brown, 1979).

[54]Richard Harris, *Decision* (New York: E. P. Dutton, 1971), p. 110.

This "over-the-shoulder" posture for the general public is aggravated by the justices' unwillingness to conform to the current standards of public communication—press releases, news conferences, mass mailings, and so on. In an era when members of other political institutions utilize these methods, the justices' failure to do so magnifies the perception of distance.

The message of aloofness is communicated in the lack of access to the justices and their public proceedings. For cases of high public interest, only a privileged few are able to secure seats in the visitors' section of the courtroom. Unlike the Congress, the Court has resisted attempts to broadcast its public proceedings. The justices may perceive that appearance on national television would weaken the message of distance between them and the public.

Beyond the indirect nature of the communication, even the content of the communication itself is fraught with symbols of distance. The language of Court writing and argument is highly technical with references to precedents and legal standards. Such language as "strict scrutiny," "important governmental objectives," and "clear and convincing evidence" is foreign to nonlawyers.

Even the tone of opinions often displays solicitousness toward the public and other political institutions, especially when direct conflict with these other players is imminent. An example is the Court's approach to *United States v. Nixon*. During the preparation of the opinion, Burger wrote his colleagues that "The more restrained and even the tone of the opinion, the greater will be the force of the holding."[55]

The substance of the opinions on some highly visible cases is designed to anticipate public opinion and send a message that will mollify public feeling. In anticipation of public reaction to the second set of segregation decisions in 1955, Justice Frankfurter proposed the option of a "bare bones" decree with the desired result that "local passions aroused by last May's decisions would thereby be absorbed or tempered."[56]

In the segregation cases, the Court sought to achieve compliance and worried about how to accomplish it through the writing of the opinion. Frankfurter wrote Warren that "the most important problem is to fashion appropriate provisions against evasion."[57] In writing the Court's opinion in the *Brown v. Board of Education* case, Earl Warren urged the justices to make the opinion "short, readable by the lay public, non-rhetorical, unemotional, and, above all, not accusatory."[58]

[55]Memorandum to Conference, July 20, 1974, William O. Douglas Papers, Box 1659, Library of Congress, Washington, D.C.

[56]Memorandum to Conference, April 14, 1955, Earl Warren Papers, Box 574, Library of Congress, Washington, D.C.

[57]Memorandum to Conference, July 5, 1954, Earl Warren Papers, Box 574, Library of Congress, Washington, D.C.

[58]Memorandum to Conference, May 5, 1954, Earl Warren Papers, Box 571, Library of Congress, Washington, D.C.

Public education and cultivation of public support for the Court's position is one factor in opinion writing. Earl Warren once wrote of the *Miranda* decision: "I am hopeful that it will have the effect of making the public realize the importance of good police work...."[59]

Message construction by the Court is designed to promote the objectives of the Court in its relationship with the public. But the vehicle for communication of the message is equally important.

THE PRESS AS LINKING MECHANISM

The messages of the Court to the general public are communicated via several channels—the legal system, personal observation of visitors to the courtroom, and texts on the Court for the general audience. But the primary linking mechanism between the Court and the general public is the press.[60]

The role of the press is even more salient here than in the relationship between the public and other national political institutions due to the absence of any alternative methods of direct communication. Members of Congress interact with their constituents through mailings, town meetings, and district offices. Presidents deliver nationally televised speeches. Those modes of communication are not utilized by the justices of the U.S. Supreme Court. Even when justices deliver speeches, they rarely address nonlegal groups.

The justices perceive the press as the main educational tool about the Court for the public. Earl Warren argued that the issues the Court handles should be "well understood and intelligently apprised by the public. Since the public cannot be expected to read the opinions themselves, it must depend on newspapers, periodicals, radio, and television for its information."[61]

The press is nearly the exclusive medium for the Court's communication with this constituency and, in that sense, the Court's relationship with the press is not a superfluous association that the justices engage in merely for good government. The relationship is critical for the Court. The justices, unlike elected officials, lack other nonmedia mechanisms for interaction with this constituency, such as town meetings, newsletters, and frequent campaigning. For most people, knowledge of the activities of the Court comes exclusively from the press.

The press serves two roles for the Court. One is as a gauge of the outside world. As such, the press transmits reactions to specific decisions, but also, in a broader sense, informs the justices of the larger political environment. Secondly, the press is a public relations tool for the Court specifically for the task of reinforcing deference toward its decisions.

---

[59]Letter to Louis H. Pollack, June 23, 1966, Earl Warren Papers, Box 617, Library of Congress, Washington, D.C.

[60]See, for example, Berkson, *The Supreme Court and Its Publics*, pp. 102–103.

[61]Statement on Special Committee of Supreme Court Decisions, September 12, 1966, Earl Warren Papers, Box 665, Library of Congress, Washington, D.C.

The Press as Gauge

One component of the gauge is the justices' awareness of public reaction to the Court and its decisions. The justices do take an interest in the news coverage of their opinions, the Court generally, and the justices as individuals. The justices have sent clippings of news articles to each other, particularly those from their home states. Referring to an opinion of the time and attaching a news clipping, in 1956 Justice Harold H. Burton wrote to Chief Justice Earl Warren: "This shows that the opinion is being understood and taken as it was intended to be taken—at least by the writer of this editorial."[62]

Accepting a linkage, in at least some cases, between public opinion and judicial decision making and the Court's intent to retain a majoritarian posture, the question arises: How do the justices discern public opinion? Although the Court does rely on a variety of means of assessing public opinion (including the legislative acts of Congress, lower court rulings, and the results of elections), the press constitutes one means.

The justices are exposed to the press regularly. According to Chief Justice William Rehnquist, the justices "read newspapers and magazines, we watch news on television, we talk to our friends about current events."[63] Moreover, the advantage of the press as a gauge is its availability and regularity as a news source. The justices make no special efforts and incur no additional costs to follow public opinion through the vehicle of the press.

The gauge function of the press also acquires a broader role. As a regular, highly credible, and in some cases exclusive source of information on the larger society, the press shapes reality for the justices. The justices' cognitions about societal developments are affected by the press, for the justices, like others, receive their news about events and developments in society at large from the press.

Even some of the justices confess that they do not live in a vacuum. In April 1986, prior to his appointment as chief justice, William Rehnquist delivered a speech admitting the power of public opinion on the justices:

> Judges, so long as they are relatively normal human beings can no more escape being influenced by public opinion in the long run than can people working at other jobs. And if a judge on coming to the bench were to decide to hermetically seal himself off from all manifestations of public opinion, he would accomplish very little; he would not be influenced by current public opinion, but instead by the state of public opinion at the time that he came onto the bench.[64]

---

[62]Memorandum, April 15, 1956, Earl Warren Papers, Box 349, Library of Congress, Washington, D.C.

[63]William Rehnquist, *The Supreme Court: How It Was, How It Is* (New York: William Morrow, 1987), p. 98.

[64]R. W. Apple, Jr., "Justices Are People," *New York Times*, April 10, 1989, A1.

This function becomes more important given the recent debate over whether the Court as a policymaker is fundamentally majoritarian or anti-majoritarian. Recent research has lent support to the conclusion that the Court, in most cases, reflects national public opinion. For example, David G. Barnum has concluded that the Court's activism in the 1960s on minority rights was prompted by public opinion. Moreover, Barnum found the Court reticent to act in areas such as busing and legalization of homosexual activity where their decisions would be antimajoritarian.[65]

If the Court is majoritarian and this posture is not merely coincidental but is based on the justices' perception of the majority will, then how is that perception shaped? The justices' vision of majority opinion will be shaped much like that of other policymakers—partly through the prism of the press. In fact, the press may be even more important since justices lack other avenues for interaction with the public—mail, town meetings, district offices, privately commissioned polls, and so on.

Although many of the justices retain strong ideological commitments throughout their tenure on the Court, others, particularly those who approach decisions on a case-by-case basis are more likely to adjust their views over time. Justices who are politically moderate may be more inclined to agree with public opinion.[66] Their lack of strong ideological conviction may enhance their vulnerability to other factors, such as public opinion, as an anchor for decision making.

One example is Harry Blackmun, whose longtime friendship and ideological affinity with Warren Burger prompted the title "Minnesota Twin" to be affixed to him after his appointment in 1970. The same Blackmun, however, became the author of the *Roe v. Wade* decision, and by the end of his term he was labeled a liberal. Blackmun had gravitated from a member of the conservative majority to a frequent critic of and bête noire for the conservatives. During this evolution, Blackmun commented that "...I think, clearly, this is an educational process—and I would hope that one matures as the years go by."[67]

Another type of justice who may be more receptive to public opinion is one who has worked closely with a president while on the bench.[68] Examples of such justices include Abe Fortas (with Lyndon Johnson), Fred Vinson (with Harry Truman), and Felix Frankfurter (with Franklin Roosevelt).

[65]See Thomas R. Marshall, *Public Opinion and the Supreme Court* (Boston: Unwin Hyman, 1989); David G. Barnum, "The Supreme Court and Public Opinion: Judicial Decision-Making in the Post New Deal Period," *Journal of Politics* 46 (1985): 652–666; and Richard Funston, "The Supreme Court and Critical Elections," *American Political Science Review* 69 (September 1975): 795–811; For an opposing view, see Jonathan Casper, "The Supreme Court and National Policy Making," *American Political Science Review* 70 (March 1976): 50–63.

[66]Marshall, *Public Opinion and the Supreme Court*, pp. 109–124.

[67]Quoted in Lawrence Baum, *The Supreme Court*, 4th ed. (Washington, D.C.: CQ Press, 1985), p. 154.

[68]Marshall, *Public Opinion and the Supreme Court*, pp. 114–124.

The evidence for the causal relationship between specific decisions and public opinion is often anecdotal or circumstantial.[69] However, the justices themselves have made reference to the salience of public opinion in decision making. In explicating the rationale for certain decisions, sitting justices themselves occasionally have placed their decisions in the framework of public opinion.[70]

Publicly the justices are reticent to include public opinion as a variable in their decision making. When asked in a television interview what impact public opinion has on the Court, Justice William Brennan emphatically stated "none."[71]

Anonymously, some have acknowledged the sway of public opinion in their deliberations. The decision whether to grant a writ of certiorari can be a response to public opinion. One justice commented in a background interview that the "people just demand that the Supreme Court resolve an issue whether we really ought to or not. That does affect us sometimes."[72]

Some make reference to other justices' responses to public opinion. For example, Chief Justice Rehnquist attributed the Court's decision in the steel seizure cases in 1952 to public disenchantment with the Korean War and the Truman administration. He speculated that had those two factors not been present, the decision could have gone the other way.[73]

For some decisions, such as those where the issue is one of high visibility and compliance is problematic, the linkage is more explicit. But even for other cases, the specter of a lack of public support always exists.

The press influences judicial decision making by relaying societal reaction to specific decisions. But the press' influence also occurs through the process of helping shape the justices' view of the social and political environment in which they operate.

The Press as Deference Reinforcer

The press also serve as a vehicle for transmitting messages about the Court designed to enhance public deference for the Court and compliance with its decisions. This is the key function in the Court's communication with the public.

An anecdote by Chief Justice Rehnquist demonstrates the justices' concern about press coverage and their attempts to manipulate it to maintain the institution's

[69]See for example, David R. Manwaring, *Render Unto Caesar: The Flag Salute Controversy* (Chicago: University of Chicago Press, 1962). In chapter 7, Manwaring implies negative press reaction to a decision contributed to the Court's subsequent reversal.

[70]For examples of specific references in opinions, see Marshall, *Public Opinion and the Supreme Court*, pp. 48–51.

[71]Lawrence Baum, *The Supreme Court*, 3rd ed. (Washington, D.C.: CQ Press, 1989), p. 129.

[72]Quoted in H. W. Perry, Jr., *Deciding to Decide: Agenda Setting in the United States Supreme Court* (Cambridge, Mass.: Harvard University Press, 1991), pp. 259–260.

[73]William Rehnquist, *The Supreme Court: How It Was, How It Is* (New York: William Morrow, 1987), p. 98.

image and reinforce deference for it. He relates that in 1980 Justice White suggested the justices change their form of address on the opinions from "Mr. Justice" to merely "Justice." According to Rehnquist, White suggested the change at that time due to the likelihood of a woman justice joining the Court and the need for the Court to "avoid the embarrassment of having to change the style of designating the author of the opinion" at the time of appointment.[74] However, Rehnquist confesses the ploy did not work because Linda Greenhouse, the *New York Times* reporter assigned to the Court, spotted the change and devoted a whole story to it on the day it occurred.

The function of maintaining deference requires the cooperation of the press specifically in achieving the Court's objectives. Despite the adversarial claims of some journalists, the reporters who cover the Court have been viewed as broadly supportive of the Court's objectives through their newsgathering and reporting practices.

David Paletz and Robert Entman contend reporters serve the Court by adopting its language in their writing. For example, by calling the Court's opinions decisions rather than policies, reporters contribute to the perception of the action as the final resolution of the issue, thereby enhancing the power of the Court. According to Paletz and Entman, "journalistic language makes it less apparent to the public that nine unelected justices make policies as significant as those of the elected president and Congress."[75]

A Poor Connection

These functions of the press present a problem for the Court. The problem is the press often does not serve well as a linking mechanism for the Court, either as a gauge of the larger environment or as a deference reinforcer.

The press serves poorly as a feedback mechanism for the justices. Due to the press' prismlike rather than mirrorlike nature, it is flawed as a forum for feedback from decisions or for portrayals of reality. The justices may become misinformed about public opinion and then act based on such misunderstanding. One example Judith Blake provides is the *Roe v. Wade* decision. She argues the Court misread public views about when life begins. Justice Blackmun's references in his opinion in *Roe* to public support specifically for the concept of life not beginning at conception, and generally for the legalization of abortion, were inconsistent with extant public opinion surveys.[76]

Deference reinforcement also may not occur if it is dependent on the press' portrayal of the Court. As the public's source for the knowledge of the Court's

---

[74]William Rehnquist, *The Supreme Court: How It Was, How It Is* (New York: William Morrow, 1987), p. 301.

[75]*Media Power Politics* (New York: Free Press, 1981), p. 105.

[76]Judith Blake, "The Abortion Decisions: Judicial Review and Public Opinion," in Edward Manier, William Liu, and David Solomon, eds., *Abortion: New Directions for Policy Studies* (Notre Dame, Ind.: University of Notre Dame Press, 1977), pp. 51–82.

activities, press coverage is flawed. Press coverage of the Court in both quantity and quality has been derided as an inadequate medium for public understanding.

In quantity, news coverage of the Court is slight compared with that devoted to the Congress and the presidency.[77] Most decisions of the Court go unreported.[78] Those decisions covered are not representative of the totality of the Court's docket. News coverage is weighted toward certain types of issues. One favorite topic of news stories is freedom of the press. Another is criminal rights.[79]

As to quality, stories rarely advance beyond a description of the outcome of the decision. Typically, they do not expand to other critical tasks, such as explaining the decision process, placing the decision in the context of other decisions, and reporting reactions. David Ericson concluded that even a reader who relied on the *New York Times* for Supreme Court news "still would not know what really happened in more than three-fourths of the Court's decisions of the 1974 October term—not to mention why it happened and with what consequences for the reader."[80]

But this conclusion is erroneous. The press does cover some cases exhaustively.[81] Recent abortion-related cases, such as *Webster v. Reproductive Health Services* (1989), *Rust v. Sullivan* (1991), and *Planned Parenthood v. Casey* (1992) have received extensive press attention.

Press versus Court Imperatives

Why do some cases merit media saturation while others languish in obscurity? The answer lies not so much with what the Court does as with who conveys what the Court does.A legal scholar probably would not expect the press to notice all cases equally, since some cases clearly exceed others in potential impact on the law. However, such a scholar might expect the press to accentuate those cases considered important by the legal profession. But the press only covers what the legal profession considers important if the press also agrees.

The failure of such an expectation is that it is based on the imperatives of the legal system, with the Court at the pinnacle, and not on those of the press. Significantly, however, it is the press that serves as the keeper of the gate of the

[77]Richard Davis, "Lifting the Shroud: News Media Coverage of the U.S. Supreme Court." *Communications and the Law* 9 (October 1987): 43–59.

[78]David Ericson, "Newspaper Coverage of the Supreme Court," *Journalism Quarterly* 54 (Autumn 1977): 605–607; and Ethan Katsh, "The Supreme Court Beat: How Television Covers the Supreme Court," *Judicature* 67 (1983): 6–12.

[79]Jerome O'Callaghan and James O. Dukes, "Media Coverage of the Supreme Court's Caseload," *Journalism Quarterly* 69 (Spring 1992): 195–203.

[80]Ericson, "Newspaper Coverage of the Supreme Court," p. 607.

[81]See Stephanie Greco Larson, "How the *New York Times* Covered Discrimination Cases," *Journalism Quarterly* 62 (1985): 894–896; and Elliot E. Slotnick, "Television News and the Supreme Court: The Case of Allan Bakke," paper presented at the annual meeting of the American Political Science Association, San Francisco, Calif., August 30, 1990.

mass media; therefore, it is the imperatives of the press, not the legal profession's standards of significance, that govern news coverage.[82]

These imperatives are both professional and organizational. Professional imperatives inhere to the norms concerning news that reporters possess; organizational imperatives are the constraints of the news organization that are placed on the newsgathering process.

The preponderant professional criterion is newsworthiness. Although some reporters claim news is readily apparent to those in the news business, content analysis of news has revealed the existence of certain news values in newsgathering. These values include event-orientation, conflict, drama, timeliness, proximity, and unusualness.[83]

But the news organization also exerts its own pressures on the newsgathering process. The bottom line for the news business is profit. News must be produced in a manner that conforms to the economic needs of the organization. The expectations of regularized news produce regular deadlines. The assignment of beats predicts where news will occur and guarantees that events associated with those beats will be considered news.[84] Moreover, the organization is sensitive to other factors, such as its audience and advertisers.

In the case of the Supreme Court, the professional values and norms of a legal nature govern the cases to be covered. But cases of greater interest to the press, due to the presence of news values, are more likely to appear in news coverage of the Court. The product of the search for newsworthiness in reporting on the Court is, therefore, a distorted portrait of the Court's activity. Social policy—abortion, sexual harassment, racial discrimination—are covered to a degree out of balance with their quantity on the Court's agenda due to the presence in the story of news values. The result is "a Court docket that appears to be dominated by such cases to the exclusion of other types of cases."[85]

Organizational imperatives also shape news coverage, and at times misrepresent the Court. Organizational interests produce a news beat—the Supreme Court or legal beat—based on the expectation that news will be produced there on a regular basis. The organizational imperatives at times produce a portrayal of the

---

[82]For empirical support for this conclusion, see Ethan Katsh, "The Supreme Court Beat," op. cit.

[83]See Bernard Roshco, *Newsmaking* (Chicago: University of Chicago Press, 1975); and Herbert Gans, *Deciding What's News* (New York: Pantheon, 1979). For a discussion of news values in electronic media, see Joseph S. Fowler and Stuart Showalter, "Evening Network News Selection: A Confirmation of News Judgment," *Journalism Quarterly* 91 (Winter 1974): 712–715; Dan Berkowitz, "Refining the Gatekeeping Metaphor for Local Television News," *Journal of Broadcasting and Electronic Media* 34 (Winter 1990): 55–88; and Mark D. Harmon, "Mr. Gates Goes Electronic: The What and Why Questions in Local TV News," *Journalism Quarterly* 66 (Winter 1989): 857–863.

[84]For a discussion of the organizational model of newsgathering, see Edward J. Epstein, News From Nowhere (New York: Random House, 1973); Jeremy Tunstall, *Journalists at Work* (Beverly Hills, Calif.: Sage, 1971); and Gans, op. cit.

[85]Davis, "Lifting the Shroud," p. 52–53.

Court that is misleading. News deadlines, general assignment reporting, and the process of decoding decisions into lay language results in inaccuracies.

Inaccuracy of news stories announcing landmark decisions has contributed to critiques of press content concerning the Court.[86] One researcher who examined television news coverage of a highly visible case concluded that due to the propensity to personalize stories, the coverage did not tell the viewer much about the Court as an institution.[87] But since that personalization focuses on the parties in the case, and excludes the justices themselves, the coverage also says little about the individual justices either.[88]

Little is known about the professionals who cover the Court today and whose norms and values shape news coverage. Past studies of the press corps during the Warren years described a small press corps (five full-time reporters), untrained in legal issues, constrained from news analysis by the pressures of deadline and brevity, and overruled by editors who lacked the reporters' understanding of the Court. Moreover, they lacked the interaction with policymakers, even infrequently, common to their colleagues at the White House, Congress, or the executive agencies.[89] Although Chief Justice Burger was portrayed in *The Brethren* as hostile to the press, two studies of Court-press relations during the Burger years revealed Burger's efforts to ameliorate the press corps work conditions. Burger held periodic off-the-record briefings with members of the press corps and solicited their recommendations for alterations in Court procedures relating to the press.[90] However, neither study found an increased on-record accessibility to the justices.

Professional values and norms and organizational imperatives both alter the Court's ability to utilize the press coverage as a reinforcer of deference to the Court.

Managing the Message

The Court's ability to manage the message to the public via the press has been shaped by recent developments. These include Court policy decisions, the behavior of individual justices, the nomination process, and the Court's visibility as a target of criticism from the White House and presidential campaigns.

[86]Chester A. Newland, "Press Coverage of the United States Supreme Court." *Western Political Quarterly* 19 (March 1964): 15–36; David L. Grey, *The Supreme Court and the News Media* (Evanston, Ill.: Northwestern University Press, 1968); Everette Dennis, "Another Look at Press Coverage of the Supreme Court," *Villanova Law Review* 20 (1974): 765–799.

[87]Slotnick, "Television News and the Supreme Court," op. cit.

[88]Davis, "Lifting the Shroud," p. 46.

[89]Chester A. Newland, "Press Coverage of the United States Supreme Court." *Western Political Quarterly* 19 (March 1964):15–36; and David L. Grey, *The Supreme Court and the News Media* (Evanston, Ill.: Northwestern University Press, 1968).

[90]Everette Dennis, "Another Look at Press Coverage of the Supreme Court," *Villanova Law Review* 20 (1974): 765–799; and Mitchell J. Tropin, "What, Exactly, Is the Court Saying," *The Barrister* (Winter 1984): 14.

One such trend with a potentially major impact on the acquisition of that base of public support is the Court's expanding responsibility in the realm of social policy in recent decades.[91] Decisions on issues such as school desegregation, forced busing for integration purposes, affirmative action, and abortion have tested the Court's ability to perform dual tasks—legitimizing certain policy options while maintaining deference toward the Court.

On some highly visible issues, the Court has not been stunningly successful in legitimizing policy options. The Court's role in abortion, for example, did not serve to change public attitudes toward the Court's position and legitimate policy change.[92] Similarly, public attitudes about school prayer remained unchanged following the 1960s decisions.[93]

Another trend is the Court's role in major disputes between other political institutions. The Court during the past two decades has settled "political questions" involving executive privilege, the legislative veto, and separation of powers (e.g., *United States v. Nixon*, 1974; *INS v. Chadha*, 1983; and *Bowsher v. Synar*, 1986).[94] Such activity potentially jeopardizes the Court's mantle of legitimacy because it embroils the institution in a political fight with other representative institutions who are more likely to enjoy greater popular support and who possess the power to curtail the Court's power. On the other hand, these developments may have the effect of enhancing the Court's imperative of acquiring public deference and compliance. The significance for the Court is enhanced given its inherent disadvantage in cultivating public support vis-à-vis other institutions. Abraham has succinctly noted the Court's disadvantage:

> When all is said and done, the Supreme Court of the United States does not possess the political power, the arsenal of potent weapons of government, the tools of the publicity media, or the strategic position in the government or in the body politic generally enjoyed by the other two branches.[95]

However, the level of public confidence in the Court has experienced a roller-coaster ride since the 1960s as the public has responded to specific Court actions and other political events. The Court has achieved a role as critical player in social policy, but not without effect on its public approval.[96]

[91] Donald L. Horowitz, *The Courts and Social Policy* (Washington, D.C.: Brookings, 1977).

[92] See Raymond Tatalovich and Byron Daynes, *The Politics of Abortion: A Study of Community Conflict in Public Policy Making* (New York: Praeger, 1981), pp. 129–133; Larry R. Baas and Dan Thomas, "The Supreme Court and Policy Legitimation," *American Political Quarterly* 12 (July 1984): 335–360; and Charles H. Franklin and Liane C. Kosaki, "Republican Schoolmaster: The U.S. Supreme Court, Public Opinion, and Abortion," *American Political Science Review* 83 (September 1989): 751–772.

[93] Robert Weissberg, *Public Opinion and Popular Government* (Englewood Cliffs, N.J.: Prentice Hall, 1976), pp. 121–126.

[94] U.S. v. Nixon, 418 U.S. 683 (1974); Immigration and Naturalization Service v. Chadha, 462 U.S. 919 (1983); and Bowsher v. Synar, 478 U.S. 714 (1986).

[95] Henry J. Abraham, *The Judicial Process*, 5th ed. (New York: Oxford University Press, 1986).

[96] For a discussion of levels of public approval of the Court since the 1960s, see Stephen L. Wasby, *The Supreme Court in the Federal Judicial System* (Chicago: Nelson-Hall, 1988), pp. 345–353.

Tanenhaus and Murphy have argued the Court must be highly regarded in order to legitimate policy change. Like other political institutions, the Court was highly regarded prior to the 1960s. In 1974, the Court was at the peak of a period of public confidence lasting from 1966 to 1984.[97] Much of this positive evaluation was due to the Court's role in hastening the conclusion of the Watergate crisis. The Court's decisions on other issues, such as the rights of the accused and school prayer, were viewed negatively, but the Court's Watergate role won strong public approval and enhanced the legitimacy of the Court.[98]

Public support for the Court experienced a marked decline during the 1980s and early 1990s. In 1990, the percent of respondents in a Gallup Poll expressing a great or quite a lot of confidence in the Supreme Court declined to 47 percent, the lowest in ten years.[99]

Taken together, these developments have raised the Court's public visibility as well as the stakes for the maintenance of the Court's role as a political institution. The Court's vulnerability to public will has become increasingly transparent. Its relationship with the press in securing public awareness and understanding that results in public deference and compliance has become more critical.

Institutional actions are not alone in affecting the Court's press relations. The justices are becoming less bound by the Court's traditional aloofness from the press. One cause of this may be the turnover of personnel. According to Bickel, the Court's prestige benefits from the seniority of the justices. But what happens when the personnel transition on the Court is more rapid than usual? During a seven year period, 1986–1993, five vacancies occurred on the Court. That record has rarely been exceeded in the past half century. The new members, who constitute nearly a majority, have not yet acquired the mantle of wisdom implied by Bickel.

Some of the justices, such as William Brennan in the mid-1980s, have spoken out to answer the Court's critics. Also at that time, the Court as a whole sought to explicate the Court's role in the wake of public interest in the bicentennial of the Constitution. However, fulfillment of the Court's objectives becomes more problematic with the justices' own visibility.

Moreover, discussion of the procedures of the Court has moved beyond mere description, as was true in earlier forays by justices. Chief Justice Rehnquist and Justice Scalia have criticized the justices' conferences for their lack of interplay. Justice Marshall used a dissent to attack the Court's process of issuing summary dispositions.[100]

[97]Gregory Caldiera, "Neither the Purse Nor the Sword," op. cit.

[98]Joseph Tanenhaus and Walter F. Murphy,"Patterns of Public Support for the Supreme Court: A Panel Study," *Journal of Politics* 43 (1981): 24–39.

[99]Gallup Poll, August 27, 1990.

[100]See Rehnquist, "Ruing Fixed Opinions," *New York Times*, February 22, 1988, p 290; and "Marshall Assails High-Court Practice of Ruling Without Hearing Dissenters," *Philadelphia Inquirer*, April 28, 1987, p. 10–A.

Other political actors beyond the Court have altered the dynamic of Court-press relations. Some interest group activity has strained the Court's image. Mass demonstrations and mail campaigns reinforce the image of the Court as a political institution vulnerable to political pressure. While the Court was deliberating *Webster v. Reproductive Health Services* during the 1988–1989 term, interest groups on both sides of the abortion issue placed advertisements on television and radio to influence public opinion and to encourage expression of that opinion to the justices. Pro-choice groups ran full-page advertisements in major newspapers directed at the justices. Both sides initiated letter-writing campaigns to the Court. Telephone calls and mail to the justices reached more than 40,000 daily prior to the Webster decision. In contrast, the Court normally receives 1,000 letters daily.[101] Both sides claimed the support of the public, while a profusion of media-generated public opinion polls appeared to assess such support. These efforts were directed not at elected officials, but squarely at the supposedly distant justices of the Supreme Court. Some even centered on a single justice—Justice O'Connor—widely described prior to the decision as the swing justice and therefore the one most susceptible to outside persuasion.

Not only are the justices not oblivious to these efforts, but some have publicly acknowledged dissatisfaction with the efforts to sway their votes. Justice Scalia, writing a concurrence in the *Webster v. Reproductive Health Services* case, referred to the "public's perception of the role of this Court" and, in lamenting the lack of finality of the decision, continued:

> We can now look forward to at least another Term with carts full of mail from the public, and streets full of demonstrators, urging us—their unelected and life-tenured judges who have been awarded those extraordinary, undemocratic characteristics precisely in order that we might follow the law despite the popular will—to follow the popular will. [102]

In his dissent to that majority opinion, Justice Blackmun similarly expressed concern about the public esteem for the Court in the wake of the decision. Similar comments emerged from the justices in their opinions in *Planned Parenthood v. Casey*.

The justices' concern over the propriety of these efforts may be heightened because of their actual effectiveness. For example, after moving in seemingly inexorable fashion toward a reversal of its *Roe v. Wade* decision, the Court, via *Planned Parenthood v. Casey*, chose a middle path between the pro-choice and pro-life camps. Not coincidentally, this option closely mirrored public opinion on abortion restrictions.[103] A clear majority of Americans supported the provisions of the Pennsylvania law.[104]

---

[101]"Mail on Abortion Deluges Court," *New York Times*, April 19,1989.

[102]Webster v. Reproductive Health Services, 492 U.S. 490 (1989) at 532.

[103]See, for example, E. J. Dione, Jr., "As the Polls Go, So Did the Justices In Allowing Limits," *Washington Post National Weekly Edition*, July 6–12, 1992, p. 7.

[104]For public support for the Pennsylvania law, as indicated by public opinion surveys, see NBC News/*Wall Street Journal* Survey, May 20, 1992, Question ID: USNBCWSJ.052092 R39C; NBC News/*Wall Street Journal* Survey, July 10, 1992, Question ID: USNBCWSJ.071092 R26A.

The Court's image also has been tarnished by the use of the confirmation process as an ideological tool by presidents, the Senate, and interest groups. High profile, controversial judicial nominations have not reinforced the Court's self-created image. Press coverage of the Robert Bork and Clarence Thomas nominations with extensive live television coverage of committee proceedings exceeded any ever experienced in a confirmation process. However, even other less-controversial nominees—Kennedy and Souter—were scrutinized to an extent rare in the history of the confirmation process.

Democratic party control of the Senate contributed to more extensive scrutiny, particularly given the Reagan and Bush administrations' stated intent to fill the Court with conservatives. With potentially controversial nominees—Bork and Thomas—presidents appeared to be declaring war on the Senate over the confirmation process.

Unlike past appointments where a small circle of legal and political elite competed internally, the confirmation process today is an event dominated by a public struggle among the elite. The general public is invoked by interest group allusions to the value of public opinion. Such a process is tailor-made for news media involvement and carries the potential of effectively stripping away the shroud surrounding the decision-making activities as well as the human nature of the justices of the Supreme Court.

Confirmation hearings have not been the only times when the battle has been waged. The Court has been treated as a political football in presidential campaigns. In 1988, Democratic candidate Michael Dukakis raised the issue of Court appointments, particularly the failed Robert Bork nomination, in one of his debates with George Bush. In 1992, Bill Clinton promised pro-choice groups that, if elected, he would appoint a justice who would vote to uphold *Roe v. Wade*.

Articulating the linkage between electoral results and Court policy has not been left to the presidential candidates, however. Justice Blackmun contributed to the discussion in 1988 when he remarked during the midst of the presidential campaign that if the Republican candidate triumphed the Court could become "very conservative well into the twenty-first century."[105] In 1992, Blackmun again stepped into the fray when, again during the campaign, he remarked in an opinion in *Planned Parenthood v. Casey* that "I am 83 years old. I cannot remain on this Court forever, and when I do step down the confirmation process for my successor well may focus on the issue before us today."[106]

A public debate over the Court's role exploded during the mid-1980s when Attorney General Edwin Meese questioned the Court's role as ultimate decoder of the Constitution, with Justice Brennan vigorously responding.[107] Other Reagan administration officials publicly criticized the Court's rulings and the views of specific justices.[108]

[105] Stuart A. Taylor, "Blackmun Has Sharp Opinions of Colleagues," *New York Times*, July 18, 1988.

[106] *Planned Parenthood of Southeastern Pennsylvania v. Casey*, 1992 U.S. Lexis 4751, 61.

[107] See Stuart A. Taylor, "Meese v. Brennan," *The New Republic* (January 6 & 13, 1986): 17–21.

[108] Stephen Wasby, *The Supreme Court in the Federal Judicial System*, pp. 315–316.

In the wake of these developments, the Court's effort to cultivate a public image via press coverage has acquired a new importance. The objectives of securing public deference and compliance are more essential now. In turn, the press' role as linking mechanism, despite its flaws, has become critical for the Court.

How the Court seeks to use the press, while maintaining the public stance that it does no such thing, is the purpose of the rest of this book.

Chapter Two

Institutionalizing
Press Relations

When John Jay was sworn in as the first chief justice of the United States, the United States had no national news media—no CNN, *Time*, *Washington Post*, or even *New York Times*. But the Court's interaction with the press corps is hardly a new phenomenon. The Court has been an object of news coverage since its inception in 1790. Some of these earlier stories covered more than just decisions. A major story in 1795 was the struggle over the confirmation of former Associate Justice John Rutledge as chief justice. Rutledge was ultimately rejected and his alleged attempted suicide shortly thereafter was a subject of much discussion in the press of the day.[1]

The justices have had a relationship with the press since the origin of the Court. Chief Justice John Marshall, a former secretary of state, not only kept abreast of political developments through his reading of several newspapers and pamphlets of his time, but he also wrote several newspaper essays during his tenure as chief justice.[2] Justice Joseph Story was a frequent essayist in the opinion journals of his day. He wrote on aspects of the law, but also published articles on other subjects including a campaign biography of Daniel Webster immediately preceding the 1836 presidential election.[3]

The Court became increasingly politicized and acquired increasing political importance during the 1820s and 1830s as evidenced by the fight over Roger

---

[1] For a sample of editorial opinion of the day, see *The Documentary History of the Supreme Court of the United States, 1789–1800*, Vol. 1, Part 2 (New York: Columbia University Press, 1985), pp.772–830.

[2] Letter to Timothy Pickering, June 7, 1824. See also Letter to Pickering, December 11, 1828. The Papers of John Marshall, Containers 2 and 3, Library of Congress, Washington, D.C.

[3] R. Kent Newmeyer, *Supreme Court Justice Joseph Story* (Chapel Hill, N.C.: University of North Carolina Press, 1985), pp. 118, 177, 245, 275, and 284–304.

Taney's appointment in 1835 and an earlier eventually fruitless congressional battle over judicial reorganization.[4] By the 1850s, the Taney Court was thrust into the middle of the slavery debate, which culminated in the *Dred Scott* case. The case received wide-spread newspaper attention both before and after the Court announced its decision.[5]

The press animated at least one justice late in the nineteenth century. Samuel Miller, who served on the Court from 1862 to 1890, remarked about the press:

> The newspaper tyranny is the most oppressive now in existence, and the gravest problem of the age is to determine where relief shall come from. They have invaded everything sacred to human nature....They have respected the Courts longer than anything else, and lately they have combined to bring the Courts and the administration of justice under their control, by their appeals to popular prejudice, accompanied by the usual amount of lying.[6]

But it was not until the 1930s and 1940s that the justices began to formalize their relations with the press. The Court opened a public information office to serve the press in 1935. At that time a Court employee was designated to work with the press. A full-time public information officer was appointed in 1947. Between the 1930s and the 1980s, the justices cultivated closer relations with the press.

Although the justices at this period, not unlike those of earlier periods, sought to convey the image of detachment from the press, they were also not unlike their predecessors in their actual interest in press coverage of themselves.

One biographer of Abe Fortas wrote that Fortas held a "hatred of the press," labeling reporters "dirty" and "crooked."[7] William O. Douglas, who was known for his absolutist approach to the First Amendment, had little use for the press when he felt reporters violated his privacy. In his autobiography of his years in the Court, Douglas began a chapter devoted to the press with the charge that they were "depraved."[8] He concluded that during his years on the Court most newspapers used the editorial page as "a club by the publisher against the Court."[9]

These justices' attitudes about the press suggest their attention to press coverage of themselves and the Court and their concern that the Court had not been covered well.

As an institution whose personnel are unelected and unrepresentative, any accommodations to the press would appear unnecessary. The Court would seem to have no direct accountability to the press except to perform its constitutional functions well.

---

[4]Ibid., pp. 311–316.

[5]Carl B. Swisher, *History of the Supreme Court of the United States, Volume V: The Taney Period 1836–1864* (New York: Macmillan, 1974), pp. 592–622.

[6]Charles Fairman, *Mr. Justice Miller and the Supreme Court 1862–1890* (Cambridge, Mass.: Harvard University Press, 1939), p. 279.

[7]Bruce A. Murphy, *Fortas* (New York: William Morrow, 1988), pp. 229–230.

[8]William O. Douglas, *The Court Years 1939–1975* (New York: Random House, 1980), pp. 197.

[9]Ibid., p. 206.

However, as discussed in the preceding chapter, the Court does have an interest in press and public reaction. Moreover, since the press, as the primary medium for public knowledge of the Court's decisions, possesses a vital role in public understanding and appreciation for the Court's actions, the Court can ill afford to ignore it. The Court has been seen as the institution least understood by Americans. It relies on the press to correct that condition. Therefore, the Court's accommodating the press aids reporters in educating the news audience about the Court and its opinions.

Between 1930 and 1980, the justices were cognizant of this problem of poor Court coverage and sought some corrective. For example, during his confirmation hearings for chief justice in 1968, Abe Fortas, then an associate justice, in a letter to Senator James Eastland, expressed his support for increasing public education about the Court. Fortas wrote that this need would have to be met by facilitating press understanding of the Court and its opinions. Fortas also mentioned that the justices had been examining the solutions to this very problem.[10]

From the 1930s through the 1980s, the relationship between the Court and the press became institutionalized. Routines for interaction were established through both formal channels and informal channels. In fact, the process of institutionalization is still dynamic, as will be discussed in succeeding chapters.

This institutionalization process resulted from a perception that the image of the Court had been tarnished. The Court's image problems prompted the justices to exert more effort in shaping their own portrayal of the Court. The Court has done so by accommodating the press, surveying the press' coverage of the Court, and seeking to shape the image of the Court in the press portrayal.

Tarnishing the Image

The Court's image was severely threatened by events in the mid-1930s. The most potent threat to the Court's independence was the court-packing plan proposed by President Roosevelt in 1937.

The plan emerged only after a period of criticism of the Court for its unwillingness to sanction the constitutionality of the New Deal. Severe criticism of the Court's decisions arose from some prominent newspapers. Harlan Stone commented in a letter to his sister at the end of the 1935 term: "We finished the term of Court yesterday. I think in many ways one of the most disastrous in its history."[11]

Moreover, the Court itself had come under scrutiny. Washington muckraker Drew Pearson had written about "the nine old men" on the Supreme Court.[12] Pearson and his co-author had intended to remove the "veil of sanctity" from the

[10]Letter from Abe Fortas to Senator James O. Eastland, July 19, 1968, William O. Douglas Papers, Box 1429, Library of Congress, Washington, D.C.

[11]Alpheus Thomas Mason, *Harlan Fiske Stone: Pillar of the Law* (New York: Viking Press, 1956), p. 425.

[12]Drew Pearson and Robert S. Allen, *The Nine Old Men* (Garden City, N.Y.: Doubleday, Doran 1936).

Court and reveal "the very human virtues and failings of the nine old men and their astounding power over the welfare of the country and of every man and woman in it."[13] Other exposés of the justices and the Court have since followed.[14]

The president's plan was an outgrowth of this expected weakening of the public's respect for the institution. On the heels of a landslide reelection, Roosevelt perceived himself as strong and the Court as weak. However, he confused public dissatisfaction with the Court's decisions as a mandate for restructuring the Court itself. Due to a wellspring of public support for the Court's independence, the judicial branch was not as vulnerable as Roosevelt had assumed.

The justices publicly fought back. In response to the court-packing plan, Chief Justice Hughes wrote a lengthy letter to the Senate Judiciary Committee considering the president's proposal. In the letter, which was published in newspapers, Hughes denied Roosevelt's claim that the Court was laggard in its responsibilities.[15] The letter was the result of a deal between Senator Burton Wheeler, who opposed the court-packing plan, and Hughes to provide ammunition for the plan's critics.[16] Hughes also gave a speech to the American Law Institute and announced that "I am happy to report that the Supreme Court is still functioning." The speech was reported in major newspapers around the country.[17]

Apparently, the justices also attempted to portray themselves as more human in order to attract public support. They appeared for a March of Time newsreel showing the justices on their way to or at work in their offices.[18]

The Court not only changed its public relations campaign, but also it altered its direction. The Court began to rule favorably on New Deal legislation. This change brought criticism from several sources that the justices had responded to political pressure. One writer remarked that "Americans learned that judges are human, and that the judicial power need be no more sacred in our scheme than any other power...." Another derided Hughes's claim that the Court had been consistent throughout by remarking that "[w]e are told that the Supreme Court's about-face was not due to outside clamor. It seems that the new building has a sound-proof room, to which the Justices retire to change their minds."[19]

[13]Drew Pearson and Robert S. Allen, *Nine Old Men at the Crossroads* (Garden City, N.Y.: Doubleday, Doran, 1937), "A Note to the Reader."

[14]See, for example, Wesley McCune, *The Nine Young Men* (New York: Harper & Brothers, 1947); Fred Rodell, *Nine Men: A Political History of the Supreme Court from 1790 to 1955* (New York: Random House, 1955); and, a much later contribution to the genre, Robert Woodward and Scott Armstrong, *The Brethren* (New York: Simon & Schuster, 1979).

[15]"Chief Justice Hughes's Letter Denying Court is Inefficient," *New York Herald Tribune*, March 22, 1937.

[16]See Alpheus Thomas Mason, *The Supreme Court From Taft to Burger* (Baton Rouge: Louisiana State University Press, 1979), p. 103–106.

[17]Quoted in Ibid., 100–101.

[18]Pearson and Allen, *Nine Old Men at the Crossroads*, pp. 25–29.

[19]Quoted in Alpheus Thomas Mason, *The Supreme Court From Taft to Burger* (Baton Rouge: Louisiana State University Press, 1979), p. 112.

The court-packing plan was not the only threat to the Court's image of political aloofness. Some of the Court's decisions in the late 1930s and 1940s attracted widespread criticism. Prominent among those were the flag salute cases. In the *Gobitis* case, the Court approved of a mandatory flag salute in public schools.[20] The *Gobitis* case was criticized in press editorials. One hundred and seventy-one newspapers disapproved of the decision. The St. Louis *Post-Dispatch* labeled it a "terrible decision."[21]

When the Court later overturned *Gobitis* in the *Barnette* case, the editorial response was positive.[22] One editorial articulated what many probably thought— that the Court was reacting to public opinion.

> The fact is that Justice Frankfurter's majority opinion in the *Gobitis* case was vastly unpopular, among lawyers and laymen alike. Justice Jackson's new majority opinion expresses the widespread feeling that religious liberty is too crucial to be tampered with, even in matters where reasonable legislators might disagree. The Constitution, in the long run, is what the people say it is.[23]

The justices had regained popular support for their decisions by changing direction. But the cost was the perception on the part of at least some observers that the Court could be dictated by public will.

Some of the justices themselves also provoked controversy during this period. An accusation of Hugo Black's continuing connections with the Ku Klux Klan was raised immediately after his confirmation in 1937 by a story in the *Pittsburgh Post-Gazette*. Although Black recovered from the incident, it did prompt him to take the highly unusual step—for a justice—of delivering a nationwide radio address defending himself.[24] Black later became involved in a rare public fight with his fellow justice, Robert Jackson, demonstrating to the public the animosity between the two.[25]

Other news stories in the 1930s and 1940s reported sharp personal conflicts on the Court involving several of the justices. For example, Harlan Stone was the source for a critique that appeared in *Harper's* claiming Hugo Black as a new justice was not carrying his share of the Court's load and that his mistakes had shocked his colleagues.[26]

---

[20]Minersville School District v. Gobitis, 310 U.S. 586 (1940).

[21]Alpheus Thomas Mason, *Harlan Fiske Stone: Pillar of the Law* (New York: Viking Press, 1956), p. 532.

[22]West Virginia State Board of Education v. Barnette, 319 U.S. 624 (1943).

[23]*New York Symbol*, June 18, 1943, Harlan F. Stone Papers, Box 81, Library of Congress, Washington, D.C.

[24]Henry J. Abraham, *Justices and Presidents*, 2d ed. (New York: Oxford University Press, 1985), pp. 212–213.

[25]Howard Ball and Phillip J. Cooper, *Of Power and Right: Hugo Black, William O. Douglas, and America's Constitutional Revolution* (New York: Oxford University Press, 1992), pp. 93–98.

[26]Alpheus Thomas Mason, *Harlan Fiske Stone: Pillar of the Law* (New York: Viking Press, 1956), pp. 472–474.

The sources for the spate of stories apparently were justices. The rarity of this information becoming public was noted by the author of one article who, after hearing three justices on different occasions openly describe the internal tension, opined that "[t]here was a time when gossip by a Supreme Court justice about anything occurring within the court's sacred precincts was unthinkable."[27]

Other criticism of the Court stemmed from mediocre nominations. President Harry Truman appointed four of his old friends to the Supreme Court provoking the charge of cronyism.[28] Three of these four justices have had their performance on the Court ranked by Court scholars as "failures."[29]

The justices experienced another traumatic decade in the court of public opinion during the 1960s and early 1970s. These decades were punctuated with controversial extrajudicial activities of justices (one of which resulted in resignation and the other in attempted impeachment), and naked attempts at court-packing by the Johnson and Nixon administrations.

The extrajudicial activity of Abe Fortas, which became public during his confirmation hearings for chief justice in 1968 provoked a public controversy.[30] This was accompanied by a wide perception that Lyndon Johnson was attempting to pack the Court with his cronies—long-time friend Abe Fortas as chief justice and Judge Homer Thornberry, another old friend of Johnson, as Fortas's replacement. (Three years earlier, Johnson had played with the Court's personnel by persuading Arthur Goldberg to resign as an associate justice and become U.S. ambassador to the United Nations. Fortas was then named as his successor.) Newspaper editorials were critical of Fortas's close ties with Johnson.[31] Fortas subsequently withdrew his nomination when Republicans successfully filibustered. However, the tarnished image lingered.

The Court's problems continued when Fortas's financial dealings came under public scrutiny in 1969. The initiator of the scrutiny was a *Life* magazine story accusing Fortas of receiving a $20,000 payment from a foundation headed by a man convicted of illegal stock trading activity.[32]

One biographer of Fortas asserted that "the press hounded Fortas" into resignation from the Court. It was unusual coverage for a Supreme Court justice. Reporters staked out his house and tailed him at public appearances. A plethora of

---

[27]Jay G. Hayden, "Supreme Court Feud," *Detroit News*, February 3, 1944. See also Drew Pearson and Robert S. Allen, "Justice Frankfurter: A Powerful Prompter in U.S. War Policies," *Philadelphia Record*, June 1, 1942; and George Riley, "Frankfurter Dropped as F.D. Confidant," (Washington) *Times-Herald*, June 4, 1942. Copies of all three articles can be found in William O. Douglas Papers, Box 308 and Box 571, Library of Congress, Washington, D.C.

[28]Henry J. Abraham, *Justices and Presidents*, 2d ed. (New York: Oxford University Press, 1985), pp. 237–238.

[29]Albert P. Blaustein and Roy M. Mersky, *The First One Hundred Justices: Statistical Studies on the Supreme Court of the United States* (Hamden, Conn.: Archon Books, 1978), pp. 32–40.

[30]Laura Kalman, *Abe Fortas* (New Haven, Conn.: Yale University Press, 1990), pp. 337, 51.

[31]Murphy, op. cit., pp. 438–439.

[32]Kalman, op. cit., pp. 359–370.

news stories appeared about Fortas suggesting additional ethically questionable practices.[33] Editorials criticized Fortas's behavior, and soon after some called for his resignation.[34]

Other appointments tarnished the image of the Court. President Richard Nixon, who had campaigned for the presidency partly by criticism of Supreme Court decisions, made two nominations to the Court that were rejected by the Senate.[35]

In turn, the Nixon administration instigated the introduction of an impeachment resolution against William O. Douglas. Although the effort led nowhere, Douglas's extrajudicial activities—including his writings and personal lifestyle— were criticized by some as inappropriate for a justice.

Accommodating the Press

In the face of these problems, the Court sought to utilize the press to attain the desired image of an independent body governed by the Constitution and the law. Over a period of time, the Court commenced a policy of accommodating the press to foster coverage of the Court's decisions.

Initial accommodation and the commencement of the institutionalization of the Court's relationship with the press came with the construction of a new Supreme Court building. Initiated by William Howard Taft, the building was designed to be a proper housing for the third branch of the government. The first plans for the new Supreme Court building had no provisions for a press room. The ground floor was reserved for the clerk, pages, a cafeteria, and storage. But a letter from the architect describing the space requirements in the new building for various groups lists rooms for reporters, along with space for the attorney general, the solicitor general, and members of the bar. But, the Court was a laggard in offering physical housing for the press. The galleries in both houses of Congress and the White House Press Room had long since been in operation. Nevertheless, the Court was not anxious for its new accommodation of the press to be readily visible. The architect intended at least three rooms for reporters and in recommending the location for these rooms noted that they "need not be near courtroom, and preferably as far as possible from visitors."[36] (Even today, the Court discourages visitors from venturing down the corridor near the press-room.)

The justices went beyond physical facilities in aiding the press. In 1935, in the midst of public criticism of the Court's anti–New Deal rulings, the justices established a public information office to assist reporters in their coverage of the

---

[33]Murphy, op. cit., pp. 376–377; and Kalman, op. cit., pp. 370–376.

[34]Bruce A. Murphy, *Fortas* (New York: William Morrow, 1988), p.559.

[35]For a discussion of the appointments, see Abraham, *Justices and Presidents*, pp. 13–23.

[36]*United States Supreme Court Building, Letter from the Architect of the Capitol* (Washington, D.C.: Government Printing Office, 1929).

Court and to field queries from the public. According to the initial news stories on the Court, the office was created due to "the increasing prominence of the Court from a news standpoint."[37] The office was a direct response to press requests to the chief justice for assistance in covering the Court. In order to reduce attention to the addition, the Court did not even officially announce the change.

Once again, the Court was the last of the three institutions to create a special office for handling press relations. The Congressional Press Gallery served as a central point for information about Congress. The White House had established a press office in Theodore Roosevelt's administration, 30 years earlier. But in 1935 the Court still had not offered a central resource center for information about its activity.

The Public Information Office initially was not much more than a Court employee distributing the opinions from the Court.[38] The press contact officer was not to have any interpretive responsibility. Reporters were told there would be no handouts or press releases. But its very existence was an indication that the Court was concerned about its public image and that it sought to affect it.

From the creation of the Public Information Office, the Court began to shape that image by accommodating reporters' needs in ways both large and small. Sometime in the late 1930s or early 1940s, the Public Information Office began distributing copies of the conference lists to reporters, whereas before that time reporters were not allowed to see the list.[39]

The justices used to read their opinions in full and then release them to reporters after they finished. But the justices stopped reading their opinions in full, except on rare occasions, and the Public Information Office began to provide them as soon as a justice began to announce the opinion.[40]

The release of large numbers of opinions at the end of the term frustrated reporters. The Court would release opinions only on Mondays, which necessitated a large number of releases at the end of the term on a single day. In 1965, after a lobbying campaign by reporters and others, the Court changed its procedure on delivering opinions just on Mondays in order to accommodate the press.[41]

---

[37]"Supreme Court Gets a Press Contact Man; Appointment Was Requested by Newspapers," *New York Times*, January 1, 1936, p. 2.

[38]See Lewis Wood, "Press Needs Met by Supreme Court," *New York Times*, January 5, 1936, p. 7.

[39]Memo to Chief Justice from John Davis, Clerk of the Court, June 9, 1969, William O. Douglas Papers, Box 1429, Library of Congress, Washington, D.C.

[40]Elder Witt, Guide to the Supreme Court (Washington, D.C.: CQ Press, 1990), p. 713.

[41]David L. Grey, *The Supreme Court and the News Media* (Evanston, Ill.: Northwestern University Press, 1968), pp. 36–37. For samples of pressure on the Court to alter its decision days, see letters to Earl Warren from James Reston, June 4, 1959 and from Representative Kenneth Keating of New York, June 12, 1958, Earl Warren Papers, Box 666, Library of Congress, Washington, D.C. See also a copy of a journal article found in Warren's papers—Donald H. Dalton, "Public Relations of the Supreme Court," *Chicago Bar Record*, (May 1960), pp. 409–411—where poor reporting was attributed to the practice of "judicial dumping"— releasing several major opinions on a single day.

Chief Justice Earl Warren admitted to Alfred Friendly, managing editor of the *Washington Post*, that the change was intended to aid the press. "The reporting of our decisions on days other than Mondays should be helpful to the press, and I hope that it will be."[42] If not only better but also more extensive coverage of the Court was the goal of the justices, Friendly complied, because he told Warren that the change would mean the *Post* would assign a full-time reporter to the Court.[43]

One of the difficulties for reporters was predicting when a decision day would occur. Reporters complained to the chief justice that they did not know when to come up to the Court.[44] In response, the Court changed its practice of not announcing the date of decision days.[45] The public information officer began to notify reporters in advance of days when decisions would be announced.

When Earl Warren retired in 1969, Warren Burger, his successor, looked like a chief justice out of central casting because of his wavy white hair and chiseled looks. But Burger was widely perceived as hostile to the press, particularly after publication of *The Brethren*. In fact, Burger was more receptive to press coverage than his predecessors. Burger's perceived hostility was a protectiveness on his part of the Court. But he also viewed the press as a useful tool for the Court. Hence, Burger attempted to facilitate press coverage of the Court, but only for the benefit of the Court.[46]

Burger enlarged the press section in the Court by moving it from a position in front of the justices to one at the left of the courtroom. Previously reporters sat at tables directly in front of the justices. But that arrangement accommodated only half a dozen reporters, whereas the new section sat 20 to 30 reporters and offered room for even more behind the curtains in an adjoining antechamber. The enlarged press section was essential given the growth in the size of the press corps. The number of reporters who specialized in legal affairs had increased from half a dozen to 25 or 30 by 1969.[47]

Not everyone preferred the move. One of the effects of the move was that reporters could no longer eavesdrop on the justice's whispers to each other while sitting on the bench. Some reporters complained that due to the poor acoustics in the courtroom, they could not even hear the justices or counsel from the new press section.

[42]Letter to Alfred Friendly, June 1, 1965, Earl Warren Papers, Box 666, Library of Congress, Washington, D.C.

[43]Letter to Earl Warren from Alfred Friendly, April 6, 1965.

[44]Letter from Mark H. Woolsey, *The United States Law Week*; Fred Graham, *New York Times*; and James E. Clayton, *The Washington Post*, October 6, 1965, Earl Warren Papers, Box 666, Library of Congress, Washington, D.C.

[45]Memorandum for the Clerk, November 16, 1966, Earl Warren Papers, Box 666, Library of Congress, Washington, D.C.

[46]Fred Graham, *Happy Talk* (New York: W. W. Norton, 1990), p. 100.

[47]Memo to Chief Justice from Bert Whittington, June 9, 1969, William O. Douglas Papers, Box 1429, Library of Congress, Washington, D.C.

Another accommodation was the release of headnotes with the body of the opinion at the time of decision announcement in order to aid reporters in understanding the result. Previously, headnotes were attached when the opinions were bound. But the change helped reporters scan the decisions more quickly and enhanced the accuracy of reporting.

Like the change in decision days, this policy reversal came after years of lobbying. Bert Whittington, the Court's public information officer from 1947 to 1973, also joined in the lobbying when he wrote to Earl Warren that the press had been helped by some of the justices writing summaries of their holdings at the beginning or the end of opinions.[48] William O. Douglas said he felt the move "measurably helped increase the accuracy of reports" about Court decisions.[49] But other justices initially objected, and the change did not occur until after they had left the bench.

Other suggestions by the press, however, were ignored. The Associated Press proposed the Court establish a policy of off-the-record elucidations of opinions by the justices. Ironically, Frankfurter, who spoke often to reporters, opposed such a policy.[50]

The Court moved from a posture of neglect to accommodations designed to ameliorate press coverage. In each case, the accommodation was not made solely to benefit the press. The change of policy had to be perceived as beneficial to the interests of the Court.

Surveying Press Coverage

At least some of the justices remained constantly aware of the press' portrayal of the Court during this period. William O. Douglas devoted several pages of an autobiography to assessing the accuracy of various newspapers and newsmagazines and to explaining why the Court fared poorly in the press; all suggesting his intense readership of the press.[51]

At least some of the justices kept press clippings and they often exchanged clippings with each other.[52] Some were found by the justices or their staff, while others, particularly favorable editorials, were sent, along with congratulatory notes, by newspaper editors sympathetic with the Court's actions.[53] These clippings

[48]Memo from Bert Whittington to Earl Warren, October 19, 1965, Earl Warren Papers, Box 666, Library of Congress, Washington, D.C.

[49]Douglas, op. cit., p. 206.

[50]Letter to the other justices, November 10, 1944, William O. Douglas Papers, Box 329, Library of Congress, Washington, D.C.

[51]William O. Douglas, *The Court Years 1937–1975* (New York: Random House, 1980), pp. 197–211.

[52]For samples of this practice, see Tom C. Clark file and Harold H. Burton file, Earl Warren Papers, Box 349, Library of Congress, Washington, D.C.

[53]For samples, see Earl Warren Papers, Box 574, Library of Congress, Washington, D.C.

included press coverage of decisions, particularly controversial ones.[54] At least several justices followed press reaction to the flag-salute cases.[55]

Some justices surveyed press coverage to determine if decisions were being interpreted the way the justices intended. Harold Burton, like several other justices during the Warren Court, sent Warren clippings of editorial reactions to Court actions. On one such clipping Burton penned: "This shows that the opinion is being understood and taken as it was intended to be taken—at least by the writer of this editorial."[56]

At the time of Roosevelt's court-packing plan, there was a plethora of news articles about the plan and reactions to it. Some of the justices clipped articles, editorials, and letters to the editor, especially those written in opposition to the plan.[57]

Some of the justices also kept track of what the press said about them personally. Robert Jackson clipped a large collection of news stories about his public dispute with Hugo Black in 1946.[58] Within the confines of the Court, Felix Frankfurter criticized a *Washington Post* reporter's implication that Frankfurter did not write as many opinions as other justices.[59]

Some also kept track of what the press said about other justices.[60] At times this surveillance of the press was employed to see old scores settled. William Douglas, who clashed often with Frankfurter, clipped several newspaper articles speculating that Frankfurter was losing influence on the Court.[61] Douglas, or another justice who disliked Frankfurter, may even have been the source for the articles. Douglas also followed press coverage of Earl Warren, who, for a period, he intensely disliked. Writing of Warren, Douglas remarked: "The Washington press is, I think, now laying in wait for the old boy to pop off once more. The truth is, I think, that Earl Warren is a cheap politico...."[62] Charles Evans Hughes followed the press accusations that Harlan Stone was attacking Hugo Black surreptitiously through the press.[63] When Harold Burton was attacked as a poor worker on the Court by a Drew Pearson

---

[54]See Charles Evans Hughes Papers, Reel 135; Harlan F. Stone Papers, Box 81, Library of Congress, Washington, D.C.

[55]See Robert Jackson Papers, Box 26, Library of Congress, Washington, D.C.

[56]For samples of this correspondence, see the Harold H. Burton and Tom C. Clark files, Earl Warren Papers, Box 349, Library of Congress, Washington, D.C.

[57]See, for example, Charles Evans Hughes Papers, Reels 131 and 144; and George Sutherland Papers, Box 7, Library of Congress, Washington, D.C.

[58]Robert Jackson Papers, Box 26, Library of Congress, Washington, D.C.

[59]Douglas, *The Court Years*, p. 205.

[60]See Robert Jackson Papers, Boxes 228, 229, and 230, Library of Congress, Washington, D.C.

[61]See William O. Douglas Papers, Box 329, Library of Congress, Washington, D.C.

[62]Letter to Sherman Minton, May 8, 1961, William O. Douglas Papers, Box 329, Library of Congress, Washington, D.C.

[63]Charles Evans Hughes Papers, Reel 144, Library of Congress, Washington, D.C.

article in the *Washington Post*, not only did Burton take note of the article, but so did almost all of the other justices.[64]

One recurring subject of press interest and, as measured by the clippings kept by some of the justices, their subject of interest as well, was that of future political offices for some of them. During the 1940s, William O. Douglas and Robert Jackson were touted as possible vice-presidential choices. Jackson kept track of the speculation about himself.[65]

Shaping the Image

The justices during this period did more than just follow press coverage; they attempted to shape the image of the Court through it. Their attempts were not overt, but congenial with their desired image of aloofness.

Generally, the justices held to an unwritten tradition of not replying publicly to press coverage of the Court. George Sutherland remarked in a letter to U.S. Senator Tom Connally that he made it a practice, to "almost never comment upon what is said about the Court."[66] Earl Warren, ironically in the middle of a television interview, announced that he upheld this practice, commenting that "[the Court] never can answer its critics and when all the public hears is one side, one never can tell what lodges in their minds and what they think."[67]

On-record interviews and press conferences were rare. But there were notable exceptions. Earl Warren gave several interviews where he discussed the Court.[68] Hugo Black was interviewed on CBS by Eric Severeid on December 3, 1968. Black also held a news conference on the celebration of his eighty-fifth birthday.[69]

The tradition has extended to involvement in debates about current issues. Some of the justices chafed over that practice. In a speech reported in the *New York Times*, Wiley Rutledge complained that there were too many limitations on the justices' ability to speak out.[70] William O. Douglas, with his propensity for extensive writing, often violated that tradition.[71] Douglas appeared for interviews on

---

[64]Mary Frances Berry, *Stability, Security, and Continuity: Mr. Justice Burton and Decision-making in the Supreme Court 1945–1958* (Westport, Conn.: Greenwood Press, 1978), pp. 88–89.

[65]See Robert Jackson Papers, Box 229, Library of Congress, Washington, D.C.

[66]Letter to Senator Tom Connally, January 11, 1937, George Sutherland Papers, Box 6, Library of Congress, Washington, D.C.

[67]Transcript, "A Conversation with Earl Warren," Broadcast by McClatchy Broadcasting Stations, June 25, 1969, Earl Warren Papers, Box 846, Library of Congress, Washington, D.C.

[68]For samples, see Gilbert Cranberg, "The Court and Its Public: Warren's View," *Des Moines Register*, October 16, 1966; Letter to Jim Karayan, June 25, 1969; David Burnham, "The Warren Court: Fateful Decade," *Newsweek*, May 11, 1964; and John D. Weaver, "The Honorable Earl Warren," *Holiday*, April, May, and June 1966 issues. Copies of the articles are located in Earl Warren Papers, Box 666 and Box 6, Library of Congress, Washington, D.C.

[69]Hugo L. Black, *Mr. Justice and Mrs. Black* (New York: Random House, 1986), p. 257.

[70]William O. Douglas Papers, Box 388, Library of Congress, Washington, D.C.

[71]For a list of his writings, see Index, William O. Douglas Papers, Library of Congress, Washington, D.C.

several television shows. On one program he defended himself against critics who argued he should not speak out on issues by replying he should have "full-fledged citizenship and therefore participate in all public affairs that didn't involve the work of the Court...."[72]

The justices occasionally did respond to news stories about them and the Court's work. Earl Warren wrote congratulatory notes to journalists. He wrote to an ABC News reporter that he was "pleased beyond words" with the reporter's coverage of the *Miranda* decision.[73]

News coverage contradictory to the Court's or the justices' image of aloofness were discouraged. Earl Warren requested Drew Pearson not publish an article Pearson had written that discussed Warren's dislike for Richard Nixon.[74] In order to affect reporting of the Court, Warren Burger was not above bypassing the reporters and complaining directly to news executives about their reporters.[75]

On the other hand, potentially useful stories for the Court's image were encouraged. Earl Warren sat for an on-record interview with a *Newsweek* reporter after the reporter explained this would be a "friendly" story.[76]

Generally, the justices' direct interaction with the press consisted of background sessions with reporters. According to one newspaper account, Frankfurter was widely known in Washington for holding "secret press conferences with newspaper favorites."[77] Harlan Stone was widely insinuated as the primary source for a controversial article on the inner tensions among the justices that appeared in *Harper's* magazine in 1938.[78]

Off-the-record meetings with reporters were not infrequent.[79] Earl Warren occasionally met with reporters.[80] Near the end of his term, Potter Stewart lunched

---

[72]See William O. Douglas Papers, Box 848, Library of Congress, Washington, D.C.

[73]Letter to Edward P. Morgan, June 25, 1966, Earl Warren Papers, Box 617, Library of Congress, Washington, D.C.

[74]Letter to Drew Pearson, August 19, 1968, Earl Warren Papers, Box 6, Library of Congress, Washington, D.C.

[75]Bob Woodward and Scott Armstrong, *The Brethren* (New York: Simon & Schuster, 1979), pp. 281–282.

[76]Memorandum from Bert Whittington to the Chief Justice, April 8, 1964, Earl Warren Papers, Box 6, Library of Congress, Washington, D.C.

[77]George Riley, "Frankfurter Dropped as F.D. Confidant," (Washington) *Times-Herald*, June 4, 1942.

[78]Marquis W. Childs, "The Supreme Court To-Day," *Harper's* May 1938, pp. 581–588. For the insinuation, see Paul Y. Anderson, "Marquis Childs and Justice Black," *The Nation*, May 21, 1938, p. 579.

[79]For example, see Alpheus Thomas Mason, *Brandeis: A Free Man's Life* (New York: Viking Press, 1956), p. 620.

[80]See, for example, samples of Warren's correspondence with representatives of the press: Letter from Lester Velie, *Reader's Digest*, September 29, 1955; Letter from Paul F. Healy, *New York News*, October 30, 1958; Letter from Joseph Foote, September 17, 1965; and Letter from Earl Warren to Wes Gallagher, Associated Press, November 16, 1965. The above located in Earl Warren Papers, Box 666, Library of Congress, Washington, D.C.

with a *Time* reporter quarterly and regularly had luncheons, dinners, or other meetings with journalists from the *New York Times*, the *Washington Post*, and CBS News, and with columnists such as Joe Kraft, Rowland Evans, and Richard Reeves. Over a three year period, Stewart met with reporters 36 times.[81] Fred Graham considered Stewart a friend, and the justice frequented Graham's house.[82]

Another vehicle for affecting press coverage was shaping the training of journalists. Some of the justices apparently were disturbed by the quality of Court reporting. This concern was shared by others. In a 1956 speech to the National Conference of Editorial Writers, Max Freedman called the Court "the worst reported and worst judged institution in the American system of government."[83] Felix Frankfurter attempted to improve the quality of press coverage of the Court by urging reporters to acquire legal training. He successfully encouraged Anthony Lewis of the *New York Times* to study law at Harvard.[84] Lewis approached the beat quite differently from his predecessors. Lyle Denniston, Supreme Court beat reporter for the *Baltimore Sun* explained the difference between Lewis's reporting and others:

> Most of the journalists who cover the Court are covering it with their left hand while they cover Congress. They come across the street on decision day. No one before Tony tried to make a real beat out of that and really work the beat.

But Lewis also was criticized as being too sympathetic to the Court's interests. According to Denniston, Lewis worked to maintain good relationships with the justices: "Tony had good ties within the Court. Tony's copy kept those ties open. If you read Tony's copy, it isn't quite adoring but its pretty close to that. There was not a critical dimension to his assessment of the Warren Court and there still isn't."

Felix Frankfurter's assessment about Lewis's reporting reinforced the perception of coziness. Obviously pleased with Lewis's treatment of the Court, Frankfurter once remarked that "[t]here are not two members of the Court itself who could get the gist of each decision as accurately in so few words."[85]

But Lewis was not alone in highly sympathetic accounts of the Warren Court. One *Christian Science Monitor* article about the writer's interview with Earl Warren was almost fawning in tone: "A visit with Chief Justice Warren strengthens one in the belief that the American heritage of freedom will not dwindle but increase under those who comprise the judicial branch of the United States Government."[86]

---

[81]Potter Stewart Appointment Books 1977, 1978, 1979, Potter Stewart Papers, Manuscript Division, Yale Library, New Haven, Conn.

[82]Fred Graham, *Happy Talk* (New York: W. W. Norton, 1990), p. 118.

[83]Max Freedman, "Worst Reported Institution," *Nieman Reports* (1956). Quoted in Everette E. Dennis, "Another Look at Press Coverage of the Supreme Court," *Villanova Law Review* 20 (1974–1975): 765.

[84]Douglas, *The Court Years*, p. 205.

[85]Quoted in William L. Rivers, *The Other Government: Power and the Washington Media* (New York: Universe, 1982), p. 89.

[86]Max K. Gilstrap, "Warren Looks at American Scene From Vantage of High Court Post," *Christian Science Monitor*, June 3, 1957.

Sometimes this favorable reporting of a justice sparked resentment. William O. Douglas wrote to Hugo Black about a *New York Times* article about Felix Frankfurter. Douglas complained: "It makes out that of all the judges he is the only one who is objective...."[87]

The intent of legal training for reporters was to enhance their understanding of and appreciation for the Court's work. Since the primary visible product of the Court's work is the set of opinions delivered for each case, especially the majority opinion, the legal training should have facilitated more accurate coverage of that effort.

Along with legal training, the Court supported the attempt by the legal community to improve news coverage of decisions. The Association of American Law Schools (AALS) created a special committee to make recommendations for assistance to reporters. The AALS committee suggested distribution of pre-decision materials prepared by the legal community to educate reporters about the issues involved in pending decisions. Earl Warren became a strong advocate for the idea and helped arrange for law professors to receive briefs of cases as aids in writing press-oriented summaries of the issues before the Court.[88]

One development in press coverage may have hampered the justices' desire to focus coverage on their opinions. Television news coverage, like print, had primarily relied on the sources readily available at the Court or in Washington. CBS News correspondent Fred Graham decided to personalize the stories by traveling to the communities where the cases originated and by interviewing the parties in the case. This practice has now become standard for television news coverage of the Court.

There is not a lot of evidence that the decision-making process of the justices during this period was affected by the press. Felix Frankfurter once urged his colleagues to grant review of the *Rosenberg* case because of "heightened public feeling."[89]

Although the Court sought to affect the press' portrayal of the Court, there is little evidence that the relationship was a two-way street. If the justices themselves were significantly affected by what the press wrote about them, it is not obvious. The evidence of influence is difficult to obtain and somewhat speculative. For example, Harold Burton may have been wounded by the Drew Pearson article mentioned earlier because he noted the efforts of the other justices to console him.

One evidence that a justice may have been moved by press coverage about him is a remark by William O. Douglas about Hugo Black after Black had appeared for an interview with Eric Severeid on CBS television. Douglas concluded that

[87]Undated memorandum to Hugo Black, William O. Douglas Papers, Box 308, Library of Congress, Washington, D.C.

[88]Letter to Vern Countryman, Harvard Law School, June 24, 1964, Earl Warren Papers, Box 665, Library of Congress, Washington, D.C.

[89]Undated memorandum, Robert Jackson Papers, Box 183, Library of Congress, Washington, D.C.

Black had been changed by the experience—his only television interview in his life—and that the change was in the direction of increased criticism of the Court:

> Ever since HLB's TV show on December 3, 1968, he has turned the corner and become more and more critical of the Court. A few weeks after the TV show he left the Conference saying he had 2,000 letters to answer from people who had seen the show. He became, as the weeks passed, more and more critical of the Court. Apparently the public reaction he received from his TV show made him realize that criticism of the Court had become popular.[90]

Douglas went on to note that during a conference Black denounced the Court and blamed it for increased crime.

There is also little evidence to determine whether press coverage of the justices affects their relations with each other. Bob Woodward and Scott Armstrong related that in one of the conferences in 1976 an argument ensued among the justices over a newspaper article quoting two unnamed justices making derogatory remarks about two other justices.[91]

It was not editorial reaction to decisions, but the early announcement of decisions through leaks to the press that greatly disturbed Warren Burger. *Time* magazine and ABC News carried stories of pending decisions with accurate predictions of their outcome. Burger's anger over leaks during the 1972–1973 term led him to reject a suggestion for a "coffee hour" with clerks with the comment that "[b]ecause of last year's 'leaks' I was not in the mood to see law clerks generally, and if we have any more of last year's business there will be minimal interest." Though Burger did admit that the "security problem may have derived from the 'remoteness' [felt by clerks] you seek to remedy."[92]

Summary

The attempt to shape the image of the Court is not new. During the period from 1930 to 1980 the Court reacted to the press portrayal of itself by commencing a policy of accommodation with the press. It regularly surveyed press coverage, and several justices sought to shape the press' image of the Court, and of them personally.

---

[90]Conference notes on *Conway v. California*, January 1967, William O. Douglas Papers, Box 1429, Library of Congress, Washington, D.C.

[91]Woodward and Armstrong, *The Brethren*, pp. 526–527.

[92]Letter from Warren Burger to William Rehnquist, September 25, 1973, William O. Douglas Papers, Box 1622, Library of Congress, Washington, D.C.

Chapter Three

Speaking
for the Court

THE RITUAL

In the basement of the Supreme Court building, across from the cafeteria where tourists, clerks, reporters, and even justices share common meals, is the Public Information Office (PIO). Inside the four-room office are three public information officers and two secretaries.

On decision days, the hallway in front of the office is filled with representatives of law firms and various interest groups sitting on the few couches available or standing for an hour or two, shifting from one foot to the other. Most are messengers waiting to receive copies of the opinions to carry back to the legal staff or constitutional experts in their Washington offices.

The main room of the Public Information Office itself consists of an office filled with two desks and an open space no larger than 10 foot x 10 foot, where journalists gather shortly before 10 A.M. on decision days to receive copies of opinion. Three other offices, one for the public information officer and two for clerks and secretaries who handle the files of briefs and other case materials, are located nearby.

Near the end of the term, when reporters expect several opinions or at least one or two significant ones, the pressroom begins to fill shortly before 10 A.M. Thirty or more people will crowd into the available space. This number does not constitute the extent of the Supreme Court press corps because many reporters will have opted to go upstairs to sit in the press section of the courtroom and watch the justices announce the decisions. Others, especially those for the nondaily press, will not necessarily need the opinions immediately after their announcement and will pick them up later.

Those who choose to remain behind will gather around the two desks waiting for the moment of announcement upstairs. The desks of the main office are filled with papers. Reporters can speculate on the number of opinions for that day by counting the number of stacks. The nature of the opinions can be estimated by the height of the stacks, since more copies are printed when the PIO expects the decision to be highly newsworthy.

The decision day ritual begins at shortly after 10 A.M. The standing room only crowd of reporters waits in an eerie quiet, tensely punctuated by light banter but generally possessed with a sense of reverence for the procedure underway upstairs. Within two or three minutes, the phone rings on a desk in the main office. Toni House, the public information officer, picks up the receiver and listens while a clerk in the courtroom relays the number of the opinion just announced by the Court. She then announces the number to her assistants and the crowd of waiting reporters. She and her assistants then begin to dispense copies of that opinion.

With a great rustle of paper, thick packets including the majority opinion and any concurring and dissenting opinions are handed to the waiting press corps sandwiched between the desks and the door to the pressroom. Early arrivals who have positioned themselves directly in front of the desks hand packets backwards to the rest of the crowd. Nonregulars take only the opinions they have been assigned by their editors to cover. One returns a copy to House, commenting, "You can have this back."

Within two to three minutes, while reporters thumb quickly through their packets, usually in tense silence, the phone rings again and the ritual is repeated. When more than the usual time passes, light banter begins to ease the nervous tension. One reporter asks jokingly, "Someone reading a long dissent?"

Decisions are thumbed through rapidly. Someone yells, "This is the patronage case." After skimming the decision, he comments loudly, "You mean the Court just discovered there's politics."

Some think aloud as they read. "Still no lead," remarks one while thumbing rapidly. Another says, "Not page one, that's for sure." While standing, some in the crowd begin to take notes with one hand, holding the opinions in the other. The banter increases as the room grows hot and stifling with bodies packed tightly together. After reading one result, a reporter jokes, "I'll have to pull back my column for Sunday."

The crowd in the main office thins as the newsworthy cases are announced and some reporters move back to the pressroom to study them. This is especially true near the end of the term, when the short list of cases most reporters are following has been winnowed down to a few lingering decisions.

After a final telephone call, the public information officer announces, "That's it. See you Monday." Several reporters attempt to elicit more information about future decision days. "So we might be here all next week?" one queries her. "I don't know," comes the response.

As the rest of the crowd files out of the room, a buzzer sounds twice, signaling that the justices have left the bench. The PIO staff begin to distribute the rest of the opinions to the waiting line in the hallway and to prepare for a deluge of telephone calls throughout that day and the next from people asking for copies in response to the news coverage. They also save copies for the reporters who have walked upstairs to hear the opinions read in the courtroom. The Court typically prints 175 copies of the bench opinions, and the public information office usually distributes more than half of them within the first half hour.

The ritual shared by the Public Information Office staff and the press is not unlike that of the daily briefings in the White House or the State Department or the morning news briefing from the Speaker of the House. It is an attempt by the Court to focus press attention on its written product.

The frequency of the encounters differs sharply from those other offices. This ritual does not occur on a daily basis, with the occasional exception at the end of the term when the Court may sit in public session on a daily basis. But even that frequency is part of the message of the Court. It is saying, in effect, "we aren't trying to cultivate a public image. We're not out to manipulate the press." More frequent encounters might communicate a message of attempting manipulation. "We're not spin doctors, as it were," explains Toni House, the current public information officer. "It is a very different office from the other two branches."

THE MECHANICAL CHANNEL

Performance of this ritual is only one of the functions of the Public Information Office in its fulfillment of the mission to cultivate the public image of the Court. It is the job of the Public Information Office to assist in the maintenance of the public image of the Court. The PIO focuses press attention on the product by emphasizing it and hopefully by channeling press energy to the written opinions and away from the process and the individual justices. Written material is made available to reporters.

However, the Public Information Office does not ignore the Court's imperative to avoid the appearance of attempting to shape news coverage. The functions of the office are designed to reinforce the message that the Court is unconcerned about public opinion. Referring to crank calls and advocacy mail, House asserts, "People don't realize we [the Court] don't care what they think."

Even the title of the Court's press relations arm reflects its effort to disassociate itself with an image of media manipulation. While the title "press secretary" and "press office" have acquired wide acceptance in the parlance of government public relations, the Court prefers the more benign term "Public Information Office." The term connotes a mere conveyance role to the general public without specific reference to the primary mechanism of public knowledge, that is, the press.

It cannot be said that the Public Information Office is qualitatively different from any other government press office in this respect. Although the office does field requests from the public for information, it devotes most of its attention to the press corps housed only a few feet away in the adjoining pressroom. Witness, for example, the facilities provided regulars at the Court: a pressroom with certain amenities (to be described in the next chapter), as well as the priority given the press in distribution of copies of opinions.

The No Information Office

The mission of the Public Information Office is similar to that of other government public relations offices, but the tactics employed necessarily differ from those used elsewhere. The difference, according to Toni House, is that "we do not do spin."

By appearances, the office does not conform to the image of a public relations office. The common features of other government public relations offices, such as frequent press releases, advisory statements, and press secretary background briefings, are absent. News conferences are rare occasions at the Court. Access to the principal newsmakers at the Court is severely restricted. Complaints from reporters about lack of access, even to many parts of the building, fall on deaf ears. Reporters must cultivate their own relationships with the justices to obtain private access.

These differences sometimes lead to frustration over the Court's unwillingness to meet press imperatives. One reporter on the Court beat expressed this attitude about the Public Information Office:

> I don't consider it an information office. It ranges from no information to disinformation. Anybody who understands the English language can't help but be offended by the term "Public Information Office" at the Court.

Former *Time* reporter on the beat Jerome Cramer added, "It's the only beat in the federal government where if you ask them a question they just stare at you and say, 'That's your job. I'm not here to do that.'"

But the kind of information reporters expect from other government public relations offices is just not forthcoming from the Court's Public Information Office. In the sense that the Court does not offer the press substantive guidance in its work, it is a "no information" office. However, the Public Information Office does fill an important niche for reporters as a source for the documentary information the Court wants emphasized in coverage of itself.

Documentary Source

Reporters come to expect the Public Information Office to act as a "mechanical channel" but not as a repository of information beyond the mechanics of the process. Lyle Denniston of the *Baltimore Sun*, the dean of the Supreme Court press corps, explained:

> As a mechanical channel for documentary information, they're indispensable. I don't expect Toni and her staff to do anything for me other than get paperwork and answer pure process questions: Is this going to go to the conference or is an individual justice going to handle it?

The Public Information Office serves as an invaluable resource for the documentary information that reporters will use in planning and preparing, as well as writing, the stories they will submit about the Court. The ultimate written product is the opinion of the Court, which culminates the ritual described previously. However, the Public Information Office also provides other material supportive of the Court's emphasis on its written work.

A document usually highly coveted by the press is the *orders list*. Released primarily at the beginning of the term for that term, and near the end of the term for the next, the orders list announces those cases the Court will accept for oral argument. Since the Court's appellate jurisdiction offers the Court broad flexibility in its handling of cases, it typically hears only approximately 100 cases in a term from a pool of about 4,000 petitions for writ of certiorari or acceptance of review of a case.

The orders list enumerates those certiorari petitions granted as well as those denied. This list becomes the subject of stories as well as the basis for reporter preparation for stories about forthcoming arguments and decision announcements. The orders list also includes the summary dispositions of the Court. These are decisions made by the Court without hearing oral argument. These 100 to 200 decisions may be issued with a per curiam opinion by the justices. Other items included in the orders list are Court actions on stays of execution, disbarments from the Supreme Court bar, motions to file amici briefs, motions to participate in oral arguments, motions for additional time in oral arguments beyond the allotted 30 minutes, and motions for admission to the bar.

The Court also makes available to the press all the petitions for writ of certiorari, commonly known as "cert." petitions. The cert. petitions can become the basis for stories about cases appealed to the Court, especially on already newsworthy issues such as abortion or flag-burning.

Other documents the Public Information Office provides do not become the impetus for a news story, but contribute to story preparation and scheduling. These include the briefs of the parties to cases and the amici briefs.

A set of briefs on each case before the Court in the current term is available in the Public Information Office Document Room for perusal by reporters preparing for future stories. These include not only briefs from the parties in the case, but also amici briefs from various groups and organizations with an interest in the impending decision. Given reporter reliance on these briefs for understanding the facts and the issues of the cases under review, it is understandable that Lyle Denniston would call the PIO clerk who handles the briefs "the most useful person in the Public Information Office." The wire service reporters from the Associated Press and United Press International are provided their own set of briefs.

Reporters also receive a schedule of the oral arguments in order to plan argument stories. At the time of oral arguments, they are handed a sheet listing the cases to be argued that day, including the title of each case and the names and positions of the counsellors participating in argument. (See Appendix A.)

On a weekly basis during the term, the Public Information Office distributes the conference list to the press corps. Those cases to be discussed that week in the justices' conference are listed. These include petitions for certiorari, motions, applications for stay of execution, and petitions for rehearing. However, these lists do not appear in news stories because they are designed for the guidance of the press and not for publication.

The PIO offers a plethora of descriptive data for reporters to incorporate in their stories about the Court, but such descriptions also concentrate on the product of the Court's work. These statistics, which usually compare the current term with past ones, include the number of pauper cases, the number of original cases, the number of cases argued and submitted, and the number of cases disposed by per curiam opinion.

Reporting Justices' Activities

Although nearly all of the written material proffered by the Public Information Office is related to cases, some is not. Other statements or advisories to the press appear infrequently. These include the texts of speeches that justices give at law schools, bar association meetings, or before other groups, and the text of testimony on Capitol Hill by junior justices lobbying for the Court's annual budget. On special occasions, the PIO dispenses more personal information on the justices, such as statements about the resignation or the medical status of a justice. (See Appendix A.)

The Public Information Office publishes *The Docket Sheet*, a quarterly newsletter of Supreme Court activities. Although the newsletter is designed as the internal Court organ, at times it contains articles useful to the press. On occasion, interviews with the justices conducted by Public Information Office personnel attract press attention. An interview with Justice Kennedy, conducted when he was a new member of the Court, was quoted in news stories.

THE SCREEN

Another function of the Public Information Office is to act as a screening mechanism for the justices. The justices expect the Public Information Officer to ward off the inquiries of the press and the public. Officially, the justices have positioned the public information officer between themselves and the press. "I think her job is to deter people," explained Miranda Spivack of the *Hartford Courant*. "That may be what her marching orders are—keep [the press] away from us."

One example is the office's role as dispenser of trivia about the justices or the Court that is used for detail in stories or simply to satisfy public curiosity. We get questions in here like what kind of pen does Justice O'Connor use, what does she eat for breakfast? What kind of a car does she drive? Who was your role model when you were growing up? Were you a Boy Scout? Were you a Girl Scout? Stuff like that.

The screening function is designed to help distance the justices from the press corps. Hence, the PIO serves not as an extra appendage to the functions of the Court, but as a valuable buffer between them and the press corps, some of whom would attempt to humanize the justices if they possessed the information to do so.

The screening role apparently is not merely the public information officer's self-perception, but one adopted by the justices. "I've been here eight years and the justices and I understand each other," said Toni House. "They understand that I'm in the middle and that I try to shield them from the silliness to the extent that I can."

The public information officer screens out a variety of press requests. For example, press requests for explanations of refusals to hear cases. Some of the justices—Kennedy, Scalia, and Thomas—have established a policy that they will not reveal why they are out in a case. Others will do so. "If we know that they have a policy, why bother to go to them," explained House.

However, the screening function is not designed to leave the justices ignorant about the interests of the press. According to House, it is her job to keep them informed of those interests. "They prefer to know what's going on. They don't want to bump into a reporter at a reception and have the reporter say 'I'm sorry I bothered you about what kind of pen you use' and have the justice say 'what?'"

The Public Information Office does not serve the same functions for the press as other government public relations offices, and journalists who cover the Court learn not to rely on the Public Information Office for the type of information they would receive elsewhere. Tony Mauro, *USA Today* reporter at the Court, illustrates how he was reminded of this difference:

> I had heard Carl Rowan was writing a book with Marshall. I had heard the deal had broken off. I went to Toni House and said, "I need to get comment from Marshall." She said, "You're chances of getting an answer out of Marshall are as good as mine. You call."

However, individual justices, in accordance with their high degree of independence, choose the Public Information Office as a screen. Some justices, particularly the chief justice, use the office extensively, others do not. According to House, Thurgood Marshall "preferred to conduct his own press relations such as they were. So we just told people to call his chambers direct...." However, for reporters without their own personal relationships with the justices, which constitutes the majority of those who cover the Court, the Public Information Office is an initial contact.

The public information officer does play a role in arranging press interviews with justices, although the Court's policy is that the justices do not grant interviews. What that means for the public information officer is that almost every interview request will be denied. But some arranged through the Public Information Office are accepted. According to House, "the bicentennial of the Constitution [in 1987] or the bicentennial of the Court itself [in 1990] has served as an opportunity for the justices to feel more comfortable about granting interviews."

The justices have their own policies for press coverage when away from the Court as well. Whereas Antonin Scalia is opposed to television cameras recording his speeches, William Rehnquist is comfortable with cameras.

For House, inconsistency in usage can magnify press-relations problems. Some justices support the concept of the public's right to know about their personal activities, particularly their medical history. For example, on February 26, 1992, Justice Stevens provided the Public Information Office with a statement announcing his prostate cancer. Others have not been forthcoming. The hospitalization of William Rehnquist and Lewis Powell in the early 1980s was not announced, and a visit by Justice Blackmun to the Mayo Clinic was not disclosed until rumors abounded. According to House, the PIO "certainly will notify when they're hospitalized. If we know where they are and why they're there." The problem for her is the justices don't always tell her or anyone.

As mentioned earlier, the justices also choose whether to announce their reasons for a decision to recuse themselves from cases. Absent a stated reason, the press speculate on the cause of the justice's action. "We know the justices are honorable and honest people," commented Nina Totenberg of National Public Radio. "But when they refuse to explain the reasons for disqualifying themselves, the public will tend to think the worst, unnecessarily."[1]

Resignations serve as another example. The justices are hardly uniform in the scenarios of their resignation announcements. At times the PIO is left dangling without information.

One of the biggest stories on the Supreme Court beat in the 1980s was the retirement of Chief Justice Burger on June 17, 1986, and the announcement of the nomination of his successor, Associate Justice William Rehnquist, and, in turn, of his successor, Antonin Scalia. But Burger's manner of announcement circumvented the Court's own established public relations arm. "Chief Justice Burger chose to do it at the White House," House lamented, "much to my dismay because it left our own reporters flatfooted." Implicitly, House is saying it also left the PIO "flatfooted."

Justice Brennan's announcement of retirement on July 20, 1990 similarly revealed the justices' peculiaristic treatment of the PIO. Brennan's imminent resignation leaked out to several reporters during that day, but before the PIO was alerted to it. Toni House admitted to reporters that, like them, her information was limited to rumors. While Stephen Wermiel, former Supreme Court reporter for the *Wall Street Journal* and author of a biography-in-progress about Brennan, was fielding calls from reporters from Brennan's chambers about the resignation, the PIO still labored without official word from Brennan.

Others have utilized a format that clues in the PIO before others. In 1987, Justice Powell, for example, informed House prior to his resignation announcement. House explained:

> Justice Powell had the chief justice announce his retirement from the bench....He had prepared a statement. He called me that morning and told me what he was doing. A justice calls you at 9:20 and says can you stop up to my chambers, you have a pretty good idea. He had prepared a statement of his own that we had duplicated. When the

[1]Mitchell J. Tropin, "What, Exactly, Is the Court Saying?" *The Barrister* (Winter 1984): 14.

call came from the bench that the retirement had been announced, we had copies of the statement to hand to people.

Some of the justices will provide the Public Information Office with texts of speeches they have delivered or will deliver. The chief justices have done so, as have other justices, such as Justice Marshall. But others, like Justice Blackmun and Justice O'Connor have declined to do so. The Public Information Office can encourage usage, but compulsion is not possible. Public information officers past and present have sent memos to the justices constantly pleading with them to alert them of pending speeches and to provide texts for the press. They have attempted to persuade the justices to utilize the office more.

> We would like to be able to tell our press corps when the justices are giving a speech, and where, and make text available. It's been very hard to wrestle into submission. Again, because they don't think public relations. They think "I'm going out and I'm going to make a speech. And I'm going to make it as low key as possible." To the extent that we can get to them and ask them for the text, five of the nine give us texts. Some of them remember to give us speeches and some we have to inquire if we hear about it.

Since individual justices vary in their approach to the press, it becomes important to clarify each justice's policy on information dispersal. When a new justice comes on the Court, the Public Information Office attempts to ascertain their policies.

But clarification alone is not the ultimate objective. The Public Information Office seeks greater use of the office and more extensive cooperation with the press in responding to requests for information about upcoming speeches, serious medical problems, and pending resignations of the justices.

The Public Information Office does not offer the amenities of press-relations offices elsewhere. However, it does serve as a "mechanical channel" for reporters. The "care and feeding of the press corps" is directed at offering written documentary information, almost exclusively case-related, with the expectation that reporters will take the hint and follow the Court's lead in news coverage emphasis. The role of the Public Information Office is to dispense that written material while simultaneously attempting to fend off other approaches by acting as a screen for the justices.

THE PROTECTOR OF THE IMAGE

The public information officer is expected to help preserve the image of the Court and the individual justices. By screening press requests, offering the official information the Court provides, facilitating press access to the aspects of the Court's activity that the justices want known, and aiding in closing off access to other facets of the Court, the public information officer helps communicate the messages designed to foster the desired image of the Court.

This protector role can also extend to the individual justices. When he was a public information officer, Barrett McGurn was asked by Warren Burger to blunt reports that the Nixon tapes opinion was not his. McGurn called a meeting of reporters to dispute the reports by detailing Burger's work on the case.[2]

The protector role can also be carried out more quietly. In another situation, McGurn helped William O. Douglas handle media criticism. In a speech, Douglas had criticized oil companies. The speech was covered by the wire services and received broad circulation in the press. Shell Oil Company asked the Court to remove Douglas from a pending case involving natural gas rates. McGurn acted as a background source to state that Douglas had been misunderstood in his speech. McGurn's efforts resulted in a *Baltimore Sun* article referring to federal court sources that explained how "Mr. Douglas felt he had been misunderstood and misquoted by the wire services. The thrust of Mr. Douglas's criticism, according to these sources, was against a failure by public officials to prepare for an energy crisis, not against oil corporations."[3] By this method McGurn was able to get Douglas's side of the story in print without direct attribution to either Douglas or McGurn.

"We are the buffer," says Toni House. "Most of the time we prefer to be low key and provide guidance and background for people. It would be idiotic if we were quoted. We are not interested in seeing our names in the paper."

THE OUTSIDER AS PUBLIC INFORMATION OFFICER

One major difference between many press secretaries and the public information officer at the Supreme Court, is the latter's absolute exclusion from policymaking. He or she is not an advisor to the justices on decisions. He or she is not included in the justices' conferences; only the justices are present. He or she does not participate in the writing of opinions. Unlike Jody Powell, who served as a policy advisor to Jimmy Carter as his press secretary, or Marlin Fitzwater, who was included in policy-making sessions in the Bush administration, the Court's public information officer is not a public policy advisor nor is he or she even included in any deliberations. Nor is he or she an advisor on the public relations aspects of policy. By all accounts, he or she does not offer guidance to the justices on how a particular opinion would "play in Peoria."

The public information officer is an outsider at the Court. He or she cannot give regular briefings to reporters on Supreme Court decision making because he or she is not privy to that process. In fact, he or she and the staff do not know the outcome of a case until two hours before it is announced when they receive the opinions from the clerk's office, collate the majority opinion, and attach the concurring and dissenting opinions when necessary.

This outsider status is not due to the person who fills the office, but it results as a conscious decision on the part of the justices not to make the individual who

---

[2]Bob Woodward and Scott Armstrong, *The Brethren* (New York: Simon & Schuster, 1979), p. 415.

[3]See Dean Mills, "Douglas to Remain on Natural-Gas Case," *Baltimore Sun*, February 26, 1974, and Memo from Barrett McGurn to William O. Douglas, March 6, 1974. Both can be located in William O. Douglas Papers, Box 621, Library of Congress, Washington, D.C.

deals with the press, unlike the clerks, a part of the policy-making process at the Court. The public information officer acts much as does the administrative assistant to the chief justice, who handles the Court's administrative affairs but apparently plays no role in the Court's decision-making process.

At times the outsider status has its disadvantages for the public information officer. For example, when there is a high demand for information, such as when word of an imminent resignation has leaked, the outsider status becomes obvious, perhaps painfully so. Lyle Denniston offered an example of the problem when word of Justice Brennan's resignation spread:

> When Brennan resigned, first call I made was to Steve Wermiel of the *Wall Street Journal* who was then, and has been, serving in a double role because he's been doing the Brennan biography....I told Steve first and then I called Toni. At that point, Toni had been authorized to say something. The people who talked to Toni early in the afternoon got the response "I don't know anything" because, in fact, Toni hadn't been clued in. Toni got several calls from Ruth Marcus and Al Kamen [both of the *Washington Post*] and Linda Greenhouse [of the *New York Times*]. But her message through most of the afternoon was I don't have anything, I don't know. I hear the rumors, but I don't know anything.

Denniston's impulse to call a fellow reporter who was close to Brennan rather than the Court's public information officer epitomizes the expectations on the part of the press that, in a fast-breaking news situation, information actually will be obtained more quickly from other sources than the Court's public information officer.

The public information officer's outside role also means he or she can offer no behind-the-scenes guidance to reporters on decisions. Explaining the difference in reaction between the Court's Public Information Office and some other public relations office when a reporter has a leak, Henry Reske, former UPI reporter, said, "You can't call the flak and say 'confirm or deny.' They'll just laugh at you. You can play that game in [the rest of] Washington, but you can't play it here."

Moreover, the Court's public information officer adopts an arms-length attitude toward any discussion of the substance of Court decisions with the press. Members of the press corps relate that she does not discuss substantive matters of the Court with them. One long-time member of the press corp expressed near-dismay at their attitude:

> I can't imagine myself being in that job without really being fascinated with what the Court is doing substantively. But they don't seem to.... Maybe she thinks that's outside her responsibility. I can't imagine on a decision day walking into Toni and saying, Toni why don't you help me figure this out. It would be a useless endeavor.

House asserts that she does stay abreast of the Court's work since she may have to describe the result of the Court's action to someone, but it is not her role to offer guidance to the press on the substance of the written opinions on or off the record:

I would never play that role. I am the spokeswoman for the Supreme Court when it chooses not to speak for itself. Assigned opinion is speaking for itself and I would not wade in there and say 'This is what they really mean.'

Nor do the justices want House to play that role. They design their opinions to speak for themselves and not to be interpreted for the press by an official spokesperson. "They would not be remotely happy to see that Toni House said that in its action the other day the Court meant something or other," House commented. And then she added, "I could probably kiss this job goodbye."

Whether House or any public information officer is truly disinterested in the substance of the opinions or consciously avoids such discussion is not as important as the fact that the public information officer does not operate as a source for explanation and interpretation of the Court's written product. This effect well serves the Court because it minimizes the possibility of the decisions being displaced, or at least supplemented, by "quasi-official" interpretation from the public information officer. The justices retain control over the Court's information flow if the public information officer cannot offer even background guidance on its written opinions. Moreover, the justices remain the theme of the news coverage, without qualification or supplement.

Press Policy Advisor

The outsider status of the public information officer does not imply that the justices do not include her in noncase related matters. Lyle Denniston suggested that "Toni is pretty clued in with Rehnquist." The public information officer interacts with the justices frequently, especially the chief justice. She is passing on queries from the press, occasionally scheduling interviews, or arranging for the release of texts of speeches or other announcements.

The public information officer can be a vehicle for alerting the justices to the press corps' activities. Bert Whittington, PIO until 1973, sent to the chambers a list of the reporters who covered the Court. He also notified the justices when a new reporter for the *New York Times* joined the beat.[4]

The public information officer also can keep the justices informed about press treatment of the Court. Bert Whittington sent the justices memos that included recent news clippings of Court decisions.[5] One of the first things Barrett McGurn would do each day was mark the newspapers for clipping. Toni House says she does not do that.

Also, upcoming press coverage of the justices is communicated to them by the public information officer. Memos are sent to all of the justices alerting them to pending press treatment of the Court.[6] Individual justices are kept informed as well

[4]Memo from Bert Whittington, November 20, 1957, Earl Warren Papers, Box 666, Library of Congress, Washington, D.C.

[5]Memo from Bert Whittington, April 16, 1959, Earl Warren Papers, Box 666, Library of Congress, Washington, D.C.

[6]For samples, see memos from Bennett McGrun to Justice Marshall dated February 11, 1981 and December 8, 1980; Memos from Toni House to Conferences, December 3, 1986 and October 3, 1986; Thurgood Marshall Papers, Box 5475, Library of Congress, Washington, D.C.

about press coverage of them. Barrett McGurn notified William O. Douglas that an upcoming CBS documentary on the Court included clips from a press conference and an interview Douglas had previously given.[7]

The public information officer also becomes a source for the justices in their interpretation of the press. After he had given a speech on crime control, Earl Warren asked Bert Whittington why the speech had not been reported by the press.[8] At times, the justices will talk with the public information officer about television programs about the Court.

Another topic is the evaluation of Court policy toward the press corps. Toni House has kept justices informed about the progress of the Court's policy vis-à-vis the press, such as the Project Hermes experiment. Bert Whittington reported that more of the justices' opinions were appearing in the press coverage and that longer stories were being published. Whittington also used the occasion to suggest another change in Court policy—the announcement of opinions on two set days of the week. With this change, Whittington argued, "most all reporters would be apt to be here on days they know opinions are likely to come."[9] But the justices rejected his idea.

However, Whittington's suggestion is an example of the public information officer's role as an advocate of press policy reform. Toni House and the chief justice confer on policy changes relating to the Court's relations with the press. In the case of major changes affecting all of the justices, such as the introduction of cameras into the courtroom, the chief justice confers with his associates as well as with the public information officer. One example, according to House, is the Court policy on television standups from the pressroom. "The chief justice and I have consulted and we've looked at what was before. The answer being no, because it's too disruptive." Another issue is the use of cameras in other areas of the Supreme Court building. House offers an example of how she and Rehnquist established Court policy:

> There had been two instances I could document where television cameras had been allowed in the building prior to my being here. And so I went to the chief, "There have been television cameras here before, so we need to figure out what's acceptable." So working with him, it evolved to what could be done and what couldn't be done. Yes, you can film in the courtroom, but nobody can appear on camera except the justice or if someone is interviewing the justice. Yes, you can film in the conference room, but nobody may appear on camera. Journalists and narrators may appear on camera in the great hall or one of the conference rooms.

The process of deciding Court press policy apparently is based on two points: tradition and compromise. The Court's adherence to tradition usually necessitates

[7]Memo from Barrett McGurn to William O. Douglas, November 21, 1973, William O. Douglas Papers, Box 621, Library of Congress, Washington, D.C.

[8]Memo to Chief Justice from Bert Whittington, April 7, 1967, Earl Warren Papers, Box 666, Library of Congress, Washington, D.C.

[9]Memo from Bert Whittington, April 29, 1965, Earl Warren Papers, Box 666, Library of Congress, Washington, D.C.

reference to a precedent in procedure to effect a change in policy. Also, what emerges as policy appears to be a compromise between the Court's imagemaking strategies and the demands of new technology.

In effecting change, the Court must not be viewed as kowtowing to the press. In recommending a limit on the number of opinions released in any one day, House did not dwell on the benefits of this policy to the press, but she pointed out the constraints on the public information office's ability to organize the decisions.

The public information officer's support of the press' position does not guarantee policy change, but it may strengthen the press complaint since it arises from one who is also sympathetic with the Court's mission. Toni House: "My role is maybe in writing or maybe just in chatting to say 'I understand, of course, where the Court is coming from, but to the extent this is possible, this is really a good idea.'"

Some of the public information officer's recommendations have not succeeded. At the request of the press corps, House recommended that the Court run cable from the courtroom upstairs to the pressroom on the ground floor so reporters could listen to oral arguments in the pressroom. One of the reservations of the justices to that suggestion is the possibility that reporters will pick up the asides justices make to each other while they are on the bench. Presently, the poor acoustics in the courtroom make such eavesdropping unlikely.

House has encouraged the justices to set press policy rather than operate on an ad hoc basis. She has tried to "clarify areas" to establish a standard for the Public Information Office and the press corps to use. For instance, Toni House said to the press, "This is the way to cover Chief Justice Burger. We based it on the ABA standard for covering him. He wasn't being capricious." In that sense, she has acted as an advisor to the justices, especially the chief justice.

But apparently the extent of press policy advice is severely limited in comparison with that proffered by many colleagues in executive or legislative branch public relations offices. It does not extend to alterations in the Court's imagemaking strategies or, even less likely, the Court's decision-making processes.

However, House's efforts to clarify policy have resulted in a greater openness toward the press, particularly the broadcast media. She secured the cooperation of all of the justices in the making of the two-part PBS documentary "This Honorable Court." The documentary is now shown to visitors to the Supreme Court building. Lyle Denniston:

> Toni has done wonders for broadcast in getting access for them. You have to say part of the reason is Rehnquist is much more receptive than Burger. Burger had a hostility to broadcast that was highly developed. I don't think Paul Duke could have done his program ["This Honorable Court"] without Toni.

Dispenser of Process Guidance

Although Toni House, as the public information officer, does not comment on the substance of decisions, she does offer informal guidance to reporters on other matters, primarily process-related matters. The opportunities to do so are frequent.

Reporters often approach her with a variety of requests. The information sought ranges from "Where was Justice O'Connor today?" to the dates of decision announcements.

The public information office provides vague guidance on the number of opinions to be released on a given day. Journalists are warned that the opinion load will be average or heavy. The notification of "heavy" will alert news organizations to the potential need of assigning more than one reporter to the Court on that day.

One common form of guidance is squelching rumors. Since information at the Court is tightly held, rumors about information the Court does not want the press to acquire are common. For example, in June 1990, contradictory rumors were running rampant in the pressroom. One rumor asserted Justice O'Connor would resign due to health reasons. Another rumor had Rehnquist resigning and O'Connor becoming chief justice. In the midst of these rumors, Toni House moved around the pressroom informally to send a message. She had spoken to O'Connor about the rumors, and O'Connor had replied that they were absurd. "She says she is not sick, not bored, not resigning," House proclaimed to anyone within earshot.

Rumor squelching about resignations is particularly common at the end of a term. [In 1990] "Justice White was the subject of rumors [about resigning]. I walked into the pressroom and said, 'I have an announcement from Justice White.' They all perked up. 'He is not resigning.'"

On occasion, the public information officer also attempts to offer informal guidance on the announcement of decisions.

> I think we did a very good job last year when we knew pretty well that *Webster* wasn't going to come down. I had a television cameraman standing on the credenza in back of me filming our not releasing the *Webster* decision. I tried to say to people, I don't know anything, but my gut tells me it ain't over till its over. And you people are predicting out loud, in public, that *Webster* is going to come down on Thursday, and I'm telling you that you could be embarrassed. And they were. So then they had to write stories about why it didn't come down, which were wrong.
>
> You try to warn people off of something—negative guidance. I don't think we did know, but we had a strong sense the elephants were still moving around, as one of the law clerks used to say.

Some reporters attempt to plum the public information officer for information she is not authorized to give. For example, reporters would like to know the number of opinions the Court will announce. According to House, they inquire whether the load is "heavy" or "*heavy*."

However, some reporters are skeptical about the public information officer's depth of information. One reporter admitted that "I often get the sense she's pretending as if she knows more. Toni likes to have the feeling the press is trying to pull something out of her that she has and my own impression is she doesn't have it." If reporters believe the PIO is not informed about what decisions will be announced in advance, they may conclude the negative guidance House gives can safely be ignored.

The process guidance dispensed is often at a basic level, designed primarily for general assignment reporters covering major decisions but with little prior understanding of the Court. Toni House: "Some reporters are very good and they call and say we have got a case that is coming to you all. Would you please just tell me how you work so we will understand, so we can report it intelligently?"

Friend of the Press Corps

Although the public information officer is an employee of the Court with responsibility for cultivating the Court's image, he or she may also become a friend of the press corps. "I really like most of these people and for me this is a great job because I was a daily journalist myself for fifteen years," House remarks.

This friendship may become advocacy for the press in the formation of Court policy vis-à-vis the press. In 1969, there was an effort to deny reporters access to the conference list. Bert Whittington, public information officer at that time, argued against the policy change and in favor of the press corps. He wrote to Earl Warren that "it would be a very big handicap for all of them to work without it."[10]

The current public information officer also attempts to maintain good relations with the press corps. Generally, reporters in turn view her as a spokesperson who attempts to serve the press to the extent possible within the constraints of her position.

One example demonstrates her ability to perform a distasteful function while communicating a friendly message. *USA Today* printed a front-page story about a mistake by the clerk of the Court. The story recounted how an Ohio prisoner who was not scheduled for execution had been included on a list of names of death-row executions that the Court was not going to stop. The clerk, who was new to the Court, expressed his anger at Toni House. She then admonished Tony Mauro, the *USA Today* reporter on the Court beat, that "such stories don't do anyone any good." Mauro did not take offense at the criticism, but later explained that he read House's statement as a message that "if I saw the clerk and he frowned at me, I would know why. It was just for my information."

House attempts to maintain a friendly banter with most of the regulars in the press corps. She moves around the pressroom frequently. She visits certain cubicles with established regulars—such as the *New York Times*, the *Baltimore Sun*, the Associated Press—and passes on information: the orders list will be available at noon, or the Court will be in session next week on Monday and Tuesday, but not Wednesday.

She has cultivated a relationship with Lyle Denniston based partly on their experiences as former colleagues at the now defunct *Washington Star*. Members of her staff will query Denniston about events and issues preceding their tenure at the Court.

[10]Memo to Chief Justice from Bert Whittington, June 9, 1969, William O. Douglas Papers, Box 1429, Library of Congress, Washington, D.C.

Unlike Barrett McGurn, before arriving at the Court, Toni House was not a career government public relations officer. Her background was journalism, particularly legal reporting. She may communicate the attitude that her affinity is for the press corps due to her background and interests. In conversations, she speaks of "our press" or "our reporters."

That affinity may have gotten her in trouble with the chief justice on occasion. Barrett McGurn would write the chief justice memos about off-hand comments by reporters in the pressroom. One Court employee characterized him as a "kind of secretive guy." But House does not do those things. According to a former employee of the Court, Chief Justice Burger expressed a dislike for House's frequent contacts with the press and attempted to discourage those associations. She effectively conveyed the impression that she was friendly to the press corps, perhaps all too well.

But the press corps perceive that her loyalties clearly lie with the Court. The Court's hiring of a former journalist was meant to send a message that the Court wanted an effective spokesperson to the press, not an advocate of the press to the Court. Lyle Denniston contends that "Toni has had a conversion into a press officer from being a journalist that's as complete as what happened to Paul on the Damascus Road. She's a very good press officer."

Affinity for the press, but loyalty to the Court offers a useful combination of traits in a public information officer for the Court, even if that affinity may pain one or more of the justices and also the press corps. The impression is given that the public information officer is concerned about the interests of the press corps and relates well with the regulars. However, that impression is useful to the Court in conveying the image of good press relations without altering the actual substance of Court imagemaking policy.

CONCLUSION

The Public Information Office is the official press relations arm of the Court and its function is to officially keep the press at arms length while simultaneously feeding the press with information the Court seeks to make public. That information is the written product of the Court, which the Court takes care that the press receives.

In one sense, it is not unlike other government press relation offices. Officially, its task is to serve the public by providing information about the Court and its activities. But it is also designed to foster a positive image of the Court in the public mind.

On the other hand, since the institution discourages an overt press relations effort, the Public Information Office has become like "sleepy hollow" in contrast with counterparts in the executive and legislative branches. Little of the activity of such offices elsewhere occurs at the PIO of the Court.

The Public Information Office's primarily mechanistic functioning reduces press expectations to the point that reporters generally dismiss the office as irrelevant for any other purpose. The justices likely would not be displeased with that conclusion. As will be discovered in the next chapter, the result of this functioning is the maintenance of press routines revolving around the justices' output, but also the creation of a vacuum for other players to fill.

Chapter Four

On the Court Beat

The Supreme Court building is a formidable edifice often described as "the marble temple." The imposing structure and its artwork are designed to remind visitors that although it is located directly across from the Capitol, this is not another political institution, but the home of a legal body dedicated to interpreting the law above politics.

However, along with the justices, clerks, and other officials who arrive for work at the Court each morning come a group who seem to belie that image. These are the members of the press corps. For the Supreme Court is not only a legal institution, but it is also a beat for news media organizations ranging from national television networks to regional metropolitan dailies and news syndicates. But unlike other beats in Washington—the White House, Capitol Hill, the government agencies—the Court beat is marked by a press corps unlike any other, with a routine unique to it.

In this chapter, we will examine the composition of the Supreme Court press corps. We also will describe the routine of Court reporting today and analyze the social and political forces helping to shape it.

THE PRESS CORPS

Although about 50 reporters operate on the Court beat, actually they are divided into two groups—those who cover the Court on a full-time or near full-time basis and those for whom the Court beat is one of several beats to which they are assigned. The 12 to 15 regulars who cover the Court on a full-time or near full-time basis include reporters from the national daily media such as the *New York Times*, the *Wall Street Journal*, *USA Today*, and the major broadcast networks. It also includes reporters from the Washington area press, such as the *Washington Post*, the *Washington Times*, and the *Baltimore Sun*.

The nonregulars include reporters who fall in the following categories: those covering a legal beat for whom the Court is but one facet, bureau reporters for regional media such as mid-size metropolitan dailies or news syndicates, and correspondents from specialized publications, such as legal magazines and trade publications with interest in specific cases.

The mix of regulars and nonregulars places a significant cross-section of the American news media in the same room at the same time when there are cases of high national visibility. However, for the most part, the nonregulars, as their title implies, are only occasional occupants at the Court.

Since the beat of the nonregulars usually encompasses several of the more traditional journalistic beats, their attention to the Court is more limited. For example, a Washington bureau reporter for a regional newspaper may well be covering Congress and several bureaucratic agencies, in addition to the Court. As one regular describes, these reporters are covering the Court with "one hand tied behind their backs."

When major long-running stories break in unrelated areas, they are often pulled onto other beats and become even more sporadic in their attention to the Court. For example, during the Persian Gulf War in 1990–1991, nonregulars were routinely assigned to Persian Gulf stories. Since the war began and ended before the period of heaviest activity in the Court's term, there was little effect on Court coverage.

Also, both regulars and nonregulars are assigned to the additional duties of covering a confirmation process when a vacancy occurs on the Supreme Court. Fortunately for the press corps, since the retirement of Potter Stewart in 1981, vacancies have occurred at the end of the term and, with the exception of the Robert Bork, Douglas Ginsburg, and Anthony Kennedy nominations, have concluded early in the next term.

The dichotomy between these two groups sometimes creates resentment on the part of the nonregulars, who view the regulars as the dominant players in the pressroom. Some dislike a practice of allowing the regulars to get the opinions first when they are announced. "If a regular wants to be the first to get a decision," explained one nonregular, "you don't argue with that." Sometimes the frustration is directed not so much at the regulars but at the Public Information Office that, according to some nonregulars, favors the regulars.

"Whatever there is to give, it goes to big papers," complained one nonregular print journalist. But since there is not much to "give" to the regulars due to the nature of the Public Information Office, as described in the preceding chapter, the complaint is not often raised.

The Elite

Within the regulars—those whose primary responsibility is the Court beat— there are gradations of time spent on the beat. Broadcast television reporters today are assigned to a broader legal beat, rather than to the Court specifically. They cover other legal-related stories, and sometimes stories of their choosing unrelated to legal affairs. According to CBS News correspondent Rita Braver, "the Supreme Court is about a two-thirds of the time job for a television reporter." Some regulars cover both the Court and the Justice Department, for example.

Due to their media organization's emphasis on Court coverage, a few members of the press corps cover the Court full-time or nearly full-time. These reporters tend to be known as the "elite." This designation stems from their seniority on the beat, skill in interpretation and reporting, and, typically, the elite nature of their publication. "We all know who are the good reporters," said Jerome Cramer, who covered the Court beat for *Time*. "Linda [Greenhouse of the *New York Times*] reads all the cert petitions. She has an incredible knowledge. She's a very technical write. Lyle Denniston [of the *Baltimore Sun*] takes a different interpretation."

Denniston, known as the dean of the press corps due to his more than 30 years on the beat, is highly respected for his legal reporting experience and knowledge of the Court. What also attracts attention is Denniston's approach to the justices, which emphasizes the Court's political nature and the importance of the justices' personalities in decision making. "I don't think it's just because of senior status. I'm fairly provocative," remarked Denniston.

Several of the elites, such as Nina Totenberg of National Public Radio, Tim O'Brien of ABC News, Denniston, and Greenhouse, have become media personalities in their own right—writing columns, delivering speeches, and appearing as guests on the *MacNeil-Lehrer News Hour*, C-SPAN call-in programs, and C-SPAN's *America and the Courts* program.

The elite not only are accorded respect for their expertise and ability, but their position and product directly affect the work of other reporters on the beat. Since nonregulars do not follow cases with the same intensity as the regulars, particularly the elite, they often turn to them for assistance. One nonregular explained how the elite were important to him: "Once in a while you get a complex decision with no clear majority. Then I would talk it over with some of my colleagues who would have covered the case more closely." After a decision announcement, some nonregulars will attempt to determine what the elite think about the issue. One nonregular explained: "I usually hang out in the press room and listen and talk to people about it. Usually there will be a discussion going on after a big opinion."

Because the elites also are highly respected by editors at other non-elite publications, the elite become important later in the reporting process. Their stories become a standard by which other reporters measure their own work. Editors for other publications compare the work of their staff reporters against those of the elite since the elite are highly regarded for their expertise and analysis.

The Specialist

Stephen Hess found most Washington reporters exhibit a distaste for story preparation involving documentary research. Not surprisingly, the Supreme Court beat with its heavy reliance on documents rather than interviews was not a highly desirable beat.[1] Hess found the Supreme Court beat to be high in prestige among Washington reporters due to its proximity to power, but low in satisfaction.[2]

However, most of those actually on the beat were at least fairly satisfied with their job.[3] Apparently, those who serve on the beat are more likely than their counterparts on other beats to enjoy the peculiarities of the Court beat, including the legal research required. Many Supreme Court reporters thrive on such research.

The stimulation comes not from personal interaction, but from documentary interpretation. According to Linda Greenhouse, the type of person who does well on the Court beat is "someone who feels interest and pleasure in dealing with technical materials." Richard Carelli of the Associated Press saw the Court press corps as living a different life from most other reporters: "This is a more sedentary life we lead. We're more interested in substance." Miranda Spivack of the *Hartford Courant* succinctly stated one of the primary reasons for the stimulation that arises from the beat: "In the sense that you can bring to bear your own knowledge and expertise, I find it one of the more intellectually challenging beats around."

The nature of the beat is fundamentally different for its occupants when contrasted with others in Washington. Less time is spent interviewing sources than elsewhere. More of a journalist's day is devoted to reading briefs, legal summaries, and the opinions of the Court. Richard Carelli estimated he spent 50 percent of his time reading approximately 4,000 cert. petitions each term.[4]

Another character trait of the Court press corps is the ability of its reporters to operate independently. Reporters at the Court, particularly the regulars, are not the objects of constant attention from the Court itself. A reporter's day is not scheduled around photo opportunities, press briefings, and news conferences as is true on other beats. The result is an absence of continual overt guidance from the institution about what constitutes news. Reporters who enjoy the lack of "spin control" are more likely to be successful on the Court beat.

Unlike general assignment reporting where reporters move from one story to another with little carryover, at the Court beat such carryover is paramount. Issues that arise one year likely will return in successive years. Hence, longevity on the beat becomes more important than in many settings. As one reporter noted, it's the kind of beat where "your expertise over the years works for you." One-half of the journalists on the beat surveyed had been there for six or more years. (See Appendix B.)

The specialist hat has been the subject of debate within the pressroom. Most of the reporters on the Court beat surveyed had some legal training. While some reporters possess law degrees or at least some legal training, others do not and some of the latter even pride themselves on their lack of legal training. Some reporters

---

[1]Stephen Hess, *The Washington Reporters* (Washington, D.C.: Brookings, 1981), pp. 18–19.

[2]Ibid., pp. 2, 52, 58–59.

[3]Ibid., p. 141. Hess' survey included those who covered a "law" beat in Washington.

[4]Rorie Sherman, "The Media and the Law," *National Law Journal* (June 6, 1988), 33.

argue that legal training may prevent you from communicating with the general reader. A new member of the Supreme Court press corps explained:

> When my job first opened, my editors interviewed about a half dozen lawyers thinking at first they really wanted someone with a law degree. They realized these people were interested in tiny legal twists and turns of opinions and not the larger picture. When you only have 20 inches to write a story, you really need to be general and you need to grab that reader.

Although there is probably a higher percentage of reporters with law degrees on the Supreme Court beat than on any other beat, most members of the press corps interviewed dismissed the notion that legal training or a law degree was essential for the Court beat. "I think all things being equal, a good journalist without a law degree is going to do a lot better job than a mediocre journalist with a law degree," said Stuart Taylor of *American Lawyer* magazine, and a lawyer himself, who summarized a prevailing view.

Some members of the press corps argue legal training aids in understanding the legal process. Miranda Spivack saw her first year experience at Yale Law School as a substantive help: "You see the nuances." Tim O'Brien of ABC News suggested the new reporter at the Court should know "evidence, legal procedure, criminal procedure—that's a good foundation."

A legal background also enhances the interpretive role of the reporter by instilling self-confidence in the ability to move beyond the justices' words and to explain the opinion. "All too often where you see jargon in print," remarked Stephen Wermiel, former reporter on the beat for the *Wall Street Journal*, "the reporter didn't understand it and was afraid to paraphrase it or to explain it."

Those who possess legal training find it useful in their relations with sources, especially within the legal profession. "You usually get asked if you're a lawyer," Spivack related. "Then you say you went to Yale Law School. It's a status thing." Reporters who possess law degrees often experience a new respect from their sources. Stephen Wermiel: "All too often when somebody starts off a conversation they'll begin in a condescending fashion, 'Gee, you don't have a law degree, so how am I going to explain this to you.' And I say, well I do have a law degree."

But others contend a legal background can detract from the reporter's task in two ways. First, the lawyer-journalist may be more inclined to write in a technical style. Those with legal training admit that they often fall into "legalese" and are chastised by their editors. "When I first covered the Court, editors were very happy," explained Tim O'Brien. "I was leaving a lot out. After a couple of years they would say, 'wait a minute you left a step out in the thought process.' I'd say, 'Well, everyone knows that.' 'No, you've got to go from point A to point B to point C.' I'm constantly leaving out steps."

For some reporters, not possessing a legal background is viewed as an advantage. "It makes it easier to explain to lay people if I've gone through the same basic questions the reader has when I'm writing the story," said Tony Mauro of *USA Today*, who also writes a column on the Court for *Legal Times*. "I can still ask dumb questions. I feel I'm not as tempted to write in legalese."

Secondly, some reporters argue that those with legal backgrounds become too deferential toward the Court and the legal process. One of the strongest advocates of this view is Lyle Denniston. According to Denniston, some lawyer-reporters become too much like lawyers. "If a reporter hangs around judges and lawyers too long he begins to smell like them. A journalist has his own smell and he should never trade that aroma for someone else's."[5] The criticism is lodged especially at reporters who join the Supreme Court bar. "It has the appearance of being more deferential," said Richard Carelli, who has a law degree but has not joined the bar. "One swears to uphold the Supreme Court, then covers that institution." They become "officers of the Court" while they are expected to be objective observers. Stephen Wermiel described the dilemma he faced as a lawyer-reporter:

> I'm a member of the D.C. bar. I'm eligible to join the Supreme Court bar, but I've chosen not to. In theory you can fall under their jurisdiction for something you do. While I think the threat is quite attenuated and remote, I consider myself to have a fairly high ethical standard and I think Lyle may have a point there. So I considered there was no real reason to join the Supreme Court bar.

Tim O'Brien of ABC News, who is a member of the U.S. Supreme Court bar, called such accusations "nonsense." O'Brien, who obtained a law degree prior to his post on the Court beat, defended his decision by arguing it has had no effect on his aggressive style of reporting. The reaction of the justices when O'Brien was sworn in suggested they did not perceive him as an officer of the Court. "I joined the bar while I was covering the Court," O'Brien related. "Justice Byron White shook his head. Chief Justice Burger, whose decisions I had leaked on three prior decisions, grimaced."

Despite the arguments of those who do not possess legal training, for the most part, respect within the press corps is correlated with legal training. With only a few exceptions, the elites possess such backgrounds. The national newspapers such as the *New York Times* and the *Wall Street Journal* have reporters with law degrees or at least some legal training. The possession of legal training has become standard for regulars at the Court beat. Reporters such as Tim O'Brien of ABC News possessed law degrees before coming to the Court beat. Others such as Richard Carelli of the Associated Press obtained degrees while on the Court beat. Some reporters such as Linda Greenhouse and Miranda Spivack participated in a program of first year legal training at Yale Law School. By contrast, nonregulars rarely possess legal training.

Supreme Court reporters seem to have adopted the specialist label. According to Stephen Hess, the majority consider themselves to be specialists, while most on other Washington beats see themselves as generalists.[6]

Although the debate over the effect of a legal background is ongoing, the clear trend has been toward the possession of some legal training for those who cover the

---

[5]Quoted in Mitchell J. Tropin, "What, Exactly, Is the Court Saying," *The Barrister* (Winter 1984), p. 14.

[6]Hess, *The Washington Reporters*, p. 156–157.

Court on a regular basis. Given the move by the more prestigious press toward such lawyer-reporters, it is a trend that is likely to continue.

THE PRESSROOM

The workplace for the regulars who cover the Court, particularly the wire service reporters who are full-time occupants, is a narrow rectangular room housing 15 cubicles (each no more than five feet by six feet) along the walls, with long rectangular tables in the middle. Located in the northwest corner of the ground floor, the room is carpeted in an amethyst hue and decorated with pastels by courtroom artists, posters regarding the press and the law, and photographs of the justices and the press. At one end of the room is a bank of telephones, primarily for nonregulars to contact editors before returning to the bureau office.

At that end, there is also a bulletin board where the Public Information Office's handouts are pinned. These include the conference list for the next two weeks, the schedule of arguments, a copy of *PREVIEW*, and a statistical sheet for the current term comparing it with the last two at the same point in the term. The statistical information includes the number of paid cases, in forma pauperis cases, cases argued and submitted, cases disposed by signed opinion, and so forth.

At the other end are two small offices, each housing two reporters who work for the wire services. However, UPI's recently contracted status has freed one-half of that office for a nonwire service reporter. Lyle Denniston works from there.

Fifteen cubicles are assigned to the regulars at the Court, such as reporters for the three major television networks, National Public Radio, Mutual Broadcasting, Knight-Ridder Wire News Syndicate, Reuters, and several major dailies—the *New York Times*, the *Washington Post*, the *Wall Street Journal*, and the *Los Angeles Times*.

The cubicles facilitate working at the Court on decision and argument days. But an office, or at least a desk, is available to these reporters at their bureau offices as well. Each cubicle bears a nameplate with the name of the organization to which it is assigned, but beyond that they vary greatly. Some of the cubicles are barely decorated while others are more elaborate, reflecting the choice of whether to work there or at the bureau office. Some include bookshelves, telephones, computer terminals, and political cartoons about the Court.

The nonregulars who remain in the pressroom to work make use of the long rectangular tables located in the center of the room. Manual typewriters at the tables are for reporters' use, although few actually do. The tables also serve the sketch artists who, after sitting in the rear of the press section in the courtroom sketching portraits of the justices, put finishing touches on their renderings of the justices. The details of the justices' faces are enhanced by frequent reference to official Court photographs.

An extension of the pressroom is the bank of audio broadcast booths on the ground floor of the Court building directly behind the sitting statue of John

Marshall. Equipped with telephones and microphones, the booths are used to broadcast radio news reports directly following a newsworthy decision announce-ment. In major cases where the decision is announced in time for the 10 A.M. news, broadcast network reporters will walk briskly to their booth directly after receiving the opinion and immediately go on the air.

THE ROUTINE

Members of the press corps follow a work routine that mimics the Court's own schedule of cert. petitions, conferences, oral arguments, and decision days. The bulk of the work occurs at the beginning and the end of the term. At the beginning the major decision for the press is what cases to follow throughout the term.

Choosing What to Cover

For most of the members of the press corps, the process of reporting on the Court begins with the justices' decision to grant review in a case. The Public Information Office releases the orders list, the longest of which is the one on the first day of the term. The orders list is the announcement of which cases appealed to the Court will be granted review and which will not. It also includes summary decisions the Court delivers—decisions made without oral arguments and often without signed opinions.

When the orders list is released, the regulars and some of the nonregulars will file stories about what cases the Court will be hearing. These initial stories take the form of previews or curtain raisers since they examine the issues the Court will be addressing in the case. They alert the audience to the Court's pending agenda. Some interest groups attempt to shape these stories through press releases explaining the issue in the case and the group's stance in the case. (See Appendix C.)

Occasionally the list of cases the Court decides not to review provokes press interest. For example, during the 1991–1992 term the Court's decision not to review an appeal of a California term limitation law attracted a spate of press stories.

The briefs filed in cases, especially the amici or "friend of the court" briefs, may attract press attention. During the late 1980s and early 1990s, the Reagan and Bush administrations' briefs urging the Court to overturn *Roe v. Wade* were news items.

For some reporters, the culling process for news begins even earlier than the orders list. A few reporters, for instance, Linda Greenhouse of the *New York Times* and Richard Carelli of the Associated Press, read the cert. petitions the justices receive to understand which cases the Court is choosing for review.

At times, other cases are followed by the rest of the press corps as well, even prior to their acceptance for review by the Court. Appellate cases related to already newsworthy issues attract press attention. The succession of abortion cases in the early 1990s received press notice for their potential as the vehicle for the Court to review and possibly overturn *Roe v. Wade*.

Orders lists are released throughout the year, although the longest list occurs just prior to the beginning of the term in October, after the justices have spent their summer recess reading cert. petition memoranda from their clerks and determining which cases they will vote to accept for review.

As the Court accepts cases for review, reporters create files for each case they expect to cover through the term. Only the wire services will cover virtually every case. For the rest of the press corps, decisions must be made about which cases to cover. These decisions are based on the nature of the media and its audience. There is a wide disparity between media outlets. While the *New York Times* reporter will write about the vast majority of the cases the Court accepts for review, a regional metropolitan daily reporter covering the Court in addition to other beats will cover only a few cases. Miranda Spivack of the *Hartford Courant* presented a far more narrow scope of Court coverage: "My function is to pick out ten big cases of the year and follow. I will try to get all the Connecticut cases."

Broadcast network reporters are limited in the number of cases they can follow by the greater expense entailed in their coverage. Tim O'Brien of ABC News identifies between a dozen to two dozen cases a term on which he will shoot material. They discuss with producers the list of cases they will cover during the year. Broadcast reporters offer their producers a list of cases they plan to cover during the term. The memo serves as a justification for the expense. CBS News Correspondent Rita Braver said she specifies the stage of the case to be covered. The cases will not be covered at all stages. Some lend themselves to an argument story; others to a decision announcement piece.

National newsmagazines also present a limited number of stories, not due to expense but to the smaller news hole in a weekly publication. Newsmagazine reporters, like those in broadcast, are choosing stories as part of a shared editorial process with their editors.

According to Jerome Cramer, former *Time* correspondent at the Court, although the choice of stories usually results from his queries to editors, control of the final product rests with the editors:

> I suggest perhaps two a week. Sometimes I'll suggest to "Nation" [an editorial section of *Time* magazine] if there's something that's going to be very sexy and breaking, like flag-burning. It was more than just law. Then they'll come back and say we like your suggestion, or we're going to put two of your suggestions together. We're going to take one of your suggestions about a case coming and put it with a much larger look at an issue.

In still another category are the regionals who focus on cases arising out of or including issues important to their region. For example, Frank Aukofer of the *Milwaukee Journal* watches "anything that comes out of Wisconsin or Wisconsin courts and occasionally things that are of interest to people in Wisconsin. Abortion is a very big issue back there."

Reporters for specialized publications exhibit an interest in cases concerning their specialty. The *Wall Street Journal* reporter follows cases of interest to the business reader.

The process of choosing what stories to cover also is affected by interest groups who use litigation to achieve policy objectives. These groups attempt to direct press interest at the beginning of the term when reporters are writing their previews of the upcoming term. If the interest group is successful, the reporter will come to share the groups' perspective on the significance of the issues in the case and the consequences of various options before the Court.

Several interest groups, such as the National Organization for Women Legal Defense Fund, the Chamber of Commerce, and the American Civil Liberties Union hold briefings in or near Washington to acquaint reporters with the groups' interests in upcoming cases. Featuring noted Washington legal experts such as Kenneth Starr, Timothy Dyk, and William Greenhalgh, the briefings allow reporters to become educated on the legal issues surrounding cases the Court has accepted for review. (See Appendix C.)

The briefings are well timed. "We are writing preview stories at that time, " Tony Mauro explained. "They help me spot important cases to look at and what trends to look for. They also tell me the cases these groups are interested in." Mauro also saw the briefings as evidence that "the Supreme Court press corps is coming into its own as a force. These groups were trying to cater to us and feed us." These groups conduct briefings in order to gain publicity for their organization and its objectives, as well as to encourage reporters to be sympathetic in story writing.

Stephen Bokat of the National Chamber Litigation Center, the legal arm of the Chamber of Commerce, explained why his organization sponsors press gatherings:

> What we get out of it is developing those contacts and relationships with reporters so that when they have a question they call us....Being seen as an expert, being quoted or put on the news or whatever is very helpful to us. Also it's got a rub-off effect; inevitably within a week of the briefing, before or after, I will get calls from all kinds of reporters who will say, "I can't come to the briefing, but can you give me a run-through of the cases you are going to discuss?"

What Is Newsworthy?

How do reporters determine which of the cases granted review constitutes news? The reporters themselves do not provide that answer. One called the determination an "almost undefinable phenomenon of what's news." Another suggested that, of the cases he must choose from, "most of them are obvious" in their newsworthiness. However, some commonality emerges in reporters' decisions about what constitutes news.

One feature is the presence of an issue already defined as newsworthy. The flag-burning cases serve as an example. Lyle Denniston explained how these cases became news:

> Flag-burning for a year and a half was an exciting and inciteful issue. I couldn't give my editors enough on that. It was wonderful because it was kind of a residual carryover

from the campaign in '88. It was such a wonderful mix of personality and patriotism. I thought it was the best case of the lot.

Another characteristic is the potential for a case to have major impact on individuals. Cases with potentially far-reaching implications in the larger social and political environment are most likely to become one of the small number of cases to concentrate on.

The issues involved in an oral argument must be viewed as relevant to the common person. CNN Reporter Tony Collings described how he used this tactic to persuade his producer on an argument story.

> I went to [him] and said. I think we should do this one [Eastern Airlines]. Passengers on an international flight. They were scared they would die and they're suing for mental damage. Airlines say there has to be some physical harm—can't just be scared and collect some money. He and the other producers [were] interested. They were saying I've been scared on a plane. They related to it in a personal way. On that basis, I was able to persuade them to do a piece.

Even the lack of attention to the case throughout the term does not mean it will not be covered at the time of decision announcement. But the initial selection of cases to follow does predict the composition of news stories about oral arguments and decisions throughout the term.

Preparing Stories

Given the complexity of the issues and the technicality of the writing present in the opinions the Court delivers, it is essential on the Court beat to devote large blocks of time in preparation for the forthcoming argument and decision stories. Unlike their counterparts on other beats, members of the Court press corps will spend much of their time studying the documents provided by the Court in order to understand the issues involved in the case and the options available to the justices.

The briefs provided by the Public Information Office are critical to the preparation for stories. As Frank Aukofer's following comment implies, many reporters glean most of their information about the case from the briefs:

> Most of the stuff that you need is right there at the Court—you have read the briefs, the amicus briefs. There isn't much need to go out and interview anybody. Sometimes to personalize it, to make a better story out of it, I will go out and talk to the people involved or talk to their lawyers. On a big case, when you have 20–30 amicus briefs, you pretty much get the gist of what's going on from the documentation at the Court. It's a nice, comfortable way to operate as a reporter because it's all there right in front of you.

Another source is the plethora of interest groups and legal experts who have an interest in what types of cases the press follows. Jerome Cramer related that he will "follow very heavily what the groups have to say about it...what the major lobbyists, major political activists say."

Reporters also rely on legal publications. A popular source is *PREVIEW*, financed primarily by the American Bar Association. *PREVIEW* summarizes the key issues of each case, the arguments of the parties, and the arguments contained

in amici briefs. For some reporters, *PREVIEW* also becomes a listing of possible
sources on the case since the authors of the summaries are identified. Another
source is *U.S. Law Week*, which provides a brief summary of each paid case
docketed. It is helpful as reporters review the conference lists for possible
stories. Other news outlets on legal issues include the *National Law Journal*,
Legal Times, and *American Lawyer*. Reference books such as the *Congressional
Quarterly's Guide to the U.S. Supreme Court* and constitutional law books are
used in preparation.

Preparing stories is a far more simple exercise for print journalism than for
broadcast. Broadcast journalists travel periodically during the term to prepare
stories from the origin of the case. Stephen Hess found the Supreme Court reporters
among the least likely to travel on assignment.[7] Most of the traveling that occurs is
done by the broadcast network reporters.

The greater expense and the logistics of transporting camera crews and
equipment require greater coordination between the reporter and producers before
resources are allocated on covering stories. "We have considerations in gathering
news that go far beyond journalistic concerns," according to Tim O'Brien. "Telephone and typewriter are key tools of the print reporter. When I go with a camera
crew, they carry roughly 20–25 cases of equipment. We can't just pick up the phone
to get an interview." The result is enormous expense, effort, and time, resulting in,
usually at best, a two to three minute story on the evening news.

Preparation for broadcast stories includes scheduling the time for the producer
and the reporter; locating a camera crew and arranging the time of a shoot in a
network bureau office or at an affiliates' office. Freelancers may need to be hired.
Traveling to the location where the case originated may be necessary. Conducting
on-camera interviews with the parties in the case, the counsel for the parties, legal
experts, or related interest groups will then be done. Much of the time, the broadcast
reporter is concerned with technical aspects—microphones, lighting, sound levels,
make-up, camera angles, and so forth.

Moreover, all of this activity is conducted in competition with others, as all
of the major networks usually converge on the same locations and sources. An
important objective is to be the first reporter to interview a key source or, better yet,
the only one able to do so. However, on the major cases, all the reporters will be
able to get to the principals in the case.

Broadcast journalists attempt to personalize the Court stories, presenting the
cases as mini-human dramas. One example is a case arguing the constitutionality
of victim impact statements—discussion of the impact of the victim's death on
others—during the sentencing stage of a trial. To personalize the issue, Tim O'Brien
traveled to Memphis to interview the family members of a woman and her daughter
who were killed in a stabbing. O'Brien interviewed the woman's mother, who had
made the statement, during the course of the sentencing stage, about the impact of
her daughter's death on her grandson that had prompted the case. The Supreme

[7]Hess, *The Washington Reporters*, p. 10.

Court oral-argument story was personalized in the form of an ordinary grandmother being able to express in court the impact of her loved ones' deaths on their family.

But for both print and broadcast journalists, documentary research is a critical aspect of the job. Much of the journalist's time is spent researching the issues through reading briefs and cert. petitions. One journalist estimated he spends five hours researching for every ten minutes of writing.[8]

Covering Oral Arguments

The next discrete event for the press corps, after the granting of the review of a case by the Court, is the presentation of oral arguments. Scheduled throughout the term, these public sessions offer the Court an opportunity to hear the arguments of the parties to the case. But they also serve several purposes for the press corps.

Many reporters choose to use the argument story as an introduction to the issue for the audience. This is particularly true when the case was not previously covered in press stories at the time it was granted cert.

Conversely, the presence of more than one critical point during the term can work to the disadvantage of some reporters. In some cases, editors will bypass an argument piece because they know this will not be their last opportunity to address the issue. One reporter bemoaned this fact: "The trouble with the Supreme Court is we get a second crack at it. We get a chance when the decision is made to describe the issues of the case."

Oral arguments also become useful to reporters in two other ways: First, by listening to the arguments the reporter can acquire a greater understanding about the issues in the case. One reporter remarked that "sitting in on the arguments helps in writing about the decision" because the reporter gains insight through the presentation of counsel and the questions of the justices. Second, the arguments can alert the reporter to the concerns of the justices, which may be useful in assessing which way the Court will decide when it ultimately does so.

But reporters must be careful in their attempt to read in to a justices' comments a voting tendency in a case. For example, after oral arguments in the *Rust v. Sullivan* case during the 1990–1991 term, a spate of news stories from the press corps appeared speculating that Justice Souter, then the newest member of the Court, might vote against the government position due to his sharp questioning of the U.S. Solicitor General who presented the government's side. When the decision came down, Souter was lined up with the majority in favor of the government's position.

The exclusion of cameras would seem to make argument stories unattractive to television. But in one sense, argument pieces can be ready-made for television: they are predictable. "This is the only beat in the country where you know what you're getting," according to CBS News correspondent Rita Braver. "The way the Court works they tell you what cases they're going to take, and they tell you what days they're going to argue them on."

---

[8]See Thomas S. Hodson, "'Fourth Estate' Watches Over Third Branch," *The Docket Sheet*, (Fall 1987).

Argument pieces are even easier than decision stories because they can be planned in advance of the day of the argument. Preview pieces can be aired on late night programs the day before or on the morning news of the argument day.

The predictability of arguments is an advantage for print reporters as well. Unlike with decisions, they know when arguments in a case they have chosen to follow will occur and can arrange their daily schedule accordingly. Reporters who file a weekly schedule of activities for their beat can include the list of arguments. The angle for the argument piece often can be determined in advance as well.

Another advantage of argument pieces for television is the presence of clear conflict. That conflict often does not emerge in decisions, especially when the Court decides narrowly or leaves the issue muddied. Conflict is a key ingredient in newsworthy argument stories. "Some cases that are really good for argument stories are not that good for decision cases," explains Rita Braver. "I hope with an argument story you and your spouse will get into a discussion of which side is right."

For television the argument becomes a launching pad for the presentation of the issue. Unlike print, the actual arguments—the exchanges between the justices and counsel—do not dominate the story. Tim O'Brien suggested television should "do the argument pieces the night before" because the "arguments for our viewers are a bit technical, but the issue is explosive."

Other reporters, however, find arguments to be difficult to report. "Sometimes I come out of an oral argument with hardly a quotable quote," one regular admitted. "These arguments are very technical. It's sometimes hard to get the subtleties of an oral argument." Oral argument stories appear amorphous to reporters due to the lack of resolution in the story. The reporter is left with a notebook of quotes from opposing counsel and the justices but with no clear direction. "I've yet to come up with a definitive lead for an argument story," admitted Miranda Spivack. "I don't think they make good news stories."

The incompleteness of the arguments increases the likelihood of diverging reporters' interpretations within the press corps on what occurred and what it means. Such divergence among reporters is allowed by editors for elite publications since they set the tone of coverage, but it can be dangerous for other reporters whose interpretation is less trusted by editors. Some nonregulars are likely to linger after oral arguments and listen in the pressroom for the interpretations of the elite.

Interest groups also attempt to take advantage of the tentativeness of argument stories by sending news releases about the oral arguments reiterating the group's position in the case and expressing optimism that justices will agree. (See Appendix C.) In highly visible cases, interest groups involved in the issue will schedule news conferences with the counsel or the parties in the case, either at the Court or nearby, to claim victory in the oral arguments and express optimism about the final decision.

Another problem with oral argument stories is the possibility of misquoting the justices. Problems with acoustics in the courtroom magnify the opportunity for error. Reporters continually complain they cannot hear well from the press section.

The misquotation problem is especially acute for reporters—such as those from wire services, broadcast networks, or afternoon dailies—who face deadlines early in the day. When plagued by uncertainty, reporters will check with colleagues to confirm what they thought they heard.

The Court bars reporters from carrying audio tape recorders into the courtroom, but the Court itself tapes the arguments for internal purposes. Reporters are given access to both the audio tape and the transcripts taken from them, but reporters argue that deadlines prevent their actual use. The transcripts are not made available to reporters until ten days after the arguments, far too late for all but a monthly publication. Audio tape access is granted to reporters who make special requests through the Public Information Office. Some reporters see the procedure as cumbersome and not many actually request to listen to the tapes. In almost all cases, reporters are willing to rely on their own memories or those of their colleagues.

In highly newsworthy cases, such as *Webster v. Reproductive Health Services* in 1989 and *Planned Parenthood of Southeastern Pennsylvania v. Casey* in 1992, some news organizations have hired the transcription services hired by the Court to provide same day transcriptions. Their use is rare, however.

During the latter half of the term, the Court begins to announce decisions on previously argued cases on the same days it is hearing arguments in other cases. Since decisions have a finality to them, the potential exists for a decision announcement to displace an argument story. Rita Braver described the risks of oral argument pieces conflicting with decisions: "My chances of them announcing a really big decision on that day aren't so great, so I will go ahead and prepare a nice argument piece, but sometimes you get blown out of the water."

WRITING THE DECISION STORY

Except for the last day of the term, reporters do not know which decisions will be announced on any given day. Thus, when they report for work each morning, particularly at the end of the term, they do not know what they will be doing that day. The Court could announce several decisions they have been following closely and create a hectic day for them, or it could release decisions most of the press corps have little interest in—cases which, on the basis of news values, do not merit coverage. This uncertainty is characterized in a statement of humorous frustration by Tim O'Brien to Toni House one day after none of the opinions released included those he was following. He said, "I was really expecting heavy duty today. I wore my new suit and everything."

The opinions are announced at 10 A.M. in a public session that rarely lasts more than one-half hour. At one time, the justices would read the opinions in full; now they merely announce the result and offer a brief summary of the opinion and the lineup of concurrences and dissents. Occasionally, a dissenter will read an opinion in full to call public attention to it.

Some in the press corps hear the opinions first while in the press section of the courtroom. Linda Greenhouse maintained she always goes upstairs to hear the announcement from the courtroom. "The way each author chooses to convey the

holding is very enlightening. I'm always shocked that not everyone goes up there."
Others remain in the pressroom. Some reporters, such as those in the wire service
and broadcast press, stay in the pressroom in order to report the decision faster.
Reporters with more time before deadlines are more likely to observe from the
courtroom.

Another reason for avoiding the courtroom is the predictability of the events
there. Generally, the routine of the public sessions varies little. The oral arguments
rarely produce sharp verbal fireworks and only occasionally will the justices make
an announcement in public session that goes beyond the written opinion.

On occasion, the events in the courtroom become part of the story. Publisher
Larry Flynt once disturbed an oral argument by yelling obscenities at the justices.
"Sometimes a justice will read a dissent because they feel so strongly about it, and
I'll say that," Greenhouse explained.

But the events in the courtroom are rarely considered news by the press. Even
when a resignation is announced upstairs, it is simultaneously released downstairs
in the Public Information Office.

The dilemma of whether to go upstairs or down becomes acute for reporters in the spring when the justices are both hearing arguments and announcing
decisions. Some of the press corps split the difference by sitting in the back of
the press section in an overflow section separated from the courtroom by velvet
curtains in order to hear the arguments, but also to facilitate leaving quickly,
without disturbing the proceedings, if a major decision is announced. The
overflow section is used primarily on days when highly visible cases are argued
or are expected to be decided, such as on the last day of the term when the
decisions have not previously been announced. Reporters who sit there can hear,
but not see. Court security officers standing behind the curtains inform reporters
as to which justice is speaking.

When reporters are handed the opinions by Court public information
officers, the first issue for most of them is which, if any, of the decisions will
merit a story. The Court's practice of releasing most of its decisions in a
compacted period at the end of the term creates a flood of opinions on some days
near the end of the term. The Court's decision in 1965 to announce decisions on
days other than Monday was intended to disperse opinions more evenly across
several days of the week. Although the Court still follows that practice, at the
end of the term decisions pile up with seven or eight opinions in one day not an
uncommon practice. During the Burger years, the Court promised a maximum
of seven opinions a day.[9] But under Rehnquist, the Court no longer places any
limit on the number released in a day. According to Toni House, the technological capabilities of the Court's Publication Unit—the number of pages it can
handle—is the only limit on the release of opinions.

Also, the Court used to announce approximately how many opinions
would be delivered. However, Chief Justice Rehnquist, who has not evidenced

---

[9]Tropin, op. cit.

any interest in accommodating press interests, stopped the practice when he learned of it.

The Court now notifies reporters whether the opinion load will be "heavy", although the exact number is not known until the opinions are released. "Heavy" means five or more. The notification aids news organizations in determining whether to assign an additional reporter for that day. But since it is not known what decisions will be released and therefore how many are the ones followed by the press (except obviously on the last day of the term), the issue of extra help cannot be resolved until the opinions are announced. This problem engenders frustration among the press corps.

The severity of the problem for reporters this secrecy produces varies within the press corps. The elites are more likely than others to acquire space for more than one story, and in the case of the broadcast networks, another reporter will be brought in to cover the other major newsworthy case. For some reporters with more space, other decisions will be included in bullets at the end of the story. The wire service reporters are the only reporters on the beat who are not constrained by the same limitations. The Associated Press' two reporters assigned to the Court write stories on nearly all the decisions. Richard Carelli estimates that, including decision stories and other types of stories, he writes between 800 to 1,000 articles per term.[10]

But for many reporters, receiving several opinions simultaneously creates a conundrum since they will be limited to a single story for that day. Except under unusual circumstances, for most of the press corps full treatment will not be accorded for more than one decision on most days.

The choice for them becomes not one of deciding which decision is newsworthy, but rather which one is more newsworthy than the others. The choice can be an agonizing one and produces frustration among the press corps. "They might as well release them in secret and not tell anybody," suggested Tim O'Brien. "It's a real problem because we can't handle that many decisions and our viewers or readers can't digest that much."

Choosing one opinion from among several opinions that the reporter has followed throughout the term, can lead to a waste of effort. Stephen Wermiel:

> I'll prepare a lot of material I will never use. I'll prepare five cases which come out on the same day. Therefore only three of them get paragraph treatment and two of them get full treatment. There is a lot of preparation which is for naught.

Editors join this decision-making process. Reporters inform editors of the available decisions and what they feel is the main story. Typically, the editor and reporter, in tandem, agree on the decision to cover. The editor relies on the news judgment of the reporter, but is not dependent on it. The reporter's decision can be second-guessed by editors. Since editors have access to wire service copy on nearly all of the decisions, they can assess whether their reporter made the correct choice. One reporter said she didn't worry much about the decision because "if I make a

[10]Sherman, op. cit., p. 33.

mistake (in deciding whether to write a story), the editors can always take the wire story." But a pattern of such mistakes can lead editors to question the value of their staff reporter.

Reporters have been looking throughout the term, actually almost anytime after oral arguments, for certain decisions to come down. As the reporter is combing the stack of opinions issued, attention is given to those opinions already viewed as newsworthy. Others not previously identified are unlikely to merit notice, unless the Court acts in an unexpected way. One example of this is a decision announced on June 27, 1990 in the case of *Metropolitan Broadcasting Co. v. FCC*, when a narrow majority led by Justice Brennan approved affirmative action in broadcast ownership. A conservative majority on the Court was expected to form to vote down the preferences. The *Washington Post* reporter called it "the most unexpected win," which also reflected reporters' surprise at the outcome and the significance of the case.[11]

At other times, the long-awaited decision may be so narrowly decided that its significance is questionable, or it is so ambiguous in its reasoning and significance that it is not easily translatable for a general audience. "Sometimes they change my preconception", admitted Linda Greenhouse. "Sometimes they'll take what seems an uninteresting case and they'll do something quite interesting with it, or they'll take what should be an important case and they punt on it."

A primary criterion is the subject matter. On that basis, the decision has already been preselected by the reporter when the case was granted cert. The resulting preparation enhances the likelihood the decision in that case will be considered news.

However, a case may receive greater weight if the majority is narrow, particularly in a case where it was not expected to be. Dawn Weyrich Ceol, former *Washington Times* reporter on the beat, explained how she made judgments about a story based on the size of the majority:

> If it's right to die, it's not going to make any difference, it's going to be front page. If it's a mediocre case and we knew its nine to zero, it's going to get 15 inches max with bullets at the end—'in other action, the Court did this.' If it's five to four on death penalty, right to die, abortion, I'll give the dissent a great deal of room to explain why they're angry. Five to four decisions I really pay a lot of attention to.

Within the parameters of subject matter deemed as potentially news, an important factor in determining newsworthiness and placement apparently is the nature of journalistic expectations about the Court's actions. When the Court acts in an unexpected manner, the action is more likely to become news.

In summary, the choice of which decisions will receive a full story versus abbreviated mention or, in the case of nonregulars with less space, any attention at all is determined by the number and type of decisions released on any given day.

[11]Ruth Marcus, "Supreme Court Liberals Savor Win Amid Conservative Majority," *Washington Post*, July 2, 1990, p. A5.

The Time Factor

Time becomes a crucial element for most of the press corps since they meet deadlines at some point each day. "You only have a couple of hours to tell the world in eighth grade language what the Court has done," commented one reporter. Time is most critical for reporters from the wire services, broadcast networks, or afternoon dailies with late morning deadlines. "For me it's a matter of grabbing and running and filing," Jim Vicini of Reuters describes. "Literally every minute counts." One wire service reporter estimated he spent three minutes examining the decision before filing a lead for the story and only another 30 minutes before filing the whole story.[12]

Reading the decision quickly and explaining its contents, the reporters contend, is a function of good journalism not legal background. It is a skill reporters develop mainly through practice. "The time trick in reading decisions is the experience at the Court," asserted O'Brien. "I don't care how steeped you are in constitutional law or one aspect of constitutional law. I don't think you're going to read that decision in the first minute thirty and know it as well—what that decision says—as me, or Rita [Braver of CBS], or Carl [Stern of NBC]. I know how to read a syllabus."

Time is even more important when a case has attracted widespread attention throughout the term, such as the recent abortion cases—the *Webster* case in 1989, the *Rust* case in 1991, and the *Pennsylvania* case in 1992. These cases are a fraction of the total covered, but when they occur, broadcast and wire service reporters are expected by their editors and producers to announce the result in a matter of a few minutes. "When the Court upheld the constitutionality of an all-male draft, when that happened at 10:02," Tim O'Brien related. "I was on the phone by 10:02:30, and the decision was out by 10:03. That's fast."

Reporters pressed by time constraints in normal circumstances, and nearly overwhelmed by them in extraordinary situations, fear they will get it fast, but will not necessarily get it right. "You want to make sure you don't mistake the word 'affirm' for 'reverse'," O'Brien joked wryly. "It is only one word off but it can be terrible." The problem is especially acute in highly publicized cases resulting in ambiguous decisions. "The more controversial, the more newsworthy the decision, the more danger you will misconstrue what the Court has said," explained Richard Carelli. Since much of the press lacks an established structure for admitting, much less correcting, mistakes, the consequences of a mistake can be major.

Rarely do the networks interrupt regular programming to announce a Supreme Court decision. A new wrinkle, however, is the emergence of Cable News Network (CNN) as a competitor to the three major networks. As an all-news channel, CNN has become the major source of fast-breaking news. The competition with the three larger networks to be first is still present, according to Tony Collings, CNN reporter on the Court beat:

[12]David Shaw, *Press Watch* (New York: Macmillan, 1984), p. 125.

The networks can bring in at any time. They can have an anchor come on and say the Supreme Court just decided this. We're still trying to set up a live shot and we look terrible. That's what's going through our minds. We don't know when they're going to break into their programming and announce something. So we're still competing with them. Once we're on the air and they're not, then we feel we're beating them.

Reading and Culling

Once the choice is made about which decision will be covered in full, the process of reading the opinion closely and culling from it begins. The first section read is the syllabus or headnote. One reporter said he scans the syllabus to see "who's against it and who's for it." The syllabus provides a summary of the facts in the case and in outline form what the Court has held, and it announces whether the decision was affirmed or reversed, and which justices joined the Court opinion and which dissented or concurred. Additionally, the syllabus aids reporters by identifying the page numbers in the majority opinion where the separate issues in the case are addressed.

Following the syllabus is the facts section. Most reporters who have followed the case skip this section since they have already become acquainted with the facts of the case. Tim O'Brien's approach demonstrates one reporter's quick analysis of the opinions:

> I read the syllabus of the decision, and then I read the dissent. Then if time permits I'll go back and read the actual opinion and the concurring opinions. I don't have to read the facts of the case, which is in many opinions a large part of the opinion. In a forty page opinion, ten pages may be facts.
>
> If it's an opinion we've been following, I'm just as familiar with the facts as the justices are. I've been there; I've spoken with the people who brought the case.

Even the actual decision in the case and the supporting arguments usually do not come as a surprise to reporters who have followed the case. Advance preparation clues reporters to the Court's possible direction. Henry Reske:

> By the time you get the opinion...you've read the cert. petition, you've read the briefs on the merits, you've read the amicus briefs, you've gone to oral argument, and then you get the opinion. And you know half of it already. Even more, because you know the options from reading the briefs. You know they might do this or they might do that, and when you've got all that in your head it becomes easier.

The next steps vary according to the reporters' deadline. Wire service and broadcast reporters who face the earliest deadlines produce a quick story simply expressing the Court's vote and waiting until a follow-up. The initial wire story is geared to afternoon dailies with late morning deadlines. Later, a fuller story will be written. In the case of wire service reporters, the follow-up story is directed toward next day dailies with early evening deadlines.

Most of the press corps face late afternoon or early evening deadlines for broadcast news programs to be aired that evening, or for the next day's issue of the daily newspapers. The schedule described subsequently conforms to their routine.

Following the Formula

Some reporters describe the organization of the Supreme Court story as following a set formula. In many cases, especially for the non-elites, the first words in the story will be "The Supreme Court decided today...." Jim Vicini of Reuters explained how he writes a wire story:

> It's almost a formula story: Supreme Court upheld, struck down, did x, y, z. Then I try to give a sense of the vote and perhaps implications. This would include a quote from the majority, a little background of the case, a quote from the dissent, and then more background. It's not real hard to do. It's almost like a science.

One daily newspaper reporter described in more detail the formulaic writing style, which is more common for nonregulars with less preparation time and fewer column inches than regulars:

> The general formula is what did the Court say, that goes in the lead. Sometimes the lead will fold in the broader implication of the decision or sometimes that will go in the second graph. The third graph is a quote from the opinion, with the name of the person who wrote the opinion. The fourth graph is the dissent—'the dissent sharply rebuked the majority'—a quote from the dissent, usually the juiciest quote. And then, depending on whether it is a very important or emotional case, I'll quote from the majority opinion and then I'll put "Joining Chief Justice Rehnquist was...." The vote is way high, but never in the lead.

The formula is partly a product of the structure of Court opinions and partly a consequence of the establishment of press routines. Using the formula reduces story preparation and writing time and increases the likelihood of successfully meeting deadlines.

The most difficult aspect of the formula may be the lead. Leads are even more problematic in argument stories. The lead is the most important paragraph in the story. One reporter beginning the writing process remarked, "I just have to figure out my lead. It's downhill from there." Leads are important because, as one reporter explained, "we read each other's stuff." Leads often become the topic of conversation among the press corps because they manifest the priority of the reporter. A reporter whose lead diverges from that of others on the beat will be expected to defend that selection to peers as well as editors.

Remembering the Audience

Members of the Supreme Court press corps serve almost as much as translators as reporters. Unlike reporters who cover other beats in Washington, journalists on the Court beat face an institution that rarely communicates in a language directed at the press and the general public beyond it. The "legalese" in opinions must be reworded into a language acceptable to the general audience.

However, the extent of reinterpretation is an issue of debate within the press corps, and it divides the group on the basis of the natures of the different publications. While the writing of Linda Greenhouse becomes a standard for some reporters because of its wide circulation through the *New York Times* news syndicate and the pages of the *New York Times* itself, the less technical style of Lyle Denniston and others offers an attractive competing model.

Former Supreme Court beat reporter Jerome Cramer:

> Our readers don't want to know what footnote seven says about x, y, z, or about legislative history. Some of that gets into Linda's stories and some of the others—that kind of detailed legal information. For *Time* readers, they want to know why its important, they want to know what impact it's going to have.

Beyond the appeal to a general lay audience found in the tone of the writing, it is the emphasis in the content that is important. Reporters omit much of the discussion of the reasoning behind the case because they contend it is uninteresting to their audience. Former *Washington Times* reporter Dawn Weyrich Ceol:

> The way they got there—the technical stuff—is only interesting to a lawyer. The reader just wants to know what did they say and why did they say it. If the concurrence says we would have decided this a little differently, I don't care about that.

Reporters who cover the Court understand the discrepancy between what they are receiving from the Court and what they convey to the general public. They admit to the limited nature of the press role. "The press is a messenger service," argued Richard Carelli. "We're not going to give you a good idea of what they said, but you'll know they said something."

Broadcast journalists are more prone to depart from the technical style of writing and humanize the story. "I'm not writing for lawyers," asserted Rita Braver. "I hope what I'm writing would not make a lawyer wince. But I'm not going to focus on the esoteric legal point. I'm going to focus on what the law means for you and me today."

Writing for a lay audience requires journalists to remember that the salience of Court decisions is not always obvious. According to Lyle Denniston, it is essential to insert a "so what" paragraph—"so what is important about this event"—to inform the reader of the significance of the decision or argument in their lives.

Interpreting the Opinion

At times, the Court's decisions defy interpretation even for the trained reporter. The dilemma occurs when decisions are products of compromises achieved only by a resort to ambiguity, or if there is such a mixture of partial concurrences and partial dissents that the stance of the majority is difficult to discern. Attempting to explain and discern the implications of such a case becomes an exercise in guesswork. "When the Supreme Court makes a hash of a case, the press does, too," according to one reporter.[13] The task becomes especially difficult for nonregulars. One nonregular admitted that "if I'm in doubt about something, I use more quotes rather than use my own words."

[13]Ibid., p. 122.

Since they appear first and offer the most exhaustive coverage of Court decisions, the wire services' interpretations becomes the standard for much of the rest of the press corps. Confusion reigns when the AP and UPI stories offer varying interpretations. Speaking of one decision, Linda Greenhouse said: "It was literally impossible to decipher. All I could tell my readers is that the Court had done x. I could not tell them why. One wire service hailed the decision as a great civil rights victory, while the other wire service called the decision a great civil rights defeat."[14] However, with the virtual demise of UPI and the concomitant rise of AP as the primary wire service, that problem has been somewhat attenuated.

Using Sources

One solution for the unclear opinion is reliance on sources. Members of the press corps usually turn to sources external to the Court. These sources offer two services to the press corps: analysis and reaction. Reliance on sources is a byproduct of the justices' because the justices do not offer themselves as sources except through their opinions. Nor will the public information officers offer commentary or explanation.

After perusing the opinion, consulting their files on the case, and determining the angle of the story, many reporters will immediately place calls to potential sources. If they are unclear on the interpretation of the opinion, they call legal experts in the field to get both background interpretation and quotes for possible use in the story.

Unlike print journalists who can rely on telephone interviews, broadcast journalists must start the process of arranging interviews early due to the logistical constraints of getting a visual reaction from parties or affected groups in various parts of the country. Producers must arrange the reallocation of camera crews.

Many sources will not have received the opinion when they are called. "Usually I am reading the opinion to them over the phone," explained one reporter. Stephen Bokat of the National Chamber Litigation Center remarked that "the way I first find out the decision is when a reporter calls me. I will try to send someone up to the Court or ask a reporter if they can give me a copy of the opinion."

Usually, sources will choose to wait until they have the written opinion before commenting. For many legal experts and relevant interest groups in Washington, that will mean only a delay of a couple of hours. The opinions are picked up at the Court by couriers who distribute them to law firms and interest group offices in Washington. Opinions are also faxed by various interest groups, and sometimes by reporters, who are actively soliciting comment from a source, to legal experts.

Since 1990 the Court has used an electronic distribution system titled Project Hermes to transmit opinions almost as rapidly as they are delivered in the press-room. As subscribership spreads to electronic bulletin boards and universities across the nation, the problem of even a short delay in receiving the opinion will be eliminated. Potential sources for Court reporters will be able to respond more quickly to the opinions.

[14]Quoted in Tropin, op. cit.

The parties to the case also become potential sources, particularly for television stories. The parties usually are contacted in advance to comment on the decision. Following a discrimination case, Rita Braver explained that her producer called the plaintiff in the suit and asked "if he would talk to us once the decision comes down. We knew he was willing so we didn't have to worry about finding pictures of him."

Another frequent source should be the attorneys who argue the case before the Court. They have the advantage of accessibility since they are usually willing to speak to the press.

The key attributes of a source should be legitimacy, accessibility, and the ability to deliver analysis and reaction in a form suitable for the medium being used. A coterie of legal experts possessing those attributes become frequent sources in news coverage of the Court.

Legal experts are reporters' most frequent sources, according to the reporters surveyed. (See Appendix B.) Reporters seek legal experts who possess accepted credentials for legitimacy as a source. According to one reporter, he seeks "people who have a good understanding of the Court. People you've used before who know what they're talking about." Henry Reske noted that one of the most infuriating experiences is to call back a legal expert who volunteers as a source only to find "they have not seen the opinion and are not even familiar with the case's issue."[15]

The choice of sources can rest primarily on their willingness to be accessible. One reporter, not an elite, admitted that his sources are "people you can get through to." The demands of deadline require a hasty response by sources. A delay in response means exclusion. Legal experts unwilling to conform to press imperatives will be omitted. One reporter explained: "The press knows who is fastest with analysis and interpretation."

Legal experts also need to be able to offer reporters quick, cogent analysis—in other words, to be able to speak in soundbites. The expert who can meet news imperatives for pithy quotes is more likely to be used time and again.

Identifying legal experts is not a problem on most issues. Joint appearances on panels and news programs and social interaction leads to interaction who have legal scholars and practicing attorneys who have special areas of expertise. For reporters who belong to bar associations, participation in legal profession activities serves that purpose.

Some reporters will cultivate other reporters' sources. One reporter confessed that "I can look at Linda Greenhouse's article, I can look at David Savage's piece, I can look at Lyle's [Denniston] work. I can see who they talk to, who they thought was interesting, go to them and get their opinions."

Reporters maintain a list of possible sources by issue. New reporters are disadvantaged in their lack of a lengthy expert source list. One new reporter on the beat predicted that "I'll have a much better list three years from now."

Interest group spokespersons are a frequent source. In fact, finding interest groups willing to offer analysis or reaction to Court decisions is hardly an onerous

[15]Henry J. Reske, "A Reporter at the Supreme Court," *ABA Journal*, (May 1991): 69.

task. Especially for the elite, interest groups are pleading for the opportunity to serve as sources. Linda Greenhouse: "I don't make too many calls. People call me. Usually the fax machine starts churning out. Usually it's having to fend off the phone calls." One reporter related that "people are falling all over themselves to offer you information, offering stories, offering access to major players. Would you like to come to lunch with Faye Wattleton of Planned Parenthood?" Following a major decision, interest groups flood the press corps with faxed press releases, notices of news conferences, and offers for interviews with group spokespersons. (See Appendix C.) The competition among interest groups, particularly on already highly visible issues allows reporters to "pick and choose." Their choices generally include established Washington groups with already high name recognition.

The most common interest group used by the Supreme Court press corps is the American Civil Liberties Union (ACLU). Most of the reporters surveyed said they use the ACLU for reaction. Since the ACLU handles an array of legal issues, it becomes a popular source for Supreme Court reporters. Use of other groups depends on the issue. For abortion-related cases, the primary groups are National Right to Life Committee (NARAL), Americans United for Life, and Planned Parenthood. The Washington Legal Foundation is a commonly used source for criminal rights issues, while the People for the American Way and Americans United for Separation of Church and State provide commentary on religious freedom cases.

But some reporters will turn to other, smaller groups with greater accessibility. One reporter admitted that "I'll use someone different just to get someone different in there and give them a shot."

The competition is intense between opposing groups, especially the pro-choice and pro-life groups. "Pro-life groups are very insecure," commented one regular. "They think we're going to ignore them." The insecurity is not unfounded; pro-choice groups outnumber pro-life groups as sources reporters say they rely on by a margin of almost two to one.

For those who are not the elite, the search for sources is more two-sided. Moreover, many of the non-elite are competing for the same sources with the elite. Well-known sources besieged by journalists covering a highly visible issue are more likely to return a telephone call from an elite.

Established interest groups acquire a privileged position among the ranks of potential sources due to their existing high profile and their tradition of meeting press imperatives like ready accessibility. The ACLU, for example, uses an office across the street from the Court for press conferences with ACLU spokespersons. These conferences immediately follow Court decisions on major issues they are following. The ACLU and other large groups possess media relations staffs who churn out press releases and press advisories to news organizations.

Another explanation for group inclusion in stories is that editors and perhaps readers and viewers expect to hear reaction from certain traditional interest groups on the issue. "The constraints of *Time* magazine are that if it's a First Amendment issue, they want to hear from the ACLU," explained Jerome Cramer. "If it's gun control, they want to hear from the NRA spokesman or an NRA lawyer. We call them the major players, the established groups—the people who follow these kinds of issues."

A frequent meeting place for interest group representatives and the press is the plaza in front of the Court building. On one side of the plaza, several television crews set up a bank of microphones—a "stakeout"—where the counsel in the case and sometimes the parties—will appear in front of cameras to comment. Television reporters and print reporters will gather around them in an outside mini-press conference.

On the other side of the plaza, on major cases, several network crews will have set up their own interview posts and will have invited interest group representatives and legal experts who will come to hear the case and offer instant analysis and reaction. On high-profile cases, several television crews will be lined up in a row, taping or broadcasting live.

Meanwhile in the middle of the plaza, some interest group representatives will mill about offering reporters the groups' reaction. Usually a crowd of journalists will gather to listen in on the impromptu interview and to ask questions.

Regulars, especially the elite, often avoid the plaza since sources chase them rather than the other way around. One nonregular admitted that she won't use plaza interviews because "it's such a mob scene you can't hear anyway. It's better to get people on the phone." Many go to the plaza just to make sure no dramatic statement is made there that they would miss otherwise.

Some interest group representatives have adapted to the system by making themselves available on the plaza immediately following a decision on their issue in order to assure that their group's view is included. One reporter who occasionally uses the plaza interviews concluded:

> The pro-choice groups are pretty smart. They figured out essentially when [a decision] was going to come due. They were in the courtroom for a couple of days before. They were just hedging their bets. Interest groups are very shrewd. They know the best thing they can do is be there [in the plaza] afterwards. It's the old spin control thing . I swear I looked around and I didn't see any anti-abortion people I recognized. They came out later with news releases, but it's not the same as being there.

Nonregulars who need a quick reaction to a decision and lack independent access to well-known sources or a list of experts to contact find the plaza interviews and stakeout useful. One reporter who has a legal background commented that the plaza interviews "help reporters who are not as legally educated, which is the bulk of journalists covering these cases. They're looking for someone to tell them what it means."

A frequent source on the plaza is conservative columnist and legal expert Bruce Fein. On decision days near the end of the term, Fein positions himself in the hallway outside the Public Information Office until decisions are announced at 10 A.M. When he receives his copy, he peruses the opinion and then walks outside to the plaza to be interviewed. Fein is attractive to the press because, as one reporter described him, he "looks like Mister Peepers."

According to Fein, he is a popular source because he knows how to be very epigrammatic and speak in lay terms. "Most reporters want to make the opinions more earthbound," Fein explained. His presence on the plaza with opinion in hand and a working knowledge of the issue serves the needs of the press corps. "Their basic need is to find someone who is knowledgeable, someone who has read the opinion and doesn't have to be warmed up," Fein explained.

Another popular source is Professor Laurence Tribe of the Harvard Law School, who also occasionally argues before the Court. Other well-known pundits include Arthur Miller of the Harvard Law School, Walter Dellinger of Duke, and, particularly for First Amendment cases, New York attorney Floyd Abrams. These pundits acquire high media visibility not only for their expertise, but also because they return calls quickly and on account of their ability to translate the opinions into a language suitable for the general audience. One reporter commented: "We go through periods when we are not going to quote Larry Tribe anymore, but we're like chocoholics. Tribe is really a wonder at explaining something to you in an incredibly orderly way."[16]

Many interest groups will send press releases, especially through faxes, to reporters. These express the group's viewpoint on the outcome of the case and allow some reporters easy access to quotes from group leaders. General assignment reporters are benefitted most by this practice since they have more difficulty obtaining the exclusive interview or even having established sources able to react to the opinion. "A lot of small newspapers around the country and weekly journals respond more to the press releases," Stephen Bokat explained. "They will call or just pick something out of it."

In highly newsworthy cases, most regulars have a plethora of sources available to them—plaza interviews, solicitations to news conferences, press releases, fax and telephone offers to provide statements. By the middle of the afternoon, the sources who have solicited in the late morning are returning calls after reading part if not all of the opinions handed down that day. However, by that time typically the reporter has gathered more than enough source material for the story, and begins fending off calls. For broadcast reporters, the question is how to mix all of the Washington sources with the interviews conducted outside of Washington.

When reporters contact their sources, the intent is to extract interpretation and reaction. Interest group spokespersons provide the official reaction of the group. However, some interest group media relations officers will connect the reporter to their legal staff. The group's attorneys offer greater legitimacy and can offer both interpretation and reaction. Rene Cravens of NARAL speculated that reporters know what they want from sources before they contact them. "Reporters pretty much have a clear idea where they are going. When they come to us, they're looking for information that will back up whatever they want to say."

[16]Quoted in Charles Rothfeld, "On Legal Pundits and How They Got That Way," *The New York Times*, May 4, 1990, p. B7.

How do reporters get sources to talk? "I generally will call people, depending how well I know them; I'll say the x, y, z case was just decided; I'll say what do you think of the outcome," Jerome Cramer related. "Were you surprised with this justice's ruling or with the dissenting opinion? I'll ask questions about that. I'll try to get their feel for it. Then I'll call other people. Then when I sit down to write the story I have a variety of views."

One dilemma for reporters is when sources disagree on the significance of the case. One reporter said that "sometimes I'll get conflicting analysis. Some will say the case means nothing; others say it's very important."

Reporters solicit strong rhetoric from interest groups on the effects of decisions to enliven their stories. They plumb their sources for the perfect quote or soundbyte. One newsmagazine reporter said he is limited in the number of quotes he can use, so he is selective about the types he uses. "I try to get a key quote to illuminate the issue—a quote that is funny or sexy or unusual, or in a slightly off beat way illuminates the whole case." One reporter, talking with his bureau chief following an abortion decision, inquired, "What does Molly [Yard, president of NOW] have to say? She must have some good rhetoric."

The reliance on sources for interpretation and reaction has sparked criticism of the press' coverage. Critics claim that by choosing legal experts who are ideological and who will offer opinions on complex legal issues in bite-size doses, the reporters trivialize the issues. Kenneth Geller, a former deputy U.S. solicitor general is a critic of this practice: "There aren't many blacks and whites in law, but the gray shades in the middle don't work for the press. That leads to oversimplification and polarization, and to a certain disparagement for the process."[17]

Sometimes reporters bridle at the extensive use of interest groups as sources. Miranda Spivack criticized the process of reliance on groups for interpretation of the opinion: "You know you have to depend on people who have a vested interest. So you know you have to take what they say with a grain of salt. I figure everyone is giving me their own gloss, and I just have to sit through it." However, editors have come to expect the inclusion of sources, particularly traditional sources.

Given the interest groups' success at meeting press imperatives in a way that the Court does not do, the role of interest groups as sources is not likely to diminish.

Information Sharing

Information sharing is a common practice among journalists, and the Supreme Court press corps is no exception. Their proximity gives rise to the issue of consensual journalism or, more pejoratively, "pack journalism." The commonality in the determination of news on the Supreme Court beat is one indicator of consensual journalism.

Lyle Denniston described an unintentional similarity in reporters' choices of what cases constituted news. Denniston said one year he chose a term and

---

[17]Quoted in Rothfeld, op. cit.

unobtrusively watched the process of press corps selection of cases to cover during the term.

> It became apparent there were only about a dozen cases that I could honestly say were really candidates for the best cases of the day in newsworthiness. Without any cabal, it became obvious that these were the same cases, give or take one or two, that had newsworthiness to my colleagues. It was obvious that I and Linda Greenhouse and Stephen Wermiel and Dick Carelli and Ruth Marcus [former *Washington Post* reporter at the Court] all wound up, without ever having consulted with each other, with a tight little circle of cases.

The environment exists for pack journalism, although not as certainly as it does in other settings, such as a presidential campaign. Journalists at the Court do interact with each other frequently. The close proximity of reporters' carrels, the shared experience of frequent routines, and the social interaction offer the opportunity for exchange of perspectives. Moreover, almost all of the journalists surveyed said they were satisfied with their relationship with their colleagues in the pressroom. (Although many in the press corps work primarily in the bureau office not at the Court.)

Although reporters do talk to one another, over lunch or in chance encounters in the pressroom, they are protective of their interpretation of what constitutes news. This protectiveness diminishes the tendency toward story selection by consensus. That may explain why two-thirds of surveyed reporters said the influence of their colleagues in the pressroom is not important in their writing. (See Appendix B.)

But they are influenced by one another's stories and, in their discussions, by each other's evaluations of the cases. Lyle Denniston: "My tentative conclusion is there is no cabal, there is no pack journalism in the way I understand pack journalism, but there is a lot of exchange of evaluations and assessments of stories on the basis of news merit, and that, I think, seems to account for the parallelism."

The phenomenon of information sharing also includes helping someone else do their job. For example, Denniston admitted that he had missed the first flag-burning case—*Texas v. Johnson*—until "Linda Greenhouse said to me, as a friend, I'm going to tell you you better look at this case." Information sharing also occurs regularly in covering arguments. Reporters operate without transcripts and query each other on the exact wording of a justice's statement or question.

Information sharing also exists between the regulars and nonregulars. The most irregular of the nonregulars, those who cover the Court only rarely and therefore invest little time on the beat, may need to rely on the regulars and more frequent nonregulars for assistance. As I sat in the pressroom observing after a highly newsworthy decision, one reporter rushed into the room and announced that she had been covering another story on Capitol Hill but had been detailed to the Court to report on this decision. Assuming I was a regular, she asked me who she should talk to as sources. There was the clear expectation that another reporter would help her. In another case, a nonregular from a regional daily admitted that a regular periodically directed him to cases appearing on the orders list pertinent to his home region.

The Role of the Elite

When decisions have been released or a newsworthy oral argument has been completed, reporters discuss the case. There are plenty of opportunities as they move from the courtroom down the broad marble stairs and back to the pressroom or as they filter out of the Public Information Office after a decision release, or as they gather in small knots in the pressroom. The pressroom is small enough that any conversation in the middle of the room can be picked up by others nearby and lead to more reporters joining the circle.

This setting becomes the forum for reporters' critiques of the justices and their decisions. The critiques include the justices' performances on the bench: The questions they asked of counsel in the arguments, the intensity of the justices' response to counsellor's answers, and the nuances, such as the justices' expressions and glances.

The hostility they feel some of the justices hold toward them is expressed at these times. After a decision announcement in a libel case, one reporter in the midst of a small circle observed: "When Rehnquist read [the majority opinion] he turned and smiled at us." Another joked bitterly: "If one of us fell down and broke a leg, that would just make his day."

The interaction is not purely social; it is also productive as a mechanism for gauging others' responses to the Court's actions. Reporters ask each other what they think about the cases argued or the decisions announced. One queries another: "Do you think it's a significant hit on the First Amendment?"

The influence of the elite is most apparent in the case of an ambiguous or highly complicated decision. One nonregular explained what he does in such situations: "Once in a while you get a complex decision with no clear majority. Then I would talk it over with some of my colleagues who would have covered the case more closely."

The Influence of the Wires

The wire services possess a significant influence on the rest of the press coverage of the Court. And it is an influence that has grown with the development of more rapid transmission of news.

In the most benign sense, the wire stories expand a news organization's coverage of the Court beyond the effort of the news organization's staff reporter on the beat. The wire stories can be used by newspapers to supplement their own staff reporter's coverage, thus increasing the number of decisions actually reaching print.

But the wires also shape the writing of the stories produced by others in the press corps, especially the non-elite. They do this because of their speed and the ready availability to reporters and editors, usually long before others on the press beat have filed their stories.

Immediately following the decision announcement, the wires—especially the Associated Press—have two opportunities to influence the decision coverage by others on the beat. The wires release a bulletin about the decision—the lead—within the first hour after its release in the morning. The wire stories are the first to appear with word of the decision. While others in the press corps are still contacting sources and determining the angle of the story, the initial wire story becomes available on their computer terminals. The Associated Press angle on the story, in that brief initial story, is the first glance at how another journalist, particularly a well-respected elite, has perceived the Court's action. The presence of this early indication of the AP emphasis is useful in guiding other journalists, especially nonregulars on the angle on the story. Some print journalists are required to complete a lead by early afternoon, and the wire service's angle can influence their lead. The second opportunity to influence coverage occurs in mid-afternoon when the wires produce stories for the next cycle geared to the late afternoon and early evening deadlines. The second AP story is more detailed, contains more quotes from the opinions, and reflects interest group reaction.

Most of the press corps, except those working for the afternoon dailies, newsmagazines, and the specialized publications, face an early evening deadline for filing a complete story. By the time reporters have contacted sources and acquired possible quotes, it is mid-afternoon. At this time, reporters file an early lead, which holds a place for the story in the layout, but the actual writing is still underway.

The wire service reporters, on the other hand, have already filed stories for morning dailies. Those stories by the Associated Press, United Press International, and Reuters move to news outlets throughout the nation. By mid-afternoon of the decision day, the wire service story is already available on the reporter's video display terminal. By late afternoon, other news syndicates—Knight-Ridder and *New York Times*—also have transmitted their reporter's Court stories to subscribers. At least the AP wire story, if not those of others, is available to most reporters long before they file.

Ready access to the stories already filed by other reporters presents a professional dilemma for the press corps: Do they use these stories as a guide or not in writing their own? Some reporters contend there is no dilemma for them. Glen Elsasser, who covered the Court for more than 20 years for the *Chicago Tribune*, insisted that before writing his story he "would not look at what the wires wrote." Others admit they do read others' stories before filing their own. Tony Collings of CNN said he read the AP story to "see what their lead is." Former *Time* Court reporter Jerome Cramer acknowledged that he looked at the AP story before writing his piece on a decision. Still others are not quick to admit their reference to the wires, but are likely to use it nonetheless. One reporter I followed was referring to the AP story frequently while writing. Another changed a quote from an oral argument to conform with the AP story's version. Henry Reske, former UPI reporter at the Court, suggested the power of the wires is not minimal:

> The wires have had an agenda setting influence. That still goes on. People will get it in their heads and it's hard to fight it. If both UPI and AP say it's a big civil rights victory,

it would be hard to turn back that. Unless one of the big civil rights groups got up and said this is wrong, it would be hard to turn that around.

Not only do many reporters use the wire stories for guidance, but they are forced to respond to the wires because they are not the only ones reading them. Their editors receive the wires simultaneously and pay attention to them. At least in some cases, the video display terminal technology allows users to know who has accessed the wire story. Both editors and reporters can confirm wire story access by the other.

Editors use the wire stories to assess the work of their own staff reporter. Glen Elsasser explained the problem for nonregulars:

> You get more pressure from editors because they'll see Linda Greenhouse is writing about this case. And they'll say, what about it? Sometimes editors will take stories and blow them up as more important than the reporter thinks they are.

If nonregulars use their own judgment to depart from the wires' analyses on a decision, the editor will likely challenge the staff reporter. "They'll have to explain themselves," said Reske.

Although the elite are not second-guessed as much by their editors, even they must respond to the wires. Stephen Wermiel explained that his editors "monitor the wires all day long. It's almost never to say [to me] the wires are taking this view of the case. It's more just to see if any of the cases I didn't write about were things that are worth doing."

For those reporters who want to make their own judgments about story construction and utilize their reporting skills independently, the problem of the wires' accessibility is an acute one. Since their editors are reading the wire stories, reporters must read them also to know what their editor is seeing. However, once a reporter has read the wire coverage it is difficult not to be influenced by it.

Moreover, use of the wire stories by editors as a kind of model interpretation of the decision restricts the ability of their reporters to develop alternative interpretations. The result is movement toward greater uniformity in the news product across apparently diverse news organizations.

Working with Editors and Producers

Wire service copy is not the only source of tension between reporters and their editors and producers. Stephen Hess found Supreme Court reporters had more disagreements with their editors than the average Washington reporter. And their work was more likely to be subject to editing than the copy of their colleagues at the White House, the Congress, or the State Department.[18]

From the perspective of the pressroom, editors and producers are the primarily unseen collaborators in the news process. Two-thirds of the journalists surveyed said their editor's influence was very important in their work. (See Appendix B.)

[18]Hess, *The Washington Reporters*, pp. 142–144.

The editors play this role because of their continual interaction with reporters. They are a regular point of contact for reporters from the initial decision announcement to beyond the reporter's deadline. An editor or producer is the first person called after decision announcement to alert him or her to the story of the cases announced and the story the reporter intends to write. An initial lead, known as the "early line budget" or the "preview", is chosen for the benefit of editors in identifying a story coming later in the day. The editor queries the reporter on the story. How important is this decision? Is this something for the first page? How much space is needed? The editor is searching for the reporter's assessment as to whether there is a story and how much play it should get.

Although there is a temptation to hype a story's importance in order to receive more bylines in the paper, the long-term result would be damaging to the reporter. "I don't want to lose my credibility by pushing a story just to get it on page one," explained Tony Mauro of *USA Today*.

An allocation of space is offered depending on the reporters' judgment about the salience of the decision. That allocation apparently is smaller than it used to be. One explanation is the shrinking news hole. According to Denniston, in the mid-1980s, he was allocated between 28 to 30 inches. Today, it is 16 inches. Denniston estimated he can use only one-fifth of the material he gathers.

And the process does not stop there. The process of editing in most cases is multilayered. At ABC News, for example, four or five editors review each piece before it is aired.

For some reporters it is a task of selling the editors on the value of doing the story. Newsmagazine reporters on the Court beat, for example, compete with a host of other beats for a limited amount of space and a general lack of commitment to cover the Court.

The story must be sold as important to a broad audience, which is a difficult task in many instances. Jerome Cramer related his editors' perspective on Court stories:

> They're interested in what the case says and why it's important, and the impact on the reader. They want a real sense of why is this case important, what is the immediate impact. And if it's going to involve FCC laws, that's a small group—radio operators, but if it's a case that is affirmative action, where there is a great deal of interest and concern....The larger, the more societal, and the more immediate the ruling, then the greater chance they will agree to the piece.

Editors or producers and reporters negotiate. Rita Braver explained that when she approaches a producer with a story the scenario is "you tell them how long you think you need and they tell you how long you're really going to get."

One example of this negotiating process is seen in the situation of a reporter I followed on the day of arguments in *Cohen v. Cowles*, a case involving a reporter's use of a source's name after a promise of confidentiality. That same day the Court also announced a decision.

The reporter returned to his office before noon. When he arrived, his editor came to his desk and asked: "What you got today?" The reporter explained the topic of the argument. The argument story, he says, is not a high priority news item. The editor asks whether it should be a ten inch story or a news brief, which would consist of no more than two lines. The reporter argues for a full story, but the argument is low key. He is not pressing.

The editor says he is leaning toward a brief, but the reporter then begins to lobby for a fuller piece. He argues the issue does affect people: "People have dealt with the media as sources before."

The editor then asks for an assessment of the decision. The reporter isn't really interested in covering it. The editor argues for a decision story.

Finally, the editor says: "Ten inches for both together?" The reporter agrees.

As the editor leaves, however, the reporter confesses that both he and the editor may lose at the next layer of the editorial process. "It wouldn't surprise me if it is a brief. It is not a dramatic story. You can't sell arguments as news stories." But the reporter's prediction was wrong, and a full story did appear on page 10 of the next issue.

In this negotiation, the editor's objective apparently was extraction of a decision story. The reporter, however, did not believe the decision was newsworthy; he wanted to do an argument piece. However, he knew that an argument piece would be hard to sell even after it is written. Also, he knew the issues in the argument piece would be revisited later at the decision stage. "It wasn't as if we would never come back to this," he explained.

Also, it is significant that although the editor was asking the reporter what had occurred at the Court today, the editor had already read the early wire story on the decision and was not approaching the reporter uninformed. The wire story may have even prompted him in his negotiation with the reporter to emphasize the decision, which the wires had already confirmed as news. In addition, the wire services had not emphasized or confirmed the argument story.

Editors and reporters also negotiate on the lead and emphases within the story. At times, pressure is placed on reporters to enliven stories with personalities and drama. Two-thirds of the reporters surveyed said that at least occasionally editors will alter their copy to increase audience interest. One regular described the pressure on him in writing argument stories to predict the outcome of the case: "There is a desire among editors to say, did they seem sympathetic to one side or the other? How is it going to come out? And I shy away from that. Sometimes I'll say—'four justices seemed hostile to the government's position.'"

One print journalist's story of the *Rust v. Sullivan* argument in October 1990 demonstrates the potential tension between editors and reporters. This reporter said her editors wanted her to change the lead on an argument story to emphasize David Souter's questions. "I resisted but I didn't want to make World War III over it." She finally relented. Her editors then wanted her to hype it further by saying that in his questioning, Souter, appointed by Bush, "aggressively challenged the president's representative [the solicitor general]." She was able to block that change.

Once the copy is written, the frequency of editorial alterations varies according to the level of expertise of the reporter and the editors, the seniority of the reporter, and the nature of the publication. Linda Greenhouse insisted that when it comes to editors changing her stories, "basically I call the shots. They don't change things of anybody without consulting."

But editorial tampering is not infrequent. Two-thirds of the journalists surveyed said their editors will want the copy changed to explain a technical point. (See Appendix B) Editorial control over content may be appreciated when the change improves the story through tightening or by tightening charges of bias. Tim O'Brien of ABC News explained the editor's function as protective:

> I'll go over my script with one producer. He might say why don't you change this line. Your standup close appears to be pro-choice. I had made the point about an abortion case being argued today having to do with whether federal funded clinics may be prohibited from offering abortion counseling in the clinic. We were talking about in the South Bronx. Many of the women who go there were low income and have no place else to go. I made that point in my close. And it's all true. But it sounded like it might be a pro-choice twist on the piece. So we found a way to take that out. That was the recommendation of the editor. We took that last part of the standup close out, and I redid the piece.

Editors and reporters negotiate over language on other grounds, such as the level of "legalese" injected into the story. According to Miranda Spivack, editors get involved when they don't understand something in a story. She views them as surrogates for the audience. "I figure if they don't understand it, most of our readers aren't going to understand it."

After the reporter has filed, the editor takes over. One major factor in the editing process at this point is the wire story. "The editor usually edits my story, I think, with the AP story right by its side because that's what they get earliest," one reporter speculated. Editors may add information obtained from the wire, to the frustration of reporters if the editorial change is significant. "It bothers me if AP has a fact that I have different and they go with the AP without asking me," complained one regular.

If the wire and the staff reporter's stories differ, especially in interpretation, the staff reporter bears the burden of proof. "Editors don't totally understand how the AP operates," one reporter complained. "They've got a lot to do. It's not great writing. It's just get it down and get it out."

Reporters who believe their editors pay close attention to the wire copy are more likely to do so as well. According to Lyle Denniston, the editor-reporter relationship is important in predicting the reporter's level of autonomy from wire interpretation. "A new reporter is likely not to deviate [from the wire] because the relationship is not strong."

One example of the editors' reliance on the wire stories and the subsequent pressure on a reporter is seen in a dispute between Stephen Wermiel of the *Wall Street Journal* and his editors over his story about the *Cruzan* case in June 1990. Wermiel submitted a story that differed on one significant point from others' stories—it omitted reference to the Court creating a new, albeit qualified, right to die.

I got chastised by my editors for this, but I think I was right. I ended up adding a paragraph to the version I originally turned in because I was being bugged by the editors about it. The version I turned in doesn't talk about the Supreme Court having recognized some new constitutional right. The decision says whatever right is at stake here, 'we hold the state has imposed reasonable limits on it.' And that was the approach I took to the story. I was reluctant to write a broad dramatic story with the Supreme Court defining some new constitutional right when you have to add up the opinions of several justices, including some in the dissent, in order to find that right. It seems to me, if the Court wanted to announce a new constitutional right, it knows how to do it. While it is my place to interpret and to explain, it is not my place to do their job for them.

Despite this perception of his place and job via-à-vis the Court, Wermiel, at the insistence of his editors, agreed to do just that. Editors do not feel at liberty to change wording completely on their own, especially if it is a technical decision, but they will make content revisions, such as moving paragraphs.

Just as reporters have less control than their counterparts on Capitol Hill over the selection of events to cover, so editors have less of a role in the determination of stories on the Court beat. The tension between reporters and editors is at least partly a function of the reporters' monopoly on expertise in the area. "They realize I know things they don't," Linda Greenhouse explained. "Unlike beats [like Capitol Hill] where editors feel they are an expert on what's happening,...If there's seven opinions in a day, and I choose one as the most important, they're not going to second guess me. Whereas on the Hill a dozen discrete events happen in a day. I think editors often impose their reality on the reporter because they feel they know more."

Editors are in the vulnerable position of having to place more trust in their staff on the Court beat because they don't know the beat. "They generally trust me," Mauro asserted. "I'm the expert."

But reporters like Linda Greenhouse and Tony Mauro are more likely to be granted a freer hand with stories than the non-elite and especially non-regulars. Miranda Spivack had several years experience covering the Court and attended the first year of law school at Yale, but she was often thwarted by editors when she analyzed an opinion. "There's always a lot of pressure on me to go to outsiders to contribute. I try to resist that when I'm secure about an interpretation."

The editors also may ultimately scrap a story. Although this occurrence is rare for the daily print media, it is not uncommon for broadcast news or weeklies. Broadcast reporters may be told that despite all their advance preparation prior to decision day and their work on the day itself, there is no room for a decision story on the evening news. The best coverage the story will receive at that point is a brief reader by the anchor written by editors from the wire copy. "They'll do a reader, but usually they'll tell me [early in the day]," according to Rita Braver. "Sometimes I'll work on it a little longer and around four o'clock they'll say, its looking like we just can't get it in."

Due to other competing events, the process sometimes leads to disappointing results. In the victim impact story by Tim O'Brien mentioned previously, after he had arranged for a camera crew with a van-load of equipment to accompany him for two days, he traveled to Memphis to interview some of the parties in the case. He interviewed Washington sources, and began preparations for pulling together his material for the final decision story. But the story was killed when, on the day of the decision, Justice Marshall announced he would retire. Although he was able to use the material in other ways, O'Brien's work on the decision never appeared on the most coveted slot—the network's evening news program.

This tension between editorial role and the expert status of the reporter affects the relationship between editors and reporters on the Supreme Court beat. One-third of the reporters described themselves as at least somewhat dissatisfied with the relationship with their editor.

CONCLUSION

The reporters who cover the Supreme Court, especially the regulars, are a distinctive group. Many possess a specialty—legal reporting—that other journalists attempt to shun. They enjoy a work routine dismissed as boring by their counterparts on other beats. Yet a core of this press corps has attained a longevity at the Court that currently far surpasses most of the justices.

Also, the beat is characterized by the absence of overt "spin control." The Court's lack of overt "spin control," through a flood of press releases, news conferences, photo opportunities, and other staples of Washington reporting, in one sense clearly liberates the reporter. The justices hand down opinions via the Public Information Office, but there is little visible effort to "frame" the individual Court news story for reporters as is the case elsewhere.

These attributes enhance the reporter's role in the newsgathering process. The reporter is more salient as a gatekeeper, a framer of the story, and an interpreter of the event.

The Court's practice of releasing several opinions at the same time magnifies the gatekeeper role of the reporter. If the Court spaced opinions more evenly, the Court would guarantee itself extensive press coverage of key decisions. Currently, the reporter can "pick and choose" among the Court's offerings.

Beyond the initial choice of decisions, ideally the reporter is free to frame the story about the decision as he or she wishes. The reporter has the choice of a variety of sources—the opinions (which often include several concurring and dissenting as well as the majority), interest group representatives, and legal experts.

The opinions are released, but, with the exception of the headnotes, they are not packaged. Reporters cull the opinions or their notes from arguments to organize the story. The news values must be discerned by them because, unlike with their colleagues at the White House or Capitol Hill, the institution they cover has not done it for them.

One reporter expressed great relish in the possession of this framing capability:

> This is the only place I know of where you are so entirely on your own. There is no one here to give you guidance on what the opinion means. It gives you freedom to pick and choose. I think this is important. I'm going to stress this opinion. You have the freedom to choose how to shape the coverage.

Explaining the significance and impact of the decision also devolves to the reporter. In discussing her handling of one highly technical decision, Linda Greenhouse admitted she went beyond what the opinion actually said. "The Court was clarifying the roles of the state and federal courts, but you had to go further than the Court's holding to bring this out. It wasn't clear from the opinion itself."[19]

The current process of releasing decisions creates a vacuum in the process of explication, which the press demands as accompaniment for an ambiguous event. Press releases issued by the Court simultaneously explaining and interpreting decisions probably would prove highly useful to reporters, and for most nonregulars such releases would likely outstrip the opinions themselves as sources. The closest the press gets to such a device are those press releases issued later on decision days by interest groups reacting to an opinion. But no such press releases from the Court exists.

Information sharing and identification of a journalistic consensus becomes even more vital on the Court beat precisely because the reporter is so independent and alone. For the reporter, that freedom is both exhilarating and frightening in its consequences.

The reporter's freedom to interpret, however, is constrained by the reporter's own status. Reporters who are not the elite are less capable of acting as interpreters due to their own limitations and to the low level of trust in their interpretive abilities on the part of their editors.

Another major force on the beat today, however, are those external groups and individuals who have sought to act as news manipulators in lieu of the Court. Interest groups have acquired a major role on the Court beat. They provide press advisories, news releases, news conferences, pre-term press briefings, and opportunities to meet with key group officials throughout the term.

Interest group opinion has become a major counterweight to the majority opinion. One regular explained that when writing a decision story he tried to get an interest group on the opposite side from the majority opinion. For him, the dissent acts as a last resort: "Sometimes if no one is reacting very well, I'll quote from the dissent."

The interest group perspective-as-balance approach heightens the salience of the role of the interest group in Supreme Court news. In an age of institutional and individual attempts to shape news coverage, the Court's failure to engage in the overt activities associated with such attempts—news conferences, photo opportu-

---

[19]Quoted in Tropin, op. cit.

nities, and so forth—creates a vacuum for interest groups to fill. "They're mobilized to feed us," noted Tony Mauro. "We're not getting it from the Court."

Mauro suggests the effort intensified at the time of the Robert Bork nomination. The practice of pre-term briefings has emerged since 1987. Once mobilized to affect press coverage of the Bork confirmation process, groups may have continued by redirecting their efforts to existing cases.

But the evolution of interest group role may have dated from an earlier period, perhaps during the post-Vietnam and Watergate periods, when many in the press adopted the investigative reporting of Bob Woodward and Carl Bernstein as the ideal type of journalism.

However they have emerged, interest groups now assist reporters in juxtaposing the Court's activities with the interests of a larger society than that of the legal community. By playing the role of loyal opposition to the Court's decisions, they also act to diminish the Court's claim as a superbody, and they cast it more in the light of another actor in ongoing political dramas.

Chapter Five

The Invisible Dance

Justices and reporters would seem to have little in common. The justices typically are much older and more conservative, traditional, and scholarly than the denizens of the pressroom located in the basement of the Supreme Court building. One longtime employee of the Court close to some of the justices remarked:

> There is an enormous cultural gulf between justices and reporters. Justices rewrite their opinions maybe fourteen times to get the precise nuance in each sentence. The reporters sit down in two hours and write a story that will be read by millions of people. There's a general feeling of discomfort.

Despite this "enormous cultural gulf," justices and reporters who cover the Court interact regularly. Reporters contend no such interaction exists since they are denied access to the justices through the traditional encounters of news conferences and interviews. But interaction need not be interpersonal; nor does it need to allow for a press role in setting the agenda for the encounter.

In the case of the justices, the interaction is primarily written, not oral. And the agenda for those encounters is set exclusively by the justices. The interaction may not meet journalistic expectations, nevertheless it does exist.

Both justices and reporters bring to the relationship certain objectives. However, the justices are more successful in achieving theirs. The fact that they solely determine the mode of interaction is evidence of their success. But they also succeed due to the clarity of their objectives, and due to the press' mixed objectives and attitudes toward the justices.

This chapter analyzes the objectives of reporters and of the justices in press interaction, the inherent danger for the justices in pursuing their objectives, the tactics employed to do so, and the causes of press acquiescence to the relationship established largely on the justices' terms. The relationship between these two seemingly incompatible partners is characterized as a dance, albeit an invisible one.

REPORTERS' OBJECTIVES

Certain objectives are shared by journalists who cover the Supreme Court, or any beat for that matter. The need for accurate, quick reporting is universal. Get it fast and get it right are bywords of journalism, which take on an even weightier meaning for reporters who struggle with lengthy opinions often turning on fine points of law.

Most reporters who cover the Court also remain within the mainstream of Court reporting. The pressure from peers and editors mandates such conformity in most cases, with the possible exception of the elites who establish the standard for news coverage.

At this point, the unity of purpose dissolves into two conflicting objectives. Although no individual member of the press corps will firmly place himself or herself in one of these camps, nevertheless two factions exist within the press corps.

A primary objective of one faction is the discovery and broadcast of the human dimension in the activities of the Court. According to this school of thought, the justices should be treated like people who are making decisions, not as special recipients of divine wisdom. Tony Mauro, who writes a column often featuring the more human aspects of the justices, expressed this view:

> I think the press corps here is excessively deferential. Since I started this column, I've gone on the philosophy the Supreme Court is a place where about 300 people go to work everyday and nine of them wear robes. It is an institution like any other. They're not demigods; they're just people. Some reporters treat them like they're beyond reporting about as people.

One wire service reporter asserted that it is "my job to know as much as possible about the justices." Richard Carelli of the Associated Press said he believes the reader deserves to know the personal background of the justices:

> When Justice Stevens writes an opinion about parental rights, we can put in the story that this author is himself the adoptive parent of two children. It adds something for the readers, an appreciation of where this guy is coming from.

Another faction, however, decries such an emphasis. This faction asserts that news coverage of the Court should consist of reporting the written work of the justices because the justices have spent months writing their opinions in an organized fashion. Moreover, the important news of the Court beat is what the justices decide, and that is found in the opinions the Court readily provides.

Lewis Powell, upon his retirement, was likely addressing this group when he remarked that the reporters at the Court "deserve a great deal of credit for not making efforts to ascertain information that would be very easy to obtain if one put his or her hand to doing so...."[1] It must be made clear that those who advocate this view do not necessarily avoid the justices. Interpersonal interaction with the justices, however, at receptions or other engagements, is not sought, nor is it intended to assist in explaining the justices to the news audience.

The most influential proponent of this perspective is the *New York Times* reporter on the Court beat, Linda Greenhouse. As discussed in Chapter Four, Greenhouse's role as an exemplar used by editors and her colleagues in the pressroom enhances the persuasiveness of this model of Court reporting.

The conflict between these factions, coupled with the effectiveness of the justices' efforts to achieve their objectives, seriously undermines the ability of the press corps to accomplish theirs. The real emphasis, then, must be placed on the justices' objectives and those tactics chosen to reach them.

JUSTICES' OBJECTIVES

Although reporters rely on justices for stories, the justices appear not to rely on reporters for anything. By appearances they live in a cloistered world unaffected by the imperative of reelection, impenetrable to the whims of public opinion, and unconcerned about appeals to any electorate.

The justices' strong penchant for privacy would seem to attenuate any motivation for a relationship with the press. The kind of exposure politicians experience is foreign to the justices. However, the personalized nature of an institution that consists of nine individuals, versus 535 in the Congress, exacerbates the problem of maintaining personal privacy.

Apparently then, the justices have little motive for returning the press' interest in them and entering into any kind of relationship. The result would only be a loss of their privacy with no apparent gain.

But as was noted in Chapter One, the Court is a political institution, as well as a legal institution. The Court possesses powerful motives for shaping the environment in which the justices operate, including the perceptions of external constituencies. The cloistered world of the Court is part of the mystique. Even that penchant for privacy is part of the myth. Associated Press reporter Richard Carelli argues the justices' privacy demands are "part personal and part political. They are saying 'I'm above day-to-day scrutiny by the ink-stained wretches we give part of the building to.' It serves them [to limit access]."

Not only does the Court as an institution hold such motives, but the justices also possess their own individual motives for interacting with the press. Some

---

[1]Transcript of Lewis Powell press conference, June 26, 1987, Thurgood Marshall Papers, Box 575, Library of Congress, Washington, D.C.

of these motives are separate from, while others are intertwined with, those of
the institution.

The justices as individuals possess more individualistic objectives unconnec-
ted to, and at times even in contradiction with, the institutional objectives discussed
in Chapter One. These objectives assist in the explication of justices' behavior
vis-à-vis the press.

First, it is imperative to dismiss motives common to other policymakers. The
justices rarely publicly express ambitions for other offices. No justice has ever
moved successfully from the Court to the presidency or the vice-presidency. No
justice in the past 40 years has even displayed serious interest in these offices, with
the possible exception of Sandra Day O'Connor in 1984.[2]

But the justices do have individual motives which animate their behavior on
the Court and their press relations. These motives are a desire to explicate fully their
views, to acquire external assistance for internal disputes when perceived as
necessary, and to affect the larger political environment as it touches on their role
as members of the Court. Each of these objectives will be explored in depth.

Typically, only a single justice writes the opinion for the Court. Therefore,
the justices have used their separate opinions as a major vehicle for explication of
their views on the issues before the Court. The number of dissents and concurring
opinions has soared in recent years. David O'Brien found the Burger Court annually
produced four times the number of dissenting opinions and ten times the number of
concurring opinions of the Hughes Court during each of its terms.[3] He concludes
that "individual opinions are now more highly prized than opinions for the Court."[4]

This practice has engendered criticism from within the legal community that
the justices are harming the institution for their own individual satisfaction. Richard
Posner has expressed this argument:

> From an institutional perspective it is better for the disagreeing judge not to dissent
> publicly in such a case, even though such forbearance will make it more difficult for
> someone to write the judge's intellectual biography.[5]

However, due to the shortcomings of the opinion-writing process as a vehicle
for communicating to the Court's nonlegal constituency, the justices also employ
other means for explication of their views. These other means include the press.

One drawback to the norm of aloofness of the justices has been the inability
of individual justices to publicly attempt to alter the historical record about their
particular role on the Court. Some of the justices have attempted to use the press to

---

[2]For one justice's private remarks that in the 1960s Douglas and Stewart still harbored ambitions
for the presidency, see *Mr. Justice and Mrs. Black: The Memoirs of Hugo L. Black and Elizabeth Black*
(New York: Random House, 1986), p. 206.

[3] David. M. O'Brien, *Storm Center* (New York: W. W. Norton, 1986), pp. 263–267.

[4]Ibid., p. 267.

[5]Richard A. Posner, *The Federal Courts: Crisis and Reform* (Cambridge, Mass.: Harvard University Press, 1985), p. 236.

shape that record. Associated Press reporter Richard Carelli remarked that one justice spoke to the press because "he's very interested in his historical role as he nears retirement. He is interested in getting a sneak preview of what history will say about him."

The justices also seek to shape the current coverage of themselves in a way not possible through opinion writing. Justice Blackmun used a session with a reporter to correct what he considered a widely perpetuated myth. According to Carelli, Blackmun had a reputation as a "real slowpoke [in opinion writing] on occasion; he held the other justices up. Blackmun said, 'I've had that bum rap since Potter Stewart laid it on me. I've never, ever held up the Court' and he started pounding the table. He wanted to get this out—at least off the record." Or on the record, as it has become.

Chief Justice Rehnquist apparently possesses a keen interest in his personal image. He gave an interview to the *New York Times Magazine,* and according to Stuart Taylor, he admitted to the interviewer that he was agreeing to do it because "he'd been portrayed as sort of a stick figure all these years. He wanted to explain himself in a way that wasn't adequately explained by the press coverage of his decisions."

Several of these reasons are contained in the following explanation by Stephen Wermiel of Justice Brennan's attitude toward a high profile through his last 20 years on the Court.

> In 1969, [Brennan] cut himself off from the world, including the press. He was mentioned in stories after Fortas which he was quite offended by. That also coincided with his wife having been diagnosed with throat cancer. It spread for 15 years until she died. He spent most of the 1970s going home early so he could be with her. At the end of 1982, his wife died. He remarried and regained a happy outlook on life that hadn't been there for 15 years. Also his second wife had an interest in traveling. So he began to accept more speaking engagements. Some milestones rolled around—his eightieth birthday and his thirtieth anniversary on the Court. That also coincided with the bicentennial of the Constitution. He felt, along with others, it would be a tragic irony if the branch of the government charged with the responsibility for giving the most meaning to this document remained silent during the celebration of its two-hundredth anniversary. So he was one of several who were willing to give bicentennial-related speeches and television appearances.

Some of the justices interact with reporters to some extent because they believe the press will sympathetically portray their views. Justice Brennan spoke often to reporters during his last five years on the Court because, according to Carelli, he "realizes many in the press share his philosophy of the role of government, individual rights, and the role of the Court." Apparently Justice Blackmun also is a favorite with the press and enjoys reporters in turn, as evidenced by several reporters who mentioned possessing a close personal relationship with him.

Some of the justices may just enjoy the feedback from a group intensely interested in their product. "Supreme Court justices talk to the press because we are an appreciative audience for them." Carelli explained, "Not many people follow the

Court. We understand the sweat and blood that goes into their product. They know we appreciate the ins and outs and the finer points of the game."

On the other hand, some justices apparently do not believe they will be treated fairly and do not give interviews. Some reporters on the Court beat said they detected an intense dislike of the press on the part of Justice White while he was on the bench. One reporter called him "fundamentally a mean man." White commented to a reporter for *USA Today* that he enjoys the newspaper's sports section, but does not read coverage of the Court because it only gave him "more grief." During the public sessions, White was known to glare at the press, especially during announcements of freedom of the press–related cases. On the other hand, former UPI reporter Henry Reske recounted how Justice White escorted him on an impromptu tour of the publicly inaccessible sections of the Court building.[6]

Even if hospitable to some reporters, Justice White was perceived by some of the press corps as oblivious to the imperatives of the press. For example, according to ABC News reporter Tim O'Brien, White did not consider the effects of releasing a large number of his opinions on the same day. Speaking before White's recent retirement, O'Brien noted:

> Some justices are sympathetic. As I understand, a justice can let the decision go whenever he wants. The worst offender is Byron White. He doesn't care about us at all. Not only does he not care about us, but I feel he doesn't care about what we do. That's a mortal sin. That's wrong. He'll announce five of his own decisions on the same day. He did that last year. He had some important ones. They didn't get heard. He doesn't care.

Other justices have favored a low public profile as well. Justice Stevens does not give formal interviews to reporters. Justice O'Connor does not give interviews and is not very accessible to reporters even on an off-the-record basis. Lyle Denniston relates that this shift occurred immediately after her ascension to the Court and attributes the change to the chief justice's suggestion:

> O'Connor was very accessible to me during the confirmation hearings. In fact, I did a telephone interview with her the day of the committee vote. But after she got on the court, she just shut down. O'Connor rarely sees reporters and she won't even tell us her travel schedule.
>
> She won't share with us texts of speeches that she gives. And my own personal off-the-wall speculation is that Burger got to her after she got on the court, and said 'you don't want to be dealing with those jackals in the press downstairs.'

O'Connor also may have perceived the publicity about her after she joined the Court was getting out of hand. She was frequently mentioned in the social pages of Washington metropolitan newspapers and was the subject of a vice-presidential "boomlet" in 1984. O'Connor became the subject of news stories about her extra-judicial activities. In 1987, she was criticized in the press for agreeing to provide a

---

[6]Henry J. Reske, "A Reporter at the Supreme Court," *ABA Journal* (May 1991): 69.

"private briefing" for Republican contributors who had each donated $10,000 to a political action committee. Again, criticism in the press was leveled at her in 1989 for writing a letter, to a conservative friend, lending support to a proposed party resolution declaring the United States a "Christian nation."[7] A poll conducted by the *National Law Journal*/Lexis in 1990 found that four times as many people recognized her as any other justice on the Court, including the chief justice.[8]

According to Toni House, O'Connor is not happy with the attention to her extrajudicial activity:

> Justice O'Connor doesn't wish to be known as one of the best women tennis players in Washington, even if she is. She doesn't wish to be known as one of the best foxtrotters in Washington, even if she is. She wishes to be known as a justice of the Supreme Court. And not really even the first woman.

She may have been criticized by some of her colleagues as too public for a justice, especially a junior one. In a 1989 interview about her law clerk selection process, O'Connor discussed her initial socialization to the Court. Although she implied she was speaking in a broad sense, there may have been a specific application to press coverage when she remarked that "I think I stepped on a few toes as I made my way along those first few years."[9] New justices usually maintain a low public profile in their first few years as a justice. Antonin Scalia broke that custom initially, but then adopted it. David Souter and Clarence Thomas both remained out of the public spotlight in the first two terms. When Thomas began giving speeches to conservative groups, however, some legal experts argued that Thomas was participating in fundraising for the organizations, which is a breach of the judicial code of ethics.[10]

Usage of the press for dissemination of views apparently varies according to the justice's perception of the utility of the effort and other circumstances, such as attitudes toward and past experience with the press.

Another individualistic objective is to acquire external assistance for internal disputes from press coverage. Again, dissenting and concurring opinions are the most common expressions of internal conflicts among the justices. But other forms also exist and have been employed by justices seeking public attention to the ideological cleavages within the Court. One reporter, speaking just before Justice Brennan retired, explained Brennan's willingness to grant interviews as due to the

[7] Alan M. Dershowitz, "Justice O'Connor's Second Indiscretion," *New York Times*, April 2, 1989, p. 31.

[8] Marcia Coyle, 1990. "How Americans View High Court." *National Law Journal* (February 26, 1990): 1.

[9] Barbara Gamarekian, "O'Connor's Agonizing Search for Law Clerks," *New York Times*, November 3, 1 [10] Joan Biskupic, 1989. p. B7.

[10] Joan Biskupic, "Thomas' Speech to Georgia Group May Have Violated Judicial Code," *The Washington Post*, May 8, 1993, p. A4.

fact that his views are no longer in the ascendence. "Brennan is not riding high on the majority hog anymore. He's writing a lot of dissents."

During the 1980s, Justices Stevens, Blackmun, and Marshall in speeches and in on-record interviews expressed public comments that mildly or sharply criticized the ideological direction of the conservative majority on the Court. Justice Marshall was the most outspoken during this period. He used interviews and speeches to criticize the Justice Department, current and former presidents, and his own colleagues. Marshall also was the most vociferous in his criticism of Court procedures.[11] Justice Blackmun stepped beyond the norm when he publicly speculated on the outcome of the *Webster* case when it was before the Court, even though it had not been scheduled for argument.[12] Others have participated to a lesser extent. Justice Stevens chided the Court's conservatives in a 1982 speech.[13] While Justice Blackmun offered a surprisingly candid view of his colleagues in a 1988 speech.[14]

A third motive for using the press as a forum is to affect the larger political environment within which the Court operates, especially if the debate touches on the role of the Court as a policy-making body. At critical points in the history of the Court, such as after *McCulloch v. Maryland*, the *Dred Scott* case, and the 1937 court-packing effort, the justices have felt impelled to deflect criticism of the Court by extrajudicial writings and statements.[15] Such behavior exists today.

Some of the justices have attempted to participate in public debate over nominees to the Court. Some of the justices remarked publicly on Supreme Court nominees during the late 1980s, previously a rare practice. Two of the justices made public comments supporting the appointment of Robert Bork, who was ultimately defeated.[16] Thurgood Marshall commented in a primetime television interview that he and Justice Brennan had never even heard of David Souter and said of President Bush's appointment of Souter: "I just don't understand what he's doing. I don't understand it."[17]

Public discussion over the role of the Court has drawn out the justices. Efforts by the Reagan administration to redefine judicial review brought two of the justices into a public debate. In response to public statements by Attorney General Edwin

---

[11]Aaron Epstein, "Marshall Assails High-Court Practice of Ruling Without Hearing Dissenters," *Philadelphia Inquirer*, April 28, 1987; "Marshall Faults The Justice Department," *New York Times*, December 13, 1987.

[12]"Justice Fears for *Roe* Ruling," *New York Times*, September 14, 1988.

[13]Stuart A. Taylor, Jr., "Justice Stevens Is Sharply Critical of Supreme Court Conservatives," *New York Times*, August 5, 1984.

[14]Stuart A. Taylor, Jr., "Lifting of Secrecy Reveals Earthy Side of Justices," *New York Times*, February 22, 1988.

[15]See William J. Cibes, Jr., "Extrajudicial Activities of Justices of the United States Supreme Court." Unpublished Ph.D. dissertation, Princeton University, 1975.

[16]Stuart A., Taylor, Jr., "Justice Stevens, in Unusual Move, Praises Bork as Nominee to Court," *New York Times*, August 1, 1987; CBS Evening News Broadcast, September 22, 1987.

[17]"Marshall Says He Never Heard of Bush's Nominee," *New York Times*, July 27, 1990.

Meese questioning judicial activism, Justices Brennan and Stevens delivered speeches that constituted an extended public colloquy with Meese.[18]

During the 1980s, presidential election campaigns and their effect on future appointments have drawn justices out in a way foreign to the Court for many years. In a 1984 speech, William Rehnquist, then an associate justice, responded to criticism of conservative "litmus" tests for judicial appointments by arguing that there is no reason why the president should not "appoint people to the Court who are sympathetic to his political and philosophical principles."[19] In a 1988 speech that was open to reporters and was widely reported in the press, Justice Blackmun referred to the possible outcome of the 1988 election by remarking that the Court could become "very conservative well into the next century."[20]

Even when the justices "go public" there may be some uncertainty on the part of some about whether they have done the right thing. In 1968, Hugo Black agreed to a television interview with Eric Severeid to be broadcast nationwide on CBS. After the taping, Black sought to postpone the airing of the program until after his retirement. But he finally consented to its immediate airing and, after favorable public response, concluded that it had not been a bad decision.[21]

CHOOSING THE TACTICS

Although individualistic motives for public communication via the press exist, the problem for the justices lies in the implementation of the Court's communication strategy and in the implementation of their own. The tactics the justices employ must not undermine the institutional strategy or their individual power, which is inextricably linked to the institution's power. Overt manipulative tactics would contradict the Court's message of political aloofness and disinterest in public opinion. The justices must balance their role as politicians against their role as justices. Although Supreme Court justices usually wear robes while in their public role, couch their questions to counsel and their announcements of decisions in technical legal language, and limit their expressions to the issues of the case at hand, they are not divorced from the political process.

Not only is the process by which they ascended to the Court political in nature, but most of the justices possess political backgrounds. Of the current members of the Court, one (O'Connor) is a former state legislator, one (Rehnquist) was a partisan activist in a presidential campaign and later served as a high-ranking Justice Department official, and three others (Scalia, Souter, and Thomas) had been political appointees in federal or state administrations. For those justices with

---

[18]Stuart A. Taylor, Jr., "Meese v. Brennan," *New York Times Magazine*, January 6 and 13, 1986, pp. 17–21.

[19]O'Brien, op.cit, p. 44.

[20]Taylor, "Lifting of Secrecy," op. cit.

[21]Hugo L. Black, *Mr. Justice and Mrs. Black: The Memoirs of Hugo L. Black and Elizabeth Black* (New York: Random House, 1986), pp. 202–210.

political experience, their political nature may not be that submerged. For example, Hugo Black kept close at hand a listing of his supporters from his electoral campaigns in Alabama.[22]

According to Richard Carelli, one of the most political of the justices is the current chief justice. "Anyone who has spent any time with the Chief privately knows that he is a very political being. He likes politics. He enjoys politics. He follows it carefully." The political nature of most justices necessitates a balancing act, particularly for those justices who are more political by nature. Antonin Scalia is an example of a politician-justice who has wrestled with the tension between those two roles. Stuart A. Taylor, Jr. succinctly described Scalia's dilemma:

> Scalia is one of the most interesting [of the justices] because he's a ball of energy. He writes very forceful opinions. He does the same in oral argument. On the other hand, he doesn't want to be a public figure, he's very conscious of that. When he's giving a speech, he doesn't want to be televised. He doesn't want anyone from the press to cover it. When he's making a speech somewhere if he sees a television camera, he'll go off stage and say "I'm not going back on until that television camera is gone." The explanation he gives is that he doesn't think Supreme Court justices should be public figures, out on the hustings making arguments. He can't resist doing it; he just doesn't want the image of what he's doing widely disseminated. I think there was an element that some of the other justices felt he was getting a lot of attention, he was hotdogging too much and so I think he has legitimate reasons for being concerned. But there is a certain tension between his urge to assert himself and his desire not to be perceived as asserting himself in certain ways.

Scalia's response to this criticism was to shift into a low profile position temporarily in order to pacify his colleagues on the Court. He turned down an interview at this time with Richard Carelli with a telling explanation: "I prefer to stay in the tall grass at this time."

Scalia is "schizophrenic" about his relations with the press. On several occasions he has refused to deliver speeches if television cameras were present.[23] On the other hand, one of those speeches has been devoted to the subject of the quality of press coverage of the Court.[24] He has shunned formal interviews, yet he has been available to reporters in background sessions.

In order for the image of political aloofness and detachment from the press to be plausible, some of the justices attempt to persuade the outside world that they do not know what is said about them in the press and that they could not care less. "The justices sometimes pretend they don't pay attention to the outside world," explained Richard Carelli. "It is a sweet fabrication. I remember one time talking to Justice Powell on a Tuesday, and he said he very rarely read the popular media.

[22]Hugo L. Black, *Mr. Justice and Mrs. Black: The Memoirs of Hugo L. Black and Elizabeth Black* (New York: Random House, 1986), pp. 75–76.

[23]Tony Mauro, "Justice Scalia to the Media: Go Away," *Legal Times*, December 3, 1990, p. 14.

[24]Stephen Wermiel, "Scalia's Criticism of Journalists Misses the Target, Apparently on Purpose," *Wall Street Journal*, February 11, 1991, p. B5A.

On the following day he was in the Court cafeteria reading *Newsweek* magazine. Something was amiss."

The "sweet fabrication" is especially true with television. CBS News correspondent Rita Braver commented that when she talks socially with the justices "occasionally one will admit to having seen me on television. A lot of them say they only watch PBS. Some claim not to watch television at all. Some of them say after meeting me that they will try to watch CBS so they can see me."

However, the notion of the justices avoiding the news media, particularly in a media-rich market such as Washington, is a highly improbable one. One former, long-time employee at the Court remarked that one factor that affects the justices' decision-making is the fact that "they have the *Washington Post* delivered to their doorstep every morning."

The reporters provide evidence that the justices today not only read newspapers and watch television, but more important that they also pay attention to what is said about them. Tim O'Brien of ABC News related that he has had conversations with Justice Scalia where Scalia made specific comments about O'Brien's stories. After Stuart Taylor wrote profiles on Brennan, Powell, and O'Connor, each of the justices wrote "a nice personal note." After writing a piece on a speech by Justice Blackmun, Taylor later learned (probably in a background session) that the justice thought the article was a "good, fair piece," and that he appreciated it because it rebutted the impression left in an earlier Associated Press article that Blackmun had used the speech to roast his colleagues. Blackmun's background reaction exemplifies the justices' longing to respond but also the perception they must be careful not to convey the impression that they care very much about what is said concerning them.

There is also evidence the justices have communicated with reporters to criticize their coverage. Fred Graham related that Chief Justice Burger once called him into his chambers to complain that a story Graham had done on CBS Evening News misinterpreted Burger.[25] Others have come to the edge of responding and then backed away. William O. Douglas wrote an angry letter to the editor of the *Washington Post* after the *Post* had criticized a decision of his in a case. Douglas ended his letter with a final blast: "It is amazing how little the press knows about Supreme Court procedures. A country paper that we read at Goose Prairie can be excused, but not the *Washington Post*, whose editors could find someone to give them a seminar on judicial procedure any time they choose." Douglas decided not to send the letter.[26]

The justices rarely respond publicly to press coverage in order to perpetuate the public impression that they are above that. According to one employee of the Court with close association to the justices, a justice once said, in explaining why they avoided responding to news stories, that "you convert a story that will be forgotten in three days into one that will go on and on."

[25]Fred Graham, *Happy Talk* (New York: W. W. Norton, 1990), p. 103.

[26]Melvin I. Urofsky, ed., *The Douglas Letters: Selections from the Private Papers of Justice William O. Douglas* (Baltimore, Md.: Adler & Adler, 1987), pp. 66–67.

In the past, there have been times the justices have abandoned their reticence to respond to news coverage of them and publicly commented. In 1948, Justice Frank Murphy met with reporters to deny that he was hostile to religion because of his opinion on a religious establishment case. And in the wake of the school prayer coverage in 1962, Justice Tom Clark used a speech to correct misinterpretations about him in news coverage.[27] However, such instances are rare.

The justices are constrained by a tension: on one hand there exists an institutional need for manipulation of the public image of the Court, which arises largely from its news media coverage; and there are the individual needs of justices to participate in the debate over public policy. On the other hand, the very objectives the justices pursue as the Court and as individuals would be undermined by an overt public relations effort.

The justices then engage in a dance with reporters: It is a dance that uses news media coverage to further their institutional and individual objectives, while denying that any such dance is actually taking place. Thus it is intended to be an invisible dance.

THE INVISIBLE DANCE

A dance typically involves partners. Hence, most of those who participate in the Court-press relationship would argue it is a bad analogy. Reporters suggest they are quite willing to engage in such a dance, but are always left on the dance floor alone.

Justices, public information officers, and even the press corps claim there is no dance because there is only slight interaction between the justices and the reporters assigned to cover them. Tony Mauro offered an example of the aloofness of the justices:

> We had a reception at the press room for Justice Souter. [It is a] tradition in the last five years that [we have one] when a new justice comes on the court. We invite all the justices down for wine and cheese. It was all off the record, which doesn't please me but I decided it was worth going anyway. At the very end of it, Souter turned to us and said, "Well, thank you for this. I enjoyed it. Let's do it again when I retire." We realized as he walked away, [that] you just don't see them much. Once they get life tenure, they tend to get inaccessible—until they're old and they want to adjust their obituaries.

By all appearances, there is no dance. The justices do not give on-the-record interviews, and only infrequently provide off-record sessions. They rarely socialize with the press. The reporters who cover the Court view the justices most frequently in their public role as they sit along the curved bench at the front of the courtroom in the Supreme Court building. A logical conclusion is that the justices have little to do with the press and a that a "dance", where two partners are in some regular physical proximity to one another, just does not occur.

What that conclusion fails to consider is the subtle leadership of the justices in their dance with the press. The justices have been stunningly successful in

[27]Cibes, op. cit., p. 1361.

focusing the press' attention on those aspects of the Court most beneficial to the achievement of the justices' objectives, both those in support of the institution and those that support them as individuals.

The justices shape press coverage by directing the press to their written work, by exercising selectivity in their public interaction, by providing off-the-record or background information, by shutting off other points of access to information, and, until recently, by channeling the issues of contention into minor matters of work habits.

Channeling Attention to Opinions

On decision days, for example, justices and reporters are interacting in a manner highly conducive to the accomplishment of the justices' objectives. Justices offer typically lengthy opinions—majority, dissenting, and concurring—to reporters. On some days reporters are handed more than 100 pages of material. They spend the remainder of the time before their deadline pouring over those opinions, pondering the lead and the organization of the story, contacting potential sources for explanation and reaction, and discussing the decision with colleagues over lunch and in the pressroom.

The Court makes those opinions accessible to the press at the moment they are announced from the bench. Moreover, the Court offers access to the same materials the justices use in the decision-making process—cert. petitions, briefs of the parties, amici briefs, and evidence introduced, such as videotapes. The Court's design is that these sources become the basis of the stories emanating from the pressroom.

The Court is an institution that not only speaks to the press, but that says quite a lot. As Fred Barbash, who at one time covered the Court for the *Washington Post*, concluded, the Court speaks at such "frightening length."[28]

By "feeding the press corps" with voluminous opinions, they have focused the press' attention on their product. Unlike other forms of interaction, such as interviews or press conferences, this form minimizes the press' contributions. The tactic of ready press availability to the opinions of the Court is one form of interaction; in fact, it is the favored form for the justices.

Unlike other political institutions, the Court is highly successful at defining the mode of communication with the press. The interaction is solidly on the justices' turf. According to Lewis Wolfson, "Supreme Court justices have an official's dream: reporters devote much of their time simply to reporting what they say."[29]

The Court succeeds in its intent in focusing journalistic attention on the written opinions. Content analyses of the news stories conclude that the focus of most stories about the Court is the written opinions of the justices.[30]

---

[28]Mitchell J. Tropin, "What, Exactly, Is the Court Saying," *The Barrister* (Winter 1984): 14.

[29]Lewis Wolfson, *The Untapped Power of the Press* (New York: Praeger, 1985), p. 57.

[30]Michael Solomine, "Newsmagazine Coverage of the Supreme Court," *Journalism Quarterly* 57 (Winter 1980): 661–663; Richard Davis, "Lifting the Shroud: News Media Portrayal of the U.S. Supreme Court," *Communications and the Law* 9 (October 1987): 43–58.

Once the focus of attention is on the opinions, do the justices attempt to communicate to the press, or to the public through the press? One overriding question is: Do the justices use their opinions to affect news coverage of themselves?

First, the question must be divided into two parts: the decision-making process and the opinion-writing process. A caveat should be added that the two parts are not always separate and distinct since decisions can be made through the writing of the opinion. The first question then becomes: Do the justices decide cases in such a manner as to shape news coverage? While the second question is: Do the justices write opinions with the same objective? Evidence to answer either question is extremely sketchy.

Bob Woodward and Scott Armstrong claim Warren Burger decided to change his votes on some cases in order to blunt press criticism that he was a conservative rather than a moderate. As evidence of this attempt, they point to several cases during the 1970 term where Burger voted with the liberals.[31] However, there is no other evidence that Burger or any other justice has altered decisions to affect press coverage of themselves.

The justices take cases in order to settle the constitutional issue. However, they may also do so in order to give the constitutional issue more news coverage. Richard Carelli presented the example of the flag-burning case, where the Court upheld a Texas court decision:

> Why did they take it? The Court could have denied cert. with the same effect. The Court embraced the case, agreed to hear it, then agreed with the Texas court and struck it down. I'd like to know if those who wrote dissents knew it would spark passion (from those outside the Court). The court does perceive, with great precision, what the press' role is.

The answer to this question involves an examination of the opinion-writing process. Since most of the justices do not assign the Court's opinions to themselves (only the chief justice or the senior associate justice in the majority can do so), they are constrained in the choice of opinions. Moreover, the opinion for the Court, especially in the case of a divided Court, may well be the product of a compromise. Therefore, the difficulty arises in accurately gauging the unedited contribution of any single justice.

A concurrence or dissent is more easily identifiable as the work of a single justice. Moreover, vigorous dissents probably are designed for the notice of others beyond the members of the majority. If not, the justices would dissent privately and the Court would issue a single opinion.

In some instances the justices writing dissents or concurrences appear to be speaking even beyond the legal system. For example, in the case of *Webster v. Reproductive Health Services*, Justice Scalia's remarks seemed to be directed at those who had attempted to lobby the Court; Scalia complained about the volumes of mail the Court was receiving on abortion, while the role of the Court was to follow

---

[31]Woodward and Armstrong, *The Brethren* pp. 140–142.

the law and not popular will.[32] Scalia must have expected his words would attract press attention and therefore public notice.

Overall, however, only the justices really know if they are writing with the press in mind, and they have avoided talking publicly about it. The answer to this question remains in the realm of speculation for the present. What may be significant is whether the press believes the justices are writing with them in mind. The approach reporters take to the justices' opinions may be shaped by the reporters' expectations that the justices are writing for them. For example, reporters may become more critical of an opinion that appears packaged for the benefit of the press.

On the answer to this question, there is no consensus. Some journalists think they have at least some influence. Nearly half of those surveyed said press coverage was somewhat important in influencing the justices' decision-making process. (See Appendix B.) Other reporters believe the justices' awareness of the eventuality of press coverage results in no more than rhetorical flourishes in decisions. "There are usually some quotable quotes," Miranda Spivack of the *Hartford Courant* noted. "Some of them do recognize what's going to be quoted, or their law clerks do it."

Still others argue there may be an impact that goes beyond style, but that it is still minor. According to Richard Carelli, Associated Press reporter at the Court, the more politically oriented justices are "more mindful of how their writings will play in Peoria."

Even if decision making and opinion writing are largely separate from the public imagemaking effort of the justices, do they time their opinions for maximum exposure in the press? Logically, the justices would want to space their opinions in order to maximize press coverage of important decisions. Reporters could concentrate on one or two opinions rather than attempt to handle several, especially if more than one is particularly newsworthy.

Dawn Weyrich Ceol, former reporter for the *Washington Times*, said she once held the view the justices behaved that way. "I used to think they time their decisions with us [the press] in mind, but then they announced two abortion cases and a right to die decision on the same day. There goes that theory."

The justices' failure to space the decisions has been a bone of contention between the press corps and the Court. Tim O'Brien of ABC News argued the practice of combining the announcement of several decisions, sometimes highly newsworthy ones, does not make sense. "We'll get what we call 'dogs' on one day. And then the next day we'll get a pair of blockbusters. That, to me, is irrational."

The justices have acquiesced to press demands in the past. Prior to 1965, the Court announced decisions only on Mondays. The result was a logjam at the end of the term when large numbers of opinions would be released on the same day. In response to complaints from reporters, the Court ended "Decision Monday" and began announcing decisions on other weekdays as well.[33]

---

[32]*Webster v. Reproductive Health Services* 492 U.S. 490 (1989) at 532.

[33]Elliot E. Slotnick, "Media Coverage of Supreme Court Decision Making: Problems and Prospects," *Judicature* 75 (October–November 1991): 133.

Since that time no accommodation has been made to the interests of the press corps. The justices continue to inundate the press corps with many decisions on some days at the end of the term.

The Court maintains it cannot be driven by the concerns of the press corps. According to Tim O'Brien, Justice Scalia told him: "Look, when we decide these cases, that's when they are released. We can't hold them for your benefit."

Toni House, the Court's public information officer, contends that the justices' refusal to space decisions in accordance with press requests is an illustration of their disinterest in press coverage. On the other hand, the argument for disinterest in the imperatives of journalists also can be construed as another manifestation of the Court's attempt to portray themselves as aloof. By failing to accommodate the press, the justices are communicating their attention to their duty over any interest in the value of public relations. The image is sustained.

However, the justices' failure to space probably is less attributable to imagemaking than it is to the high degree of individuality on the Court. Justices are under no formal constraints to produce opinions before the end of the term. The majority opinion may take the full term to form, or in some cases, spill over into the following term. Moreover, no Court opinion is delivered until all the accompanying concurrences and dissents are ready. The timing therefore is rarely institutional, but primarily the amalgamation of independent individual efforts, limited only by the anticipation of the term's conclusion and an annual vacation in late June or early July.

If spacing of opinion announcements were attempted, the resulting conflict would be irresolvable given the independence of the nine members. For example, if two or more opinions were ready on the same day, and if more than one of those opinions were considered of major import, one or more of the justices would have to defer on the announcement of their opinions to others.

One aspect of timing that is more controllable is that of the oral arguments. The Court may time its calendar around press coverage. For example, two of the most newsworthy cases related to the abortion issue, the *Webster* case in 1989 and the *Pennsylvania* case in 1992, were scheduled for the very end of the oral argument calendar. Fully aware that the oral arguments for these cases and the resulting news coverage would stimulate marches, demonstrations, and interest group lobbying, the chief justice may have sought to minimize the length of such a period and its impact on the other work of the Court.

Still another area under joint control is the caseload for the Court. The shrinking docket of the Court during the early 1990s was not accompanied by any public explanation from the justices, but the Court may have been sending a public message, via the press, of an overloaded Court, or perhaps of a tilt away from an activist one.

The justices effectively turn the press' attention to the written product of the Court—the opinions. But whether the contents of opinions, the timing of announcements, the scheduling of oral arguments, or even the size of the caseload are used to affect news coverage remains an open question.

Selective Public Interaction with the Press

The official policy of the Supreme Court is that justices rarely give interviews to reporters. By comparison with other national government policymakers, that statement is true. But it does not mean the justices do not give interviews. It means the justices are highly selective in their choice of interviewers and interview topics.

The justices are aware that any other interview policy would result in a flood of requests and the criteria for granting interviews would become more blatant. They argue that they would have to accept many interviews if they are not highly selective. They feel they must convey the perception they do not grant any interviews. For example, Justice Scalia agreed to an interview with *Time* correspondent Jerome Cramer, but subsequently backed out on those grounds. "He called me and said I know I promised you, but I have to beg you not to hold me to it. I have thought about it, and I've had other reporters who have called me and if I do it for one, I've got to do it for others."

Not unlike other national government figures, the justices are selective in the mediums they use to "go public." They choose highly reputable news outlets, such as the *New York Times*, the *Wall Street Journal*, and *The New Yorker*, or reporters they are familiar with. They appear to be most comfortable with public television programming. All of the justices cooperated with the PBS production "This Honorable Court." Several of the justices also agreed to be interviewed for other bicentennial-related public television documentaries. Sometimes they bypass the Supreme Court press corps entirely and give interviews to other reporters. For example, in 1990, Justice Brennan sat for an extended interview with Nat Hentoff of the *Village Voice* who is not on the Supreme Court beat. An interview with Chief Justice Rehnquist, which appeared in the *New York Times Magazine*, was conducted not with a journalist on the Court beat, but with writer John Judis. Explaining why he and NBC News correspondent Carl Stern were successful in obtaining the first interviews with Justice Brennan after he decided to speak again to the press, Stuart Taylor speculated, "I don't think Brennan said yes to me because I was Stuart Taylor. He said yes to me because I was the *New York Times*. Carl [Stern of NBC] probably knew him very well. He'd covered the Court a long time."

The justices' selectivity provokes reporters to make a session with them attractive. One method is choosing a topic of interest to the justice. Miranda Spivack, Supreme Court reporter for the *Hartford Courant*, successfully queried Brennan to sit for an interview on state constitution reform, a topic of great interest to him since he had been a state supreme court justice prior to his Court tenure. Richard Carelli approached Anthony Kennedy on the second anniversary of his appointment to the Court. "I think the fact someone was marking his anniversary appealed to him," Carelli concluded.

Another means used by reporters to obtain interviews is promising to limit the scope of the discussion. One reporter explained: "I start out by saying 'Justice so and so, I only want to ask these questions. I promise not to ask you anything else.' Sometimes you're forced to take that tack." Politics is especially taboo.

Edward R. Murrow sought televised interviews with the justices to discuss the Constitution. He promised that the series would "not mention politics."[34]

Praise for the justice's contributions have been included in a plea for an interview. One reporter seeking an interview with Douglas wrote of "my deepest gratitude for the passion, enlightenment and devotion to good causes you have brought to the bench."[35] Douglas accepted.

Others have allowed the justices some measure of editorial control over the final product in order to encourage participation. A *Christian Science Monitor* reporter who interviewed Earl Warren initially wrote Warren asking his permission for the story to run, suggesting an earlier arrangement, agreeable to Warren, prior to the interview.[36] Fred Graham of the *New York Times*, in requesting an interview with Warren, offered the chief justice the opportunity to edit the story before publication.[37]

But some interview requests may be impossible. The justice may not like the news organization or a previous reporter. William O. Douglas declined an interview with Nina Totenberg, then a reporter with the now defunct *National Observer*. Writing to Warren Burger, Douglas alerted him to an upcoming piece on Douglas, and he remarked that he had not spoken on or off-the-record to Totenberg and why:

> …I was particularly allergic about the *National Observer*. I had seen one of the reporters several years back who wanted to do a piece about me. I saw him and it was a friendly visit. But, as I suspected, it ended up my decapitation. So I made it a point never to talk to *National Observer* reporters about things as innocuous even as fly fishing or the weather.

Offering Backgrounders

The justices do not hold press conferences, except at appointment and resignation. When Chief Justice Rehnquist gave a news conference in early 1989, he claimed to be speaking not as the chief justice, but as chairman of the Judicial Conference of the United States, and he limited the questions to those related to judicial pay raises.[38]

However, most of the justices utilize another form of interaction with the press—the backgrounder. Since these sessions are not publicized as on-record

[34]Memorandum, November 16, 1955, Earl Warren Papers, Box 666, Library of Congress, Washington, D.C.

[35]Letter from C. Robert Zelnick, October 16, 1973, William O. Douglas Papers, Box 621, Library of Congress, Washington, D.C.

[36]Letter from Max K. Gilstrap to the secretary to Earl Warren, May 8, 1957, Earl Warren Papers, Box 6, Library of Congress, Washington, D.C.

[37]Letter from Fred Graham, August 26, 1969, Earl Warren Papers, Box 666, Library of Congress, Washington, D.C.

[38]Linda Greenhouse, "Rehnquist, in Rare Plea, Urges Raises for Judges," *New York Times*, March 16, 1989.

interviews are, their existence is little known outside the press corps. But journalists who cover the Court are familiar with them. Only three of the journalists surveyed said they had not spoken with a justice off-the-record. One-half said they had spoken in such a session with a majority of the justices. Two said they had had such sessions with every sitting justice. And these are fairly regular rather than one-time occurrences. Nearly two-thirds said they have such sessions with some of the justices during each term. (See Appendix B.)

The justices use these sessions to provide reporters with information that cannot be attributed to them but will affect the shaping of a story or the perception of a reporter. Toni House illustrates how Justice Stevens used this type of encounter with a reporter writing a story about Stevens. According to House, Stevens assisted the reporter by seeing him, but he didn't allow that guidance to be attributed by the reporter. Comparing that with an on-the-record interview which would be frowned upon, House suggested Stevens' role was appropriate. "I think there's a difference between seeing a reporter and letting him bounce off him 'these are my conclusions about you, what do you think'—sort of off-the-record guidance other than a lengthy interview." The key difference here is that the justice is not publicly perceived as an active participant in the newsgathering process. Stevens could direct the story while avoiding the image of involvement.

The rules of engagement for press encounters with the justices are rarely explicit, but they are clearly understood. "When I call them, they understand and I understand that this is not to be used in a story," said Lyle Denniston, reporter for the *Baltimore Sun*. As Tim O'Brien wryly explained, in Washington, "unless you say its off the record, its on the record. Some of my sources have the opposite standard."

Sometimes justices will allow the information to be used, but not with an attribution to them as the source. In fact, some of the justices insist that the reporters not even acknowledge they even spoke. In agreeing to a background interview with one reporter, Justice Scalia insisted that there be no trace of them ever having had a conversation. By attempting to bind reporters to avoid even acknowledging a contact, justices are seeking to perpetuate the convenient fiction that they do not interact with the press.

The content of these off-the-record or (at best for reporters), background sessions varies depending on the requested topic and the attitude of the justice. Depending on the justice, once in the session other additional topics can be broached. One reporter interviewing Justice Brennan found that he was willing to expand the interview far beyond the agreed-upon topic. Former UPI reporter Henry Reske described a similar experience with Justice Powell. "In his southern accent, he said, 'Since we are off the record, I'm willing to entertain any questions you may have.' He even talked about one of his decisions, why he had gone a certain way. It was a great insight into his thought process."

Uninhibited by the likelihood that their remarks will be widely disseminated, the justices are more willing to discuss a range of topics including the decision-making process, their relations with colleagues, and reactions to events and issues in American politics. Richard Carelli commented, for example, that Chief Justice Rehnquist enjoys discussing American politics.

They also are more likely to offer candid assessments of their colleagues. Justice Blackmun told one reporter in 1990 that there were "three old goats on the Court." In an off-the-record interview with another reporter, Chief Justice Rehnquist launched into an attack of judicial activism of Justice Brennan while he was still on the Court.

Lyle Denniston calls the content of these sessions "mood stuff"—information that suggests the current mood of the justices as they approach the cases of that term. The reporters who participate in these sessions appreciate the opportunity to gauge the justices' moods. Conversely, the justices know they are offering such assessments and are willing to allow their moods to become known to reporters, although not to a wider circulation.

These background sessions probably would be sources of potentially newsworthy information but for two reasons. First, the justices are bound by judicial norms not to discuss current cases. Second, reporters engage in self-censorship by avoiding the kinds of questions that, if answered, would elicit highly newsworthy information. "If I were to ask them, what did you guys say to each other at last week's conference about the big abortion case," Stuart Taylor explained, "I would wear out my welcome very quickly because there's sort of an understanding that that's supposed to be secret...." Denniston suggests sometimes the justices will even answer such questions, but "I've always understood that it isn't something you would try to plumb regularly. You do it in a way that gives them a clear indication that this isn't sufficiently unusual and that you won't infringe on their privacy."

Another form of behind-the-scenes press encounter is the bureau gathering. Several of the current or recently retired justices—Rehnquist, O'Connor, Scalia, and White—have participated in these sessions. The justices interact with groups of reporters through breakfasts and lunches sponsored by Washington bureaus of major news outlets, such as the *Los Angeles Times* and the *Christian Science Monitor*. In the sessions the justices speak on an off-the-record basis.

At times they will use the opportunity to discuss their colleagues. According to Glen Elsasser, former Court beat reporter for the *Chicago Tribune*, Justice Scalia used one session to express his disappointment at the lack of intellectual give and take in the justices' private conferences and to share his assessment that "the only person he thought had any intellectual give and take was Justice Stevens." Some of the justices have acted much like other policymakers in Washington by making themselves available on occasion for such encounters, although not on an on-record basis.

Off-the-record sessions with justices were far less frequent two decades ago, according to reporters who have covered the Court for more than 20 years. Today, these sessions allow justices to achieve one or more of the personal objectives listed previously without destroying the institutional objective of maintaining the illusion of Court apathy toward the press.

For selected regulars at the Court, these sessions seem to occur frequently. Several regulars reported regular access to at least some of the justices. Justices appear to maintain regular contact with favored reporters. Justice Blackmun apparently is a regular source for several reporters who characterize themselves as more liberal; while Scalia and Rehnquist may be closer to journalists from more conservative publications.

It is important to note that justices initiate very few of these contacts, according to the reporters who participate in them. They do not solicit interviews or backgrounders. But, like other top-level policymakers in national politics, such as presidential candidates who are front-runners, congressional party leaders, and presidents, there is no need for them to do so. In the marketplace of information, the justices possess a high level of supply and thus face great demand from the press. The task is to sort through the plethora of press requests.

Closing Off Other Access Points

Concurrent with efforts to provide information that is official and public, as well as that which is quasi-official and private, the justices restrict press access to other sources of information. Other sources might highlight the decision-making process, specifically political compromises, or a human side to the justices. Leaks are usually successfully avoided through the efforts of the justices to inoculate clerks and other Court employees against the temptation to engage in such behavior.

According to several reporters who cover the Court regularly, the clerks are warned about the "20-second rule."[39] This rule states that if a clerk is caught speaking to a reporter, he or she will be fired within 20 seconds. "Most won't even say hello to you until the end of the term," explained Henry Reske, a former UPI reporter at the Supreme Court. "If you say hello to them in line at the cafeteria they get scared."

Moreover, during Warren Burger's term as chief justice, he suggested on more than one occasion that clerks be subjected to lie detector tests to determine who had been leaking to reporters.[40] The suggestions were not pursued by the other justices.

The Court remains successful at preventing information from leaking to the press. Only rarely do leaks occur. And even more rarely do those leaks occur in cases of major interest to reporters, as evidenced by a list of some of those leaks during the Burger and Rehnquist Courts. While the Court was initially deliberating *Roe v. Wade*, the *Washington Post* printed a story on the Court's internal disputes over the case, including quotes from one of William O. Douglas' memos.[41] In 1973,

---

[39]Woodward and Armstrong also note the existence of the admonition that clerks will be fired on the spot if they are seen talking to reporters. See Bob Woodward and Scott Armstrong, *The Brethren* (New York: Simon & Schuster), p. 417.

[40]Ibid., pp. 174–175, 280–281.

[41]See Melvin I. Yrofsky, ed., *The Douglas Letters: Selections from the Private Papers of Justice William O. Douglas* (Baltimore, Md.: Adler & Adler, 1987), pp. 185–186.

Time magazine leaked the result of the *Roe v. Wade* case before its announcement. A source at the Court tipped some reporters to the timing of the Bakke case in 1978.[42] Thirteen years later, the outcome of the decision over the constitutionality of the Gramm-Rudman-Hollings Act, *Bowsher v. Synar*, was leaked by ABC News. Leaks about the writing of the majority opinion in *Webster v. Reproductive Health Services* were also reported.[43]

Due to the Court's success at plugging leaks, reporters on the Supreme Court beat learn not to expect leaks and most do not attempt to cultivate them. Stuart Taylor accurately expressed Supreme Court press corps frustration with the search for leaks:

> You go back a few years and there were some significant leaks. Nina Totenberg had some of them. And occasionally Tim O'Brien has had one or two. Usually they're half wrong by the time they're broadcast. I think Al Kamen [of the *Washington Post*] had one significant leak during the three years he and I were both covering the Court, which I doubt came from a justice. That was Bowers and Hardwick–Powell switching his vote, which Powell later confirmed. That was a good story. But I don't think the very small number of stories that came out during my time which had the earmarks of inside dope would have warranted the investment of very much time. I don't think those stories came from justices anyway.

However, the justices also have successfully minimized the value of leaks by casting doubt on their reliability. The best source for leaks besides the justices themselves would be the clerks. But reporters are unsure of the reliability of these sources. They doubt their maturity and become reticent to stake their professional reputation on such sources. Henry Reske explains:

> Here you only have one source—it's not likely that two or three clerks are going to be leaking in one year. So you're left with one guy, one guy who's 24 years-old, doesn't know anything about the real world, who's worked for one justice and that's his entire experience. I don't think that's very reliable, and I would be very nervous to go with the story."

Reporters also question the motive of the clerks. They ask: Is the clerk attempting to use me to further their or their justice's interests? Tony Mauro summarized a general attitude toward clerks' motives, saying "clerks will do whatever serves their justice." Reporters fear that clerks who are willing to talk with them are not to be trusted. UPI's Henry Reske:

> The clerks are not in the conference. No one is in that conference except the nine justices. The clerks get gossip. Their justice comes out and says, "Well I really put it to what's his name." "I got them over on my side today." It's all one-sided. They only get one-ninth

---

[42]Elder Witt, *Guide to the United States Supreme Court*, 2d ed. (Washington, D.C.: CQ Press, 1990), p. 714.

[43]See Bob Woodward and Scott Armstrong, *The Brethren* (New York: Simon & Schuster, 1979), pp. 237–238; Al Kamen and Helen Dewar, "A Court Ruling That Wasn't," *Washington Post*, June 17, 1986, p. A1; and Martha Sherill, "On Abortion, a Delayed Reaction," *Washington Post*, June 30, 1989, p. 1.

of the picture. By the time you end up, you wonder how much is reality how much is fiction. How much is layered on to get a good story.

Moreover, the justices can mitigate the value of leaks by proving them wrong. Since the justices control the scheduling of announcement of opinions and no previous notice is given of that schedule, they can withhold an opinion if a leak occurs about it.

ABC News reporter Tim O'Brien obtained a leak concerning the decision over the constitutionality of the Gramm-Rudman Budget Balancing Act. He knew what the decision was going to be and when it was going to come down, and he reported it. The opinion did not appear on that day. Toni House affirmed that the opinion was still in process and was not held back, but some in the press corps believed the Court had reacted. Henry Reske offers the evidence:

> At that time, the Court had been telling us how many opinions would come down on a certain day. That day we had all written about Gramm-Rudman. You didn't have to be a rocket scientist to realize Burger was ticked off and just wanted to stick it to Tim O'Brien. They had held back one opinion they had said they would release.

O'Brien concluded that the Court can "make you look foolish if you say decision on such and such a day....The Court doesn't like it when someone announces their decisions before they do."

Reporters also contend that the fact the opinion will be released eventually reduces the value of leaks. Unlike the CIA or the Pentagon, the Court does "go public" with its decisions eventually. The risks of getting it wrong usually outweigh the benefits of breaking—using a leak. "You get a leak over here, you can sit back and say—'I don't know, maybe I'll just wait till next week when I get the opinion,'" Henry Reske explained. "When you realize you are going to get the final word, it's so important not to be wrong."

Thus, reporters' interest in leaks varies greatly. Some reporters like O'Brien contend that the press should exploit leaks. "I feel very strongly if its news and its correct, unless there is some compelling reason not to put it on the air, it is our job to put in on the air." Others, however, would never solicit a leak nor accept one if proffered. Linda Greenhouse of the *New York Times* placed practically impossible conditions on her use of a leak:

> What I would require in reliability is almost affidavits from all nine justices. A clerk could see a majority opinion. Two days later it could be a dissent. The chances of being wrong are so great and the benefit is so slight in terms of what you're informing people of. I could hardly imagine a situation where I would be tempted to use [a leak], especially something which is going to come out anyway.

Still others, who are inclined to agree with O'Brien, fail to pursue leaks because of the difficulty of obtaining and verifying them. "I think all of us have at one time or another attempted to breach the veil. I have and others have," Henry Reske lamented. "After awhile, you realize its futile. It only parts so far. You can spend your time doing other things."

The justices' success at the diminution of leaks, both in terms of number and value, shapes the news coverage by removing sources potentially capable of challenging the Court's control of the information flow to the public. Absent reliable alternative sources, reporters continue to devote their attention to the Court's chosen theme—its written work.

Emphasizing Minor Points

Until recently, one form of off-the-record encounter has been an annual meeting between the chief justice and the regulars in the press corps, euphemistically referred to as the "wages and hours session." Warren Burger initiated the sessions with reporters when he became the chief justice in order to solicit advice from reporters on the amelioration of long-standing problems they had encountered in covering the Court.

Henry Reske described the sessions:

> We would sit with him—eight or nine of us—and we would have coffee, tea, and cookies. A servant would bring them out. We'd talk about the nuts and bolts of working conditions here. The first time I went to one, I said, "This guy's just so accessible; he seemed so interested and he wants to make changes and everything." One of the old timers said, "Nothing will happen, we've been going to these things for years." We're talking about little things like bringing a tape recorder into oral arguments.
>
> One reporter complained about the writing tables in the press section where the regulars sit up in the courtroom. You have to lean way forward to work at them and its kind of uncomfortable. You either have to write on your leg, which is difficult or you have to lean forward. He said, "Can we have the carpentry staff extend them?" Burger was really into that idea. Of course, nothing happened. The tables are exactly the same as they were.

The purpose for the sessions appeared to be demonstrating the chief justice's interest in press concerns, but not in resolving them. The sessions also had the effect of channeling press' problems into the minor issues of work tables and tape recorders.

Chief Justice Rehnquist continued the sessions briefly. But he may have begun to share the press' frustration at the futility of the sessions. Any discussion of issues with greater substance such as more notification of justice's personal activities, especially those involving medical problems, was clearly not the intent of the sessions as evidenced by the following account provided by Reske:

> In this session, right after one of the justice's illnesses, Lyle [Denniston] asked the chief if they could make some kind of accommodation to tell us when they're hospitalized. He did it in a very deferential tone. Rehnquist just flipped out. His whole expression changed. And he called us vultures. "You people are really vultures when it comes to that sort of thing." Rehnquist just blew up at us. The sessions are off the record and we're not supposed to repeat them. It was a very strange thing, and it just shows the depth of feeling about the thing.

Somebody mentioned tape recorders and it just didn't go anywhere. He listened very attentively. He wasn't as polite as Burger was. We got coffee, but not cookies. It ended on a very sour note.

The "wages and hours" sessions have been discontinued since. However, their purpose of channeling the press corps' frustrations into the hope of small improvements was temporarily achieved.

LEADING THE DANCE

Not only is there a "dance" involving justices and reporters, but it is a highly structured exercise in which the justices clearly lead. Their success in maintaining this role is attributable not only to their tactics, but also to the nature of the press beat. The press corps exhibits attitudinal and behavioral characteristics supportive of dominance by the justices in the dance.

Reporters who occupy the pressroom in the basement of the Supreme Court building have not been immune to the attitudinal changes among the press generally toward political institutions. Like their colleagues on other beats, they have adopted an approach somewhat divergent from that of their predecessors.

Lyle Denniston, who has covered the Court since the 1950s, sees the most recent groups of reporters as profoundly different from their predecessors:

The people who are on the beat now are not as awe stricken as people who were on the beat in the 1950s. There is a skepticism, a cynicism at times, about the Court as an institution. Tony [Lewis] was absolutely worshipful about the Court, and that was not unusual.

A lot of the young people are very acerbic. Maybe that's because the Court has changed and most of us in the news business are leftist. But there isn't this kind of reverential attitude. I'm not sure very many would verbalize it this way, but I think most of them believe the Court is just another powerful institution.

Richard Carelli succinctly expressed this attitude when he described the Court as "plainly a political institution. Behind the black robes and the legal mumbo-jumbo are nine politicians who are making public policy as well as law."

However, abandonment of the "reverential attitude" has not produced a press corps seeking to openly challenge the institution of the Court. Denniston adds that this cynicism is limited to pressroom banter and does not extend to relations with justices.

You don't get the feeling, however, when there's a social encounter that this attitude toward the justices prevails—when you're dealing with the justices directly. The kind of obsequious relationship exists.

The chief justice has this annual party. And the chief wanted the press corps to put on a skit. I wound up with the assignment to make what was supposed to be a humorous speech. My attitude is I'm not very awe stricken, and I'm not awe stricken by the justices. My sense of humor is kind of bitter. So it was the kind of speech where no one was spared. It just went over awful. It was a total bust. People were embarrassed. There was a shuffling of feet. There was a quiet in the room. Reporters were amused by it later, but they were embarrassed by it when they were with justices.

Many reporters who cover the Court have come to accept the Court's rationale for its secrecy and mystique. They take the Court on its terms, not on their own. One reporter's defense of the Court's secretive practices illustrates reporters' protectiveness toward the institution:

> It's the one institution set up to defend minority rights. It's the only one that really depends totally on popular will. It doesn't have the power of the purse strings; it has no army. To demystify it, to start covering the bickerings of the justices in their private meetings—it might lower the Court's esteem in the eyes of the public. And if it doesn't have the public's support, then it won't remain an institution very long, even though it's provided for in the Constitution.
>
> So I'm not all that upset with the way it operates. I'm almost in agreement with them that it shouldn't be televised. I'd love to sit in on a Friday afternoon conference, or I'd love to be able to buttonhole the justices in the hall and find out who's sticking it to who. I'd love to do those kinds of stories. But I'm not sure it would be so good for the institution.

Concern for the institution's best interests was not always so clearly articulated in interviews with reporters, but it was generally implied in discussions of several issues facing them as they cover the Court. On occasion, this attitude may result in an unwillingness to investigate and report stories that might cast the justices in an unfavorable light. One reporter exhibited this attitude when, before Justice Marshall's retirement and death, he described a story he could have written, but didn't want to.

> A story that should have been written but hasn't been by me or anyone else is that Justice Marshall doesn't seem to do much work, seems to leave it largely to his clerks to write his opinions, seems unprepared in oral arguments, and in general is old and past his prime—isn't really a very active participant in the Court's processes, and therefore there is a legitimate question that somebody like him ought to retire. That story hasn't been written at all for a variety of reasons. It's sort of hard to prove it in a journalistically satisfying way. A lot of it rests on rumor and impression, which is widespread. I think one reason it hasn't been written is that he is the first black justice in the history of the Supreme Court. He's a nice man; he's a man with a great and distinguished career. I'm not going to be the first journalist who decides to make his career as a hatchet meister by questioning Thurgood Marshall's competence. He's a nice, distinguished old man. What would you accomplish by writing about him being a doting, noncontributing member? It's not as if he is the secretary of defense and handling the nuclear button. He's largely voting the same way he's always voted, and his opinions are not badly written because they're written by very competent clerks. That's a story—I can imagine a real hot, exposé-oriented journalist thinking it's an outrage that somebody hasn't exposed Marshall. But I frankly don't think it's an outrage.

One manifestation of this adoption of a concern for the institution's interests is in the approach to leaks. Some reporters view leaks as bad not only because they may be proven wrong, and thus harmful to one's reputation, but also due to their potential harm to the institution. According to one reporter, one of the most powerful opinion leaders among the members of the press corps shares that view: "Linda [Greenhouse] thinks its outrageous that anything gets leaked. She's someone who really defers to the institution."

One reporter who has obtained several leaks of pending decisions is Tim O'Brien. O'Brien is not highly popular with other members of the press corps who oppose leaking. One reporter explained that "some people shun Tim a little bit. They question his operation, his modus operandi."

Some reporters are reluctant to attempt to obtain leaks, even from justices, for the good of the institution. A regular on the Court beat explained that "justices can't go around spouting about cases. It is a disservice to the institution. The advantages [the Court has] are lost if you try to get justices to trust a reporter with that information."

This attitude produces a willingness to allow the institution to define itself in terms most favorable to itself. One reporter, in explaining why he eschewed off-the-record interviews with the justices in favor of relying on the justices' written opinions, implied a greater concern for the justices' interests than the press' in getting a news story:

> The product speaks for itself. If Brennan doesn't like what they did in a certain decision, then he writes a dissent saying exactly why he doesn't like it. So going to him off the record and asking him why he didn't like the decision is sort of a silly exercise. What he gives you off the top of the head isn't going to be nearly as thought through as what he gives you in his dissent.

Even the practice of background sessions with the justices is a point of dispute. Some reporters favor the sessions. Lyle Denniston contends this kind of encounter "produces information and it produces background and sooner or later it shows up in a story." Denniston cites an example of a story he wrote about Justice O'Connor's ambition to be vice-president in 1984. "I got that information from a reliable source inside the Court," he related cryptically. One reporter provided an example of how he uses the information: "You can say 'Chief Justice Rehnquist is known to believe,'... As long as you don't say: 'I interviewed Chief Justice Rehnquist and here's what he said to me.'"

Some reporters say they don't expect to use the information obtained at that time, but hope the encounter will reap benefits in information they can use in the future. Richard Carelli explained this motive when he noted that he does it "just for good relations. Just so if I need to get them, I have established good relations."

But others reject this justification, arguing that the sessions produce no news and, even if they did, the reporters would be constrained by the limits placed on the encounter. One reporter emphatically argued that "a reporter who never in his life had spoken to a single member of the Supreme Court probably wouldn't suffer very much in his coverage compared to someone who was spending lots of time sort of chatting them up." Tony Mauro implied the background sessions would limit his role as a journalist. "A lot of reporters have off-the-record interviews with the justices. I'd just as soon not do those things. I think it's harder if you have an off-the-record tea with one justice—it's harder to toss a grenade at them the next day."

Even without a concern for the institution's best interests, the reporter can become passive toward the Court's practices because it is in the reporter's best interests to do so. Strong disincentives exist for violating the traditional norms of reporting on the Supreme Court.

One disincentive is the allure of the Court's predictability. The Court's routine can become numbing to reporters. Not unlike the White House with its daily press briefings and news releases designed to "feed the press corps regularly," the Court adheres to a schedule uncharacterized by surprises.

In expressing his appreciation for the Court's schedule, one reporter revealed this numbing effect:

> It makes it very easy to cover the Court once you've figured it out. You can look at a schedule. I know what I'll be doing next April, next March. There are going to be orders and opinion days. They gave us the schedule for the next year four months ago. After being here for awhile, I like the system.

Reporters come to accept the Court's schedule of activity as their own without much questioning about whether the Court beat ought to be approached in some other way. The possibility that stories about the Court may originate from a source other than the Court's Public Information Office is not explored.

Another disincentive to more aggressive reporting is the loss of the level playing field on which all reporters on the Court beat currently play. Unlike the White House, where leaks are parceled out to elite publications on a regular basis, the Court beat is characterized by a general evenhandedness in the dissemination of news. All of the reporters at the beat receive exactly the same access to the orders list, written opinions, summary decisions, and all other material disseminated by the Public Information Office. As one junior member of the press corps explained, "Lack of leaks puts a person like me, without a law degree or legal experience, on an equal basis with reporters from the *New York Times*."

Subtle differences abound as justices interact more frequently with the regulars at the Court than with others, and particularly those regulars with seniority and widespread acceptance as leaders on the beat. But, for most of their work, even those favored reporters use such information in a small fraction of their written work.

Hence, aggressive attempts by some reporters would upset the level playing field. If some reporters obtained leaks and moved beyond the Court's standard handouts, it would place others under obligation to act similarly.

One explanation for the deference in behavior by most reporters is the longevity on the Supreme Court beat of several regulars. The seniority of the press corps presents opportunities for relationships to develop between justices and reporters.

"People hang around here a long time," Tim O'Brien commented. "So we get to know [the justices]. Instead of a healthy adversary relation, I think sometimes there is a natural predisposition to be defensive of the Court and the justices. I don't know if that's healthy."

Another explanation may rest with the legal training of some reporters. An emphasis on legal background has produced certain journalists who understand the legal process and constitutional law, but who simultaneously acquire an acceptance of the Court's role.

The Court itself has encouraged the development of lawyer-reporters who are less susceptible to errors in interpreting the legal process for the layperson. For example, Justice Frankfurter urged the *New York Times* to send to the Court beat reporters possessing some legal training. What followed was a succession of *New York Times* reporters who were lawyers or who had received legal training.

For those reporters who do not acquire a deference toward the Court, their freedom to pursue an independent course in reporting on the Court is still severely restricted. The Court does not cooperate, and as discussed previously, leaks are difficult to obtain.

Moreover, support also is lacking from most editors who compare their own reporter's work against that of the wire services or Linda Greenhouse. Setting the standard of press coverage by using the wires or the *New York Times* precludes an approach that veers sharply from the institution's written products.

The press' attitude toward its role in covering the Court is not likely to change significantly. "What do you do when half the people feel it's not their job to get their leak," complained Miranda Spivack. "You're never going to have a movement toward getting anything. I don't know what someone like that would do if they got something. Would they run it or would they not run it? Look at the *New York Times* and the Bay of Pigs. They had it ahead of time and they didn't run it. It's easier to just sit there and cover it."

CONCLUSION

The justices not only are "dancing", but they are leading the "dance" by choosing the steps both partners will take. By limiting press access with one hand and simultaneously feeding the press with the other, the Court is acting much like other political institutions, especially the presidency, in attempts to use its power to control the information flow to its own advantage.

The justices have long known what some presidents and presidential candidates have only recently learned. In order to shape news coverage, it is imperative not to upstage oneself. The Court's reliance on private, off-the-record sessions with the press and its avoidance of other public encounters with the press is designed to channel the press' attention to its written work. Although the justices could communicate with the press via news conferences and interviews, their written work—the opinions—would be upstaged. Press attention would be turned to the latest interview with a justice or their response to an opinion or an issue or event. Because these other modes more nearly fit news values and allow the journalist to participate in defining the agenda, they would become the staple of news stories, not the opinions.

The justices seek to convey the impression that they are disinterested in news coverage about them and that they would be satisfied if the press would just go away. In the standard speech on press coverage of the Court that Justice Scalia has delivered to various audiences, he closes with the following: "I hope to have explained however the wisdom of the judge's ancient reluctance to engage in public debate over the rightness or wrongness of their decisions and their ancient belief that by and large no news is good news."[44] But, for the justices of the U.S. Supreme Court, no news is not good news. Rather, controlled news is good news.

---

[44]Speech dated August 9, 1990. Transcript in possession of author.

Chapter Six

The Supreme Court as News

Baltimore Sun reporter Lyle Denniston says when he writes stories about the Court, he imagines a hypothetical "Dave and Martha"—ordinary Americans—reading them. This technique helps him visualize how the average layperson would react to the Court.

When "Dave and Martha" read, watch, or listen to news stories about the Court, they are seeing the final product of an interaction between the justices and the journalists who cover them.

The justices possess the power to affect the agenda of news coverage. They decide which cases they will hear. By establishing their docket, they are determining what stories will emerge from that term. Moreover, they direct the timing of those stories through their announcements of decisions and the scheduling of oral arguments.

The justices are not necessarily making these decisions with the press in mind, but on some occasions, the relationship does appear strong. In 1989, the justices announced their initial flag-burning decision in the same week as Flag Day. The *Webster* and *Casey* abortion-related decisions were announced on the last days of their respective terms.

In turn, reporters participate in the interaction. They must choose which cases on the Court's docket will become the subject of news stories. The nature of the selection process varies from medium to medium. At one end of the media spectrum are the Associated Press, which is responsible for conveying the most news about the Court's activity, and the national newspapers, which accord a relatively large newshole for activity of the Court. On the other end of the spectrum are the broadcast news organizations and the newsmagazines, who are limited to covering stories constituting perhaps one-tenth of the Court's docket.

Once stories are selected, the angle of those stories can be shaped by reporters. The oral argument story has the greatest potential for reporter interpretation due to its inconclusiveness. (However, that very tentativeness for most media is likely to lead editors to assign an argument story a low priority as news. The opportunity to wait for the decision that inevitably will come later reinforces that attitude.) Reporters decide what to emphasize as the lead, who to cite as sources, and what will be the focus of reaction.

The process then is an interaction with the justices leading the "dance," but the press corps participating as partner.

Following the Rhythm

Reporters accept the lead of the Court by following the rhythm of the Court's activity. The most active periods at the Court are in October, which is the beginning of the term when the Court issues orders lists, and in June and early July, which is at the end of the term when large numbers of decisions are released. (See Table 6–1.)

TABLE 6–1 Number of Stories Throughout the Term

	Sept.	Oct.	Nov.	Dec.	Jan.	Feb.	Mar.	Apr.	May	Jun.	Jul.
1984–1989											
CBS	2	20	8	9	11	3	11	6	3	27	12
Time	1	3	3	4	2	1	7	6	9	12	14
Total	3	23	11	13	13	4	18	12	12	39	26
1989–1990											
AP	6	92	37	22	65	39	36	35	37	55	–

Note: For both studies, the month of August, when the Court does not meet was excluded. For the 1989–1990 term, the month of July also was not included because the Court finished its term that year before the end of June. (For a discussion of the content analysis, see "A Note on Methodology."

The press stories followed that routine. Seventy-seven percent of CBS stories during the term aired during October, June, and July. *Time* coverage, which is more decision oriented, was weighted toward the end of the term; 55 percent of *Time* stories appeared during the last three months of the term. (For both CBS and *Time*, the June and July counts were high as well due to two vacancies occurring during those months in 1986 and 1987.)

Associated Press stories were more evenly spread throughout the term. But one-half of the stories occurred during three months—October, January, and June. The October and June rise is explainable through the Court's rhythm—those months are the beginning and the end of the term. In January, the coverage would have focused on the oral argument calendar. Several highly newsworthy cases were argued that month including one on political patronage and another on Bible groups' use of public school meeting rooms. In addition, other highly controversial cases were decided, including one involving the Yonkers city council's refusal to adopt a housing desegregation plan and another on the confidentiality of a college's faculty tenure decision process. Also, the Court celebrated its two-hundredth anniversary that month.

Minimizing the Justices as Personalities

The Court has long sought to direct press coverage to its cases. Even with the increased exposure discussed earlier, the Court has been stunningly successful at focusing press attention on its product and deflecting attention away from the individuals who produce it.

Only 4 percent of the AP stories focused on an individual justice rather than on one or more cases. The CBS and *Time* stories were almost as devoid of discussion of the individual justices as the AP stories. Eleven percent of *Time* stories and 12 percent of CBS stories were primarily about the justices. Usually, the justices were only infrequently mentioned. (See Table 6–2.)

TABLE 6–2   Average Percentage of Case Stories in which an Individual Justice is Mentioned. CBS and *Time* (1984–1989); AP (1989–1990).

	CBS	*Time*	AP
Blackmun	09%	34%	15%
Brennan	06	37	17
Burger	14	60	—
Kennedy	16	36	15
Marshall	07	25	17
O'Connor	10	36	17
Powell	09	39	—
Rehnquist	15	52	16
Scalia	12	32	17
Stevens	04	27	16
White	06	32	13

Note: The percentage of CBS and *Time* stories for those justices who served for only part of the period 1984–1989 (i.e., Burger, Kennedy, Powell, and Scalia) were calculated using only stories during those terms in which they served.

CBS News stories, with limited time for each story, were the least likely to make reference to an individual justice. No justice was mentioned in one-fifth of CBS News stories. AP stories, with far more description, also accorded justices little mention. The *Time* stories did mention justices. Typically, a justice appeared in one-third of *Time* stories about the Court. Warren Burger and William Rehnquist were mentioned most frequently. Burger's resignation and Rehnquist's new status as chief justice during this period increased news coverage of them beyond normal.

Moreover, Burger received attention due to his chairmanship of the Bicentennial of the Constitution Commission.

The absence of references to justices can be attributed primarily to the justices' attempt to remain behind the institutional shroud. In issuing the orders lists, the justices almost always remain anonymous. Justices rarely announce a dissent on granting review or a summary decision.

If a justice fails to ask questions in an oral argument, no mention is likely to be made of that fact. Antonin Scalia may gain more notice than other justices due to his frequent participation in argument.

The issuance of opinions is the time when justices are most frequently mentioned in the press. But even then, justices who join others' opinions often are not mentioned. Justices who write concurring opinions, except in highly newsworthy cases, are also less likely to receive notice.

Justices will appear in the press when they issue written opinions, especially when writing for the Court or when issuing a vigorous dissent. But mention in the press occurs only rarely early in the term. Since a large proportion of opinions are delivered at the end of the term, the justices are more likely to acquire some level of newsworthiness at that time. But, unlike presidents, cabinet members, or congressional leaders, the justices return to obscurity during most of the rest of the year. No wonder the justices do not become household names.

When the justices are mentioned, it is in conjunction with the issuance of a written opinion or, less frequently, a question during an oral argument. Factors in the decision-making process leading up to that opinion are not part of the story.

Press stories rarely make references to a justice's own personal relationship to a case. One AP story, on October 2, 1989, about the Court's decision to let stand a ruling that state officials could deny a tax break to a country club that refused to admit women, mentioned at the end that two of the justices once belonged to male-only clubs. But such allusions are rare. Generally, due to the absence of such references, the justices are portrayed as personally aloof from the issues they handle.

Portraying the Docket

In another aspect of the news portrayal, however, the dance is a more equal arrangement. The Court sets the agenda for the press portrayal by the cases it accepts and hears. For example, by refusing to grant review to an appeal of California's stringent term limitations for state legislators in 1991, it reduced the level of press coverage devoted to the issue. Rather than a series of stories throughout the year on the term limitation issue, the Court's decision removed the issue from the press agenda. It is not my argument that this is a primary motive of the Court in determining its docket. But the effect is the same: press portrayal is affected.

However, within the confines of the docket set by the Court, reporters can determine what cases to follow. Not all decisions are treated equally by the press. Press imperatives are salient in the determination of what constitutes news.

Some issues acquire greater press interest and, consequently, more attention in the press portrayal.

Sometimes other events shape news interest in a decision. The issue of the Pledge of Allegiance during the 1988 presidential campaign spurred interest in the decision in *Texas v. Johnson* (1989). New appointments on the bench create greater attention to the Court's handling of issues on which the Court appears to be shifting. The abortion issue gained a high degree of attention especially following the appointments of Reagan and Bush appointees expected to overturn *Roe v. Wade*.

The reporter's role can be shown through an analysis of the portrayal of the docket by the copy of the Associated Press. The Associated Press wire service is considered the most descriptive and comprehensive general news sources about the Court. The wire service coverage of all general public news sources probably constitutes the coverage most in conformity with the docket of the Court. Associated Press coverage attempts to report, as completely as possible for a general news source, the Court's activity.

But as Table 6–3 demonstrates, the coverage by the Associated Press also varies somewhat from the docket itself. Cases involving First Amendment and civil rights were over-reported compared with their proportion of the total docket, while those on economic or federalism issues were somewhat under-reported. The reader may be surprised that the coverage of two abortion-related cases was not greater. However, no major abortion case surfaced during that term.

For the Associated Press at least, the portrayal of the docket is a combination of the Court's lead through the cases it takes and news imperatives. Other news sources, such as the network television news, because of the limitations on the number of stories covered, may be more inclined to place news imperatives far above comprehensively representing the Court's agenda.

TABLE 6–3   The Docket and News Portrayal: Proportion of Policy Issues on the Docket and in AP News Stories During the 1989–1990 Supreme Court Term

Policy Issues	% of total docket	% of total stories
First Amendment	8.7	15.4
Civil Rights	5.0	12.0
Abortion	1.5	2.6
Criminal Law	27.5	21.1
Economy	25.4	21.6
Federalism	2.2	2.6
Environment	2.2	3.1
Other	27.5	21.6
Total	100.0%	100.0%
	(N=138)	(N=389)

Source: Policy Issue categories: *National Law Journal*, August 15, 1990.

THE INTERACTION IN ONE STORY

The process of constructing news about the Court is not a Court-dominated or a press-dominated occurrence. The major finding of this study has been the interaction between the justices and the reporters in the portrayal of the Court.

While the justices offer the written opinions, orders lists, and oral arguments to the press, the reporters who cover the Court contribute to the shaping of the news stories. Reporters are not copper tubes offering merely a conduit for the justices' words.

Especially in the absence of the "helps" for press coverage—visuals for broadcast and authoritative sources offering interpretation for print media—reporters possess the opportunity, and are even called upon by necessity, to explain the Court's actions in lay terms and to provide interpretation of the potential effects of a decision.

There is more freedom. But the question is whether that freedom necessarily produces different products across media outlets? Are reporters inclined to varying portrayals of the Court given their greater freedom from the overt packaging of the institution's presentation such as they would get at the White House or at a bureaucratic agency?

One means for answering that question is by examining the forming of a news story. Our case study will involve four different media treatments of one oral argument story. It examines coverage in three similar print media; daily newspapers—two with national circulation, the *New York Times* and the *Washington Post*, and one regional, the *Baltimore Sun*—as well as coverage in the wire service copy of the Associated Press.

Our sample of coverage concerns the oral argument in the case of *Rust v. Sullivan*. The case involved regulations imposed by the Reagan administration in 1988 that prohibited family planning clinics that were receiving federal funding from including abortion as an option in the counseling of pregnant women. Planned Parenthood of New York challenged the rulings and the case was accepted for review by the Court during the 1990 term. The case was argued on October 30, 1990.

Covering an Oral Argument

First, a word of explanation about oral arguments should be added before continuing to our case study. Oral argument stories are unlike the vast majority of opinion stories because there is an element of drama in the Court's public session that is usually absent from the written opinions themselves or from their announcement. Usually opinions are announced in summary form with only rare attempts to read opinions from the bench.

For almost all arguments, however, there is a byplay within the courtroom that sometimes attracts press interest. Stories will make note of some of the questions asked by justices. Antonin Scalia, the most colorful and energetic of the justices during oral argument, often dominates the sessions from the bench with his frequent questions and his attempts to clarify the counsel's position for his colleagues. Sometimes Scalia will even use a question to answer another justice's question. But this element of Scalia's activity is rarely noted in press accounts of oral arguments.

Counsellors in the *Rust* case were Laurence Tribe of the Harvard Law School, representing Planned Parenthood of New York, and Solicitor General Kenneth W. Starr, speaking for the Bush administration. The involvement of the U.S. solicitor general demonstrated the importance the Bush administration gave this case in affirming its anti-abortion stance. Similarly, Tribe's presence suggested that the pro-choice groups defined the decision in this case as a precursor to an eventual test of *Roe v. Wade*.

With the protagonists clearly defined, the personalities well known, and the issue simply defined, the oral argument received more than the usual attention from the press. The press section was full and demand was high for seats in the auxiliary press section behind the curtain.

Even before the argument, Tribe had been making calls throughout the Supreme Court building. That morning he circulated around the Court cafeteria shaking hands with reporters, clerks, and Harry Blackmun, who happened to be enjoying breakfast with his clerks.

The courtroom is packed and the level of anticipation high as the justices enter and take their seats. Tribe, representing the plaintiff, presents first. In the course of his argument, he makes reference to Scalia's past opinions. Scalia smiles at mention of his own opinions as support for Tribe's argument. Tribe is questioned by several justices including Anthony Kennedy, Byron White, and, most critically, by Antonin Scalia.

The solicitor general's presentation follows. Approximately midway through the solicitor general's argument, Justice Souter asks a question which appears to challenge the government's position. Doesn't this rule limit professional speech? As the only Bush appointee on the Court, Souter's question causes great interest in the press section. Other justices also raise queries that appear skeptical of the government's position.

Following the argument, as the reporters file down the marble stairs to the ground floor, argument analysis begins. The discussion continues in the pressroom as some reporters pause to elicit reactions from each other while others eavesdrop. One reporter confidently remarks that "the government is not going to win this case." (It did.)

Many in the press corps, including the three reporters for the three newspapers under study, attend a news conference sponsored by the ACLU at their office directly across from the Supreme Court building.

The Associated Press reporter, Richard Carelli, is beginning to compose the initial wire story, which will become available to afternoon dailies and broadcast news outlets. The story will be filed shortly after noon. As the first to file, the Associated Press reporter can set the tone for stories by others. But the AP reporter has little time to get reaction from other reporters before filing.

The slug for the story is "Supreme Court Scrutinizes Federal Ban on Abortion Counseling." Carelli's lead reads: "The Supreme Court, in a spirited session featuring numerous questions by the justices, today scrutinized a federal ban on abortion counseling at government-subsidized family planning clinics."

In the fourth paragraph, Justice Souter's questions are discussed. Of the 18 paragraphs, two consist of Souter's questions.

At the news conference across the street from the Court, Laurence Tribe; Rachel Pine, an ACLU lawyer; and Dr. Irving Rust, the clinic director and the main plaintiff, are speakers. One reporter explained that he went to the news conference "for PR purposes. These are sources I rely on. I will probably not use it." Subsequently, however, he does use one quote. Tribe and Pine take the questions. Although, neither are willing to predict the outcome, Pine does say she is "guardedly optimistic." Tribe is more colorful. When asked by a reporter the inevitable effects question—what does it mean if this decision goes against you—Tribe provides soundbites: "Doctors will be paid to lie." "Doctors must commit malpractice if they want to stay in compliance with the statute." These comments are interspersed by applause from the audience. The applause apparently is made by ACLU and Planned Parenthood workers who have packed the back of the room.

A news conference by the Right to Life Committee was scheduled simultaneously, but was located further from the Court building. None of the four reporters is in attendance.

Various interest groups begin to distribute press releases—primarily by fax, but some send couriers to distribute them in the pressroom to each carrel and to each box of reporters not assigned carrels. The pro-life groups are most active. In advance, Planned Parenthood has already distributed a large press packet explaining the case and the organization's position.

All four reporters, plus others in the press corps, gather for lunch in the cafeteria and discuss the argument and the coverage they will give it. Each of them share their lead and the angle they will use, and then a debate ensues on what the best lead is. Denniston says his lead will be the Souter questions because they give a clue to the leanings of Souter. The others ask why he chose that lead. Some argue he is going too far; it isn't possible to make that prediction based on Souter's questions. Denniston responds that he is writing for his readers, not his editors. He imagines the hypothetical "Dave and Martha" and writes about what they are interested in. He explains they are interested in Souter.

Walter Dellinger, law professor at Duke and an advocate for the pro-choice position in the case, is also in the cafeteria lunching with two reporters in the press corps. Other reporters move to Dellinger's table to ask him questions about the case.

The reporters then file off to their carrels or their bureau offices to begin writing. Since all, except the wire service reporters, face early evening deadlines they will spend the afternoon writing, checking and rechecking quotes, contacting sources, and, at least in some cases, comparing their copy with the wire stories. The wire service reporter will write and file a lengthier story for the morning dailies.

The Stories

Each of the three newspapers ran stories of the argument in the next day's edition. Another, lengthier wire story on the argument was filed at 4 P.M. on the day of the decision. Given the topic and the left-over interest in the Court from the recently completed confirmation process for David Souter, editorial interest in such a story is predictable.

Placement varied slightly. The *New York Times* and the *Baltimore Sun* began their respective stories on the front page. The *Washington Post* story appeared on page nine. The *Post*'s reporter may have lost the front page designation because of the tentative nature of arguments compared with the ultimate nature of decisions. Or the junior status of the *Post*'s reporter, Ruth Marcus, may have limited her ability to get front page treatment for her stories or to have her judgment not second-guessed by editors. Whatever the cause, the *Post*'s departure from the priority coverage accorded by the other two indicated a small misstep for the *Post* that surely was noted by its editors. In a media-rich community like Washington, where each of these newspapers is widely distributed, news consumers can make comparisons of coverage that may affect their evaluations of the news outlet's capability to inform them adequately.

The headline in the three newspapers was uniform. Each emphasized the Souter question: The *Washington Post*, used "Souter Questions Federal Defense of Abortion Counseling Limits," the *New York Times*, "Souter Questions A Curb on Doctors," and the *Baltimore Sun*, "Souter Questions U.S. 'Gag Rule.'" The first two also included a photograph of Souter with the continuation of the story on an inside page. The Associated Press slug had changed from emphasis on the Court to the Court and Souter. It read: "Court, Souter Hear Debate on Ban on Abortion Counseling."

The lead paragraph in all four stories also emphasized Souter's role in the argument. The AP story lead also now included mention of Souter. It read: "The Supreme Court began scrutinizing a ban on abortion counseling at federally subsidized family planning clinics Tuesday in arguments punctuated by pointed questions from new Justice David H. Souter and his fellow members." Lyle Denniston led with Souter because he felt that was the news. "The average reader is probably more interested in how Souter is going rather than the Court."

The angle of each story was Souter. The first six paragraphs in the *Washington Post* story discussed Souter's questions including some of the byplay between the justice and Starr. The *Baltimore Sun* devoted its first five paragraphs to the angle and devoted most of the rest of the story to Souter's questions. The *New York Times* emphasized Souter in the first four paragraphs, and then returned to Souter's role later.

The Souter angle was more muted in the AP story, but devoted more attention to Souter than the earlier version. Of 24 paragraphs, Souter was the subject of five.

Whether Denniston's argument at lunch changed the intended angle of the others or merely confirmed existing predilections cannot be known with certainty.

Moreover, Denniston's argument may have been reinforced by each reporter's editors. One of the other reporters later said she initially did not want to use the Souter angle, but was persuaded by her editors.

The lunch also had an influence on Denniston as well. His lead paragraph originally read: "The newest Supreme Court justice, David Souter, finally reveals in public some of his perceptions about abortion.... His questions strongly implied doubts about the broad sweep the government appears to be giving to rules forbidding doctors to even mention abortion to pregnant women at federally funded clinics." He admitted he changed the lead because of the reaction of the other reporters to his intended angle.

The stories varied in their analysis of the meaning of Souter's questions. None explicitly stated that Souter's questions indicated he would oppose the government's decision. But the *Baltimore Sun* story's first sentence announced that "the newest Supreme Court justice, David H. Souter, finally broke his silence on abortion yesterday, putting on public display some doubts about sweeping government rules forbidding doctors at federally funded clinics from even mentioning the subject." Later in the story, Denniston relates that Souter "openly wondered whether the government rule had gone beyond what Congress had authorized—a conclusion that, if embraced by the court could scuttle the rule altogether."

The other three stories were more restrained. The *New York Times* story, in the seventh paragraph, warns the reader not to jump to conclusions about Souter's position. The reporter stresses that Souter did not indicate his position "nor do his questions necessarily mean he will vote to strike down the regulations." Then, a further caveat is added with the explanation that Souter had a reputation on the New Hampshire Supreme Court as an "aggressive questioner of lawyers." The *Washington Post* story only emphasized that Souter "expressed concern" about the rules and that he "appeared troubled" by the government's position. The AP story related that Souter had "voiced doubts." However, the story did not speculate which way Souter would go, only that his was considered "a pivotal vote for the future of legalized abortion."

Although Souter's questions led the stories and constituted the angle, other justices were mentioned. But discussion of the other justices' questions varied considerably. The *Washington Post* and AP stories reported questions by Anthony Kennedy and Antonin Scalia that were critical of Tribe's position. (The AP story even mentioned that two of the justices—Harry Blackmun and Thurgood Marshall—remained silent.) But the *New York Times* excluded the line of questioning critical of Tribe's position and mentioned only the exchange between Starr and several justices. The *Baltimore Sun*, in a short reference in the second to last paragraph noted the other line of questioning by stating that Justice Scalia "used his questions to make comments generally favorable to the government controls on the clinics."

All of the stories used the argument to explain not only the issue in the case, but also the dynamics of the Court on the abortion issue. The *Washington Post* and the *Baltimore Sun* stories named justices, in addition to Souter, who may be swing votes in the case.

Rarely does courtroom activity beyond the verbal exchanges between the justices and counsel receive any notice from the press. But the *New York Times* noted that Souter's questions and comments "drew particular interest in the courtroom."

Use of Sources

The oral arguments were not the only sources. The AP, *New York Times*, and *Washington Post* stories included background on the case providing a brief history of Title X and the regulations at issue. The *New York Times* noted that Title X is "the biggest source of Federal financial support for family planning" and the *Washington Post* story and AP stories stated that Title X provides money to clinics serving "5 million women annually." The AP story also said "some 4,000 family planning clinics nationwide" were given federal funding. These figures were available in the brief filed by Planned Parenthood and may have been drawn from them.

Only one of the three stories used the press conference and that one then failed to identify it as such. The *Baltimore Sun* story close with a quote from Rachael Pine noting only that it was made "after the hearing."

The efforts by the pro-life camp—news releases, a press conference, and availability of interviews—were for naught in the coverage by these four news outlets.

Technicality versus Human Interest

The conflict between the reporter as legal specialist and the reporter on general assignment cannot be more vividly demonstrated than in the general approach to the story. The *New York Times* story expresses a form of technical writing preferred by Linda Greenhouse. The *Rust* story, like others in the *Times*, includes the full name of the cases, case numbers, quotations from the relevant statute, and the previous decisions by lower courts on the case. Such information is irrelevant to the casual reader but establishes the *Times'* stories as the most comprehensive daily press account for the legal community.

The closest Greenhouse came to the humanness of the justices in the story was the linkage between Souter's questions and his service on a New Hampshire hospital's board and as an overseer of the Harvard Medical School.

The *Baltimore Sun* story, reflecting Denniston's own style, avoids the technical details of the case and targets the general interest aspects. Denniston takes more risks in his writing, preferring to link small steps in the Court's work or the justice's questions to larger issues. The rationale is that the small steps are interesting only as they are related to the issues important to general readers. Early in his story of the *Rust* argument, Denniston explicitly connects Souter's questions with the Court's consideration of abortion and his role in the eventual outcome of the case.

Homogeneity or Variety

Is the press coverage of the Court homogeneous? In Chapter Four, the conditions favorable for a high degree of homogeneity were presented—physical proximity in the pressroom, frequent opportunities for social interaction, and a shared sense of newsworthiness.

Our case study of the AP's and three newspapers' coverage of the *Rust* argument offers evidence of both homogeneity and variety. The stories shared the same angle, similar headlines, and lead paragraphs. The reporters who discussed their pending stories apparently were influenced by each other. The other reporters and Denniston responded to each other—they by adopting the Souter angle, and he by moving away from the more extreme pronouncements about Souter's position. The effect was a leaning toward the mean—an effort not to be too different from others' approaches.

However, the construction of the story differed from medium to medium. Not all reporters used the same sources or viewed the arguments in the same way. Differences existed in the treatment of the justices' questioning, external sources, case background, and the question of whether to discuss the eventual outcome of the case.

The greatest problem for the coverage was the underlying tone. In varying degrees, the stories suggested Souter would take a position in opposition to the government's position and that the regulations would be discarded by the Court. None of the stories made that point explicitly. However, if there was a consensus evidenced in the press corps by statements of reporters after the decision, it was that Souter would vote for the plaintiff, Rust. That conclusion may have magnified the decision to attend the press conference of the likely victor, Planned Parenthood.

It also probably shaped the writing of the stories. The critical comments of the government's position made by other justices in addition to Souter—O'Connor and Stevens—may have appeared more important in the outcome of the case than the sharp questioning of Laurence Tribe by some of the justices. The *New York Times* story mentioned Souter's medical ties, which presumably would make him more sympathetic to the doctors' position than the government's. The *Baltimore Sun* used adjectives suggesting Souter's position: Souter and other justices engaged in "rigorous questioning" of the government's representative, and Souter "openly wondered" about the regulations' legality. And the *Baltimore Sun* story noted that as the only abortion case that term, this case gave Souter an "opportunity to start taking a position." The general reader should not be faulted for believing that, on the basis of the information in the story, Souter was doing just that.

Given the outcome of the case—Planned Parenthood lost by a vote of five to four, with Souter siding with the majority—the presumption of Souter's position was flawed. The reporters could not have known that at the time. But restraint on the part of those who doubted whether Souter's questions indicated anything at all, especially in the face of subtle pressure from colleagues and editors, may have been difficult to maintain.

CONCLUSION

News of the U.S. Supreme Court is the product of the interaction between the justices and the reporters who cover them. The Court offers the news it wants the press to cover, and it is successful at setting the agenda for press coverage. News stories are dominated by coverage of the Court's cases. The public stages of the Court's activity are the news events generating stories.

Press attention is successfully diverted from the individuals who decide the cases. The ongoing decision-making process in each case, of which the events are merely regular public displays, remains hidden behind the veil the Court holds around it. The discussion about whether to grant review, the conference following oral arguments where the justices' initial positions are staked out, and the process of forging or keeping a majority through opinion writing are all absent from the news.

The justices decide what cases will be granted review. By so doing, they affect their own coverage. The justices knew that acceptance of the *Rust* case, for example, in the climate of sign-watching for an overturn of *Roe*, would attract press attention.

Reporters intervene in coverage by deciding what cases on the Court's docket will attract their attention. The number of cases to be covered in any given term varies according to the medium.

Reporters also affect the angle of the story. That freedom is greater in an oral argument story than in a decision story due to the inconclusiveness of the oral argument.

In sum, the justices offer the public a record of their activity. In turn, reporters concentrate on that public record. In that sense, the justices have succeeded in shaping a portrayal that reinforces the Court's role in American politics.

Chapter Seven

Shroud or Soundbyte: The Court in the Media Age

In 1992, the United States Supreme Court faced a serious dilemma. The justices had accepted for review a case that would be decided in the midst of an election year on an issue that divided the country. If decided in one direction, it would require that the justices state that their predecessors for most of the past 19 years had been in error, and if decided in the other direction, it would betray the presidents and interest groups who had furthered the appointments of a majority of the justices.

The conundrum did not end there. A decision to return the abortion issue to the state level carried the potential of the massive civil disobedience that had been promised by women's groups. On the other hand, a reaffirmation of the *Roe* decision would reenergize the pro-life movement and possibly continue the terrorist bombings by its most extreme element. The likelihood of continued civil unrest was real. Such activity would undermine the Court's ability to function as the final arbiter in American government.

The current Court is not the first to address such volatile issues with significant consequences for public policy, competing presidential candidates, political parties, and respect for the Court itself. However, the relative rarity of these situations has been a blessing for the Court, but hardly a mere stroke of luck. The justices are keenly aware that entrance into politically charged questions, especially ones perceived by most Americans as laced with strong moral overtones, is potentially dangerous for the Court. The likelihood of resolving such issues is remote, whereas the damage to the Court in public legitimacy is high. The Court treads carefully through the minefield of public opinion. This must be so, especially since that minefield has become larger as the Court has become enmeshed in a host of social policy issues during the past half century.

Without the legitimacy bestowed by the public, the Court's efforts to resolve these issues would be futile. The Court's ability to affect public policy would be weakened.

CHANGING ATTITUDES TOWARD THE COURT

The press has been a tool in the Court's arsenal for shaping its own image. However, in recent years external groups have not remained faithful to the mystique the Court seeks to create about itself. For the press, interest groups, and the mass public, some recent perceptions about the Court are not what the Court would want.

Some evidence already suggests the Court's "shroud" has frayed considerably with the press. Acceptance on the part of some of the press corps of the Court's image of political distance has been challenged. In recent years, calls have been made for the Court to be covered more as a political institution. According to Bob Woodward, "the courts are a political institution, and we [the press] don't cover them as such."[1] One press critic suggested the press should "peek under the robes and report on Court politics."[2] Nearly half of the reporters surveyed expressed agreement with the view that the Supreme Court is primarily a political institution.

The image of a Court driven by adherence to the law already is not shared by journalists who cover the Court. Other factors—personal and political—are important determinants. Two-thirds felt a justice's personal ideology is a very important factor in decision making. Also, two-thirds said the potential reaction of Congress or the White House was also at least somewhat important to the justices. And a majority believed another factor at least somewhat important in the Court's decision making is the legal community's potential reaction.

Whether a justice's personal life, unrelated to the job, should be considered potentially newsworthy is now a matter of debate. A slim majority of the reporters surveyed felt a justice's personal life is not news unless it affects his or her job. But in the wake of the Clarence Thomas confirmation hearings, it remains to be seen whether a justice's personal affairs will remain out of the limelight. Editors and producers, who are less likely to have personal ties to justices, may even be more committed to abandoning a line of privacy for justices. One reporter admitted that he and one of his editors had argued over whether a justice's house should be staked out to corroborate rumors of homosexual activity. The reporter refused to participate and the issue was dropped.

Interest groups apparently have abandoned all but the rhetoric of the Court as a less political institution than the Congress or the presidency. And sometimes even the rhetoric is gone. Molly Yard, in the midst of an abortion demonstration in front of the Court, remarked that the justices "are all political creatures, and they do

[1]Quoted in David Shaw, *Media Watch* (New York: Macmillan, 1984), p. 120

[2]John Kenneth Vinson, "'Ruling Elite' Spreads False Image of Supreme Court," *Legal Times* (January 10, 1983): 10.

understand political opinion." Another marcher said, "This is all for Sandra Day O'Connor. One signal for one justice: I hope she gets the message."[3]

Interest groups have long lobbied the Court via amici curiae (friend of the court) briefs. But in recent years the application of pressure has "gone public" with demonstrations, full-page newspaper advertisements, and mass mailings.[4] Although abortion has been the dominant issue, there is no reason for the precedent not to extend to other potentially volatile issues in the future.

Moreover, one of the implied arguments groups have employed to lobby the Court is that the Court should follow the majority opinion of the public. Those groups have then attempted to cultivate the perception that the majority of the public shares their stance on the issue.

The image of a nonpolitical Court also is undergoing change among the general public. The mystique may be gone already. According to a 1990 *National Law Journal*/Lexis survey, 47 percent of respondents believed that the justices decide cases on other factors, such as political and personal beliefs or political pressures, instead of on the basis of the facts and the law.[5] Simultaneously, the factors determining the justices' decision-making process are important because the Court is perceived as salient to Americans. In the same survey, 31 percent of the respondents considered the Court the most powerful institution, while 38 percent said Congress and only 21 percent said the president.[6]

Approval of the way the Court is doing its job has been affected. According to a succession of *Washington Post* surveys, while 66 percent approved of the way the Supreme Court was doing its job in 1986, in 1989 only 53 percent approved. In 1991, the percentage approving had moved up to 59 percent but still had not reached its earlier level.[7]

In July 1989, in the wake of the *Webster* decision, 53 percent of the public believed the Supreme Court was out of touch with what was going on in the country.[8] But in the spring of 1990, a calmer period, when respondents were asked whether the Rehnquist Court was "in line" with American values or "out of step," 49 percent agreed with the former view, 38 percent with the latter.[9]

If the public perceives the Court as political in its decision making, yet quite powerful in its reach, then the next step may be support for increased checks on the

---

[3]R. W. Apple, Jr., "Justices Are People," *New York Times*, April 10, 1989, p. A1.

[4]For a discussion of lobbying on the abortion issue, see W. John Moore, "Lobbying the Court," *National Journal* (April 15, 1989): 908–913; and James Hirsch, "Media Become Newest Weapons in Battle for Support on Abortion," *New York Times*, April 26, 1989, p. A25.

[5]Marcia Coyle, "How Americans View High Court," *National Law Journal* 12 (February 26, 1990): 1.

[6]Ibid. p. 1.

[7]See ABC News/*Washington Post* Survey, August 14, 1991, Question ID: USABCWP.434 R01; ABC News/*Washington Post* Survey, June 18, 1989, Question ID: USWASHP.89825E R01; ABC News/*Washington Post* Survey, June 24, 1986, Question ID: USABCWP.866542 Q15A.

[8]Harris Survey, July 1989.

[9]"Illawteracy: Public Perceptions of the Supreme Court," *Trial* (May 1990): 17.

Court's power. One of those checks may be a more aggressive journalistic approach to Court reporting.

Recognition of the Court as an institution significantly affected by political considerations should not be confused with external groups' ideal. An underlying expectation, or hope, that the justices will be nonpolitical still manifests itself at times. This expectation was made explicit in a 1941 editorial when the editor complained about two of the justices giving speeches on aid to Russia. "Once a man is enshrined for life in the lofty recesses of the United States Supreme Court he is no longer an ordinary citizen—he should be the incarnation of EXACT AND IMPARTIAL JUSTICE uninfluenced by the clamor of controversy that divides the people."[10] A correspondent to Harlan Stone complained about the activity of justices. "I have a feeling, which I believe is shared by many of my fellow citizens, that speeches and radio addresses by members of the Supreme Court are not to the best interests of the dignity of the Court."[11]

Some still prefer the human side of justices to remain veiled. When William O. Douglas appeared as a guest on "What's My Line?" in 1956, he received critical letters from viewers. One letter writer asked rhetorically, "I wonder how undignified a Supreme Court justice can get?" Another chided him as a poor successor to the great justices of the past: "Can you imagine a Brandeis a Hughes a Taft a Stone (sic) doing such a thing—It just couldn't happen and wouldn't happen."[12]

These attitudes are not antiquated. When Thurgood Marshall appeared on ABC's "Primetime Live" in 1990 and made derogatory statements of President Bush and his chief of staff, John Sununu, he was criticized in newspaper editorials.[13]

One of the arguments for maintaining distance from the press is to preserve the mystique of the Court in the eyes of the public. The public, interest groups, and, to some extent, the press itself, however, may already be questioning the reality of the mystique.

ACCOMMODATIONS—PRESENT AND FUTURE

The justices have not been oblivious to the changes that have occurred in external groups' perceptions of the Court. As mentioned in Chapter One, some of the justices have used their opinions as forums to express frustration with these developments.

The Court has attempted to adjust to these expectations by meeting the communications revolution halfway. The Court has responded by instituting accommodations to press demands. But the Court has responded with changes that do not impair the Court's ability to control its communications but attempts to prevent

[10]Editorial, *Hudson Dispatch* (Union City, N.J.), August 21, 1941.

[11]Letter from H. H. Schrader, July 30, 1941, Harlan Fiske Stone Papers, Box 80, Library of Congress, Washington, D.C.

[12]Letter from G. C. Jones, Jr., May 7, 1956 and letter from John C. McClure, May 7, 1956, William O. Douglas Papers, Box 846, Library of Congress, Washington, D.C.

[13]See, for example, "Justice Marshall's Regrettable Comments," *Hartford Courant*, July 29, 1990.

decay in public support. Project Hermes, the electronic transmission of opinions is one example of such accommodation.

Project Hermes

"Project Hermes...was developed in response to requests from the *New York Times* and the Associated Press that we do something," Toni House related. "The only requests for it came from news organizations." Initiated in the spring of 1990, Project Hermes allows same-day electronic access to Supreme Court opinions for news organizations and others with on-line video-display terminal access. Project Hermes also includes the orders lists the Court releases.

Electronic bulletin boards around the country have included Project Hermes and have expanded access. However, the project is still expanding and someday will deliver even more. "We have discovered that it is inadequate in its scope," Toni House explained. "So we are moving to double the number of on line direct reports, and I hope it will have a bulletin board out...which will create free public access to the opinions, rules of the court, calendars...."

"I hope the day will come when we will have every single solitary petition, or at least paid petition that is filed in this building [on] a floppy [disc] that goes right into our bulletin board." The day may also come when transcripts of oral arguments will be transmitted, but it will not likely happen until transcriptions are done on a same-day basis since the service is not designed to be archival. News reporters would benefit from a same-day transcription to improve the accuracy of reporting of oral argument. And electronic transmission would be a convenient way to distribute such texts. But the Court so far has not been interested in providing such a service.

Cameras in the Courtroom

But the change widely sought after is one change in the Court's attitude toward cameras in the courtroom. Three-fourths of the reporters surveyed said they want the Court to begin televising its public sessions.

The Court has never allowed cameras—still or motion—in the courtroom during public sessions. The Court has even been reluctant to allow the courtroom to be filmed while any person was present. However, Chief Justice Burger, at the time of his retirement, was interviewed on camera in the courtroom by Bill Moyers. Only a justice may appear on camera in the courtroom.

Cameras in other settings have been more accepted. These include the justices' chambers for interviews. At least one justice, John Paul Stevens, urged his colleagues to allow a Washington public broadcasting station to televise a swearing-in ceremony of the Court. Evidently a majority of the other justices disagreed because the event was not televised.[14]

[14]Memo to Conference from Justice Stevens, September 23, 1986, Thurgood Marshall Papers, Box 379, Library of Congress, Washington, D.C.

Pressure has come from news media organizations for change. Broadcast news organizations, as the obvious beneficiaries, have solicited the Court's consideration of an alteration in their policy. One of the networks most anxious for change is C-SPAN, which would air the Court's public sessions in full. Another probable beneficiary would be the newly created Courtroom Television Network or Court TV, a cable channel dedicated to covering judicial proceedings.[15]

In 1989, 13 news organizations sought the justices' participation in a demonstration of the unobtrusiveness of television coverage. Three of the justices—William Rehnquist, Anthony Kennedy, and Byron White—participated in a mock oral argument with cameras present.[16] Subsequently, however, although the chief justice himself seemed neutral on the demonstration as a trial run for the Court, he announced there would be no change in policy.[17]

Televisied coverage has already come in some form in 45 state courts and in some federal courts. In September 1990, the Judicial Conference of the United States approved a three year experiment with cameras in federal courtrooms beginning in July 1991.[18] The experiment has involved both federal district and appellate courts. The U.S. Court of Military Appeals had already allowed television cameras in their courtroom.

The justices have had mixed reactions to the idea. William Brennan, before his retirement, expressed strong support. In a magazine article, Brennan said of televising the Court: "I would love it. I'm the only one presently of the nine who would allow television broadcasts of our actual proceedings.... I am convinced that the day is bound to come when we will be televised."[19] William Rehnquist, during his confirmation hearings for chief justice in 1986, stated that "If I were convinced that coverage by television of the Supreme Court would not distort the way the court works at present, I certainly would give it sympathetic consideration." Rehnquist was one of the three justices who participated in the televised mock oral argument. [20]

But the justices also have expressed their concerns about the impact of television on the Court. John Paul Stevens said in a 1985 speech that, although he

[15]Deirdre Carmody, "A Magazine's Trials, Now on Home Video," *New York Times,* February 24, 1992, p. D8.

[16]"Three Justices Show Interest in Camera Demonstration," *The News Media & The Law* (Winter 1989): 23–24.

[17]Eleanor Randolph, "Justices Continue Ban on Courtroom Cameras," *Washington Post,* November 1, 1989. Also see Rehnquist, memo to the Conference, September 19, 1988, Thurgood Marshall Papers, Box 451, Library of Congress, Washington, D.C.

[18]"Judicial Conference Approves Cameras in the Courtroom Experiment," *The Third Branch: Newsletter of the Federal Courts* (October 1990): p. 1.

[19]Quoted in "High Court Nominee Souter No Stranger to TV Cameras," *C-SPAN UPDATE,* August 5, 1990.

[20]United States Senate Committee on the Judiciary, *Nomination of Justice William Hubbs Rehnquist to be Chief Justice of the United States,* Hearings Before the 99th Congress, Second Session, July 29, 30, 31, and August 1, 1986.

realized the limitations of the courtroom in seating all those who wish to hear argument, he felt that television cameras might have "an adverse impact on the process that cannot be foreseen."[21]

Those concerns have been made more explicit by other justices. One concern is the physical disruption of the proceedings. Rehnquist expressed opposition "if it meant a whole lot of lights that would disturb the present relationship between justices and lawyers in arguing cases..."[22] Another fear is the tendency to "play to the cameras." Anthony Kennedy said he feared that "it might make me and my colleagues behave differently than they would otherwise."[23]

Rita Braver, CBS News reporter dismissed that concern: "I don't think the issue holds water that the justices are worried that some of them would ham it up. Some of the justices ham it up anyway. I don't think you're going to change that. I don't think the argument that lawyers would act up or misbehave holds water because most of them are scared out of their minds and they don't want to do anything that makes them look foolish."

But the justices also must be concerned about their image. C-SPAN coverage, with its devotion to gavel-to-gavel coverage of legislative proceedings, is a medium that justices probably feel would conform to their desired image. However, the prospect of sharing the same channel with sensational rape or murder trials, as they would on Court TV, is likely to be quite disturbing.

According to Rita Braver, the television portrayal would humanize the justices: "You would find out.... These are people like you. Some of them are getting old and some of them are known to doze off on the bench. They don't want the world to know they're human, and that's why they don't want cameras in the courtroom."

But Braver doesn't believe that would be detrimental to the Court:

> "To a certain extent to demystify anything is to undermine confidence in it, but I watch these arguments day after day and I find them inspiring. I think people's confidence in the Court would be, rather than undermined, ...reinforced. They would see how serious these people are about their jobs, and how smart they are. When you hear constitutional principles talked about in language that you can understand, its thrilling. I think it would be much better for the public."

The justices also are concerned about how producers would edit their sessions. While C-SPAN would air the arguments in full, the network evening news programs

[21]Quoted in "What the Justices Have Said About Supreme Court TV," *C-SPAN UPDATE*, September 9, 1990.

[22]United States Senate Committee on the Judiciary, *Nomination of Justice William Hubbs Rehnquist to be Chief Justice of the United States*, Hearings Before the 99th Congress, Second Session, July 29, 30, 31, and August 1, 1986.

[23]U.S. Senate Committee on the Judiciary, *Nomination of Anthony Kennedy to be Associate Justice of the Supreme Court of the United States*, Hearings Before the 100th Congress, First Session, December 14, 15, and 16, 1987.

would not. According to Antonin Scalia what would be selected "will inevitably be an uncharacteristic question or an uncharacteristic answer...."[24]

Scalia expressed another concern that is probably widely shared by the other justices: that they would become well-known figures. Scalia commented in a question and answer session after a speech that "[t]he reason I've made a conscious effort, at least after my first year on the court, to stay off of the tube [is] if it doesn't happen on television, it doesn't exist by and large in this country. It is the tradition of common law judges not to be public figures, not to be prominent in the political process or in the process of public interest."[25]

The justices enjoy their relative obscurity as individuals. Television coverage would place their faces on TV on a regular basis across the country. The still photographs the Public Information Office distributes and the sketch artists' depictions do not threaten this obscurity since they do not conform to the medium's imperative for moving visuals. "They very much covet their privacy and their anonymity," *USA Today* reporter Tony Mauro explained. "They're very loath to lose that."

Another argument used to oppose cameras is the public's supposed disinterest in seeing oral arguments. As the reasoning goes, the result might be an initial strong curiosity but a subsequent lack of interest in most of the cases the Court addresses. In his testimony to the U.S. Senate during confirmation hearings, David Souter, when asked his feelings about cameras in the courtroom, expressed his disappointment that after an initial burst of enthusiasm about televising the New Hampshire Supreme Court, where he served as an associate justice, the cameras left. "I'm sorry to say that apparently the news media or the New Hampshire public at that point grew so bored with what they were seeing photographed that people stopped taking pictures...."[26]

Souter is the only member of the Court possessing direct experience with television coverage of judicial proceedings. But assuming Souter supports a change, his junior status on the Court and his seeming lack of passion on the subject makes it unlikely he will be a prime mover in policy change.

Reportedly, one of the strongest opponents is Antonin Scalia. Ironically, Scalia is widely known as the most colorful presence in oral arguments. He often questions counsel, states their arguments for them, and aids them in answering questions from the other justices. One reporter calls him a "thespian" in oral argument. However, Scalia may feel his frequent interaction with counsel would have to be curbed to avoid the appearance of bullying or playing to the cameras. (The other justices, however, may be inclined to support broadcasting for just that reason.) Scalia also shares the belief the public would not be interested in watching the Court's activities. Although referring to the opinions of the Court, the following

[24]"Scalia Turning Against Cameras in High Court," *C-SPAN UPDATE*, June 17, 1990.

[25]Ibid.

[26]U.S. Senate Committee on the Judiciary, *Nomination of David H. Souter to be Associate Justice of the Supreme Court of the United States*, Hearings before 101st Congress, Second Session, 1990, p. 190.

comments by Scalia could also be construed to include the oral arguments. Scalia remarked in a speech that

> One would not expect the public to be interested in it. Indeed, one would feel for the Republic if the public were to be interested in it. Since the public is not interested in it, one would hardly expect the press to report it. That is why the *University of Chicago Law Review* is not sold at Seven Eleven.[27]

Following Scalia's logic, televising the Court's public sessions would produce national boredom and lead viewers quickly to change channels to more entertaining fare. Interestingly, Scalia's quote also confirms that of all the justices, as he fears, he would likely be the most quotable and the most quoted. Since the mid-1980s, a standard question in confirmation hearings has been the nominee's attitude about broadcasting public sessions of the Court. Each of the successful nominees has expressed qualified support for the idea. But still no change has come.

With the changes in the attitude of the Federal Judicial Conference and many state courts, and the retirement of Warren Burger as chief justice, for a time there was a sense of inevitability about cameras at the Supreme Court. Anthony Kennedy reportedly told a group of high school students visiting the Court that he thought cameras at the Supreme Court were inevitable.[28]

However, that expectation has been dampened somewhat. Lyle Denniston still believes it will happen. "I don't think its more than a matter of time before the proceedings are broadcast. It's going more slowly than I thought it would. I believed Rehnquist would be able to turn the court around. Toni [House] tells me there is a clear and sizeable majority that is hostile to the idea." Like Denniston, Tim O'Brien also believes TV will come: "It is the wave of the future. Its day will come."[29]

Others disagree. *USA Today* reporter Tony Mauro doubts it will come before the end of the century. Rita Braver doubts she will see a change in her lifetime.

The confirmation hearings that have increased public interest in Supreme Court appointments have had an adverse effect on the justices' interest in television. According to House, the initial interest of the justices has waned in light of televised coverage of confirmation hearings: "The confirmation hearings, particularly the Bork hearings, had an effect on their attitude toward television cameras in the courtroom. That was the summer that the window of opportunity was slammed shut. There are a number of factors that have gone into what I see is a temporary retreat from a kind of curiosity [about television]." Justice Scalia confirmed this change, at least for himself, by confessing that "when I first went on the court [in 1986], I was in favor of having cameras in the court. I am less and less so...."[30] Thurgood Marshall, an original proponent of change, subsequently changed his mind due to the Bork hearings. According

---

[27]Transcript of speech delivered on August 9, 1990, provided by a reporter on the Court beat.

[28]David Margolick, "Federal Courts May Lift Ban on TV," *New York Times*, May 23, 1990, p. A14.

[29]Speech delivered to Washington Council of Lawyers, August 9, 1989.

[30]"Scalia Turning Against Cameras in High Court," *C-SPAN UPDATE*, June 17, 1990.

to a reporter on the Court beat, "Marshall remarked after watching the Bork hearings that 'no one's going to stick a camera up my nose.'" If the Court allowed televising, it is unlikely the C-SPAN coverage of Congress would be the model. While the House and Senate leadership retain control over the placement of cameras and can control the airing of roll call votes, quorum calls, and other procedures, it still allows nearly all of the floor proceedings to be televised.

The Court may offer the press some variation of that. One option is in-house televising of the oral arguments with the justices providing pre-packaged excerpts to the press, perhaps with the proviso that the media agree to use all or nothing. But would news organizations agree to that kind of control? "That raises serious questions of whether we would use any of it," admitted Tim O'Brien. "I would hope not. We've relinquished our editorial process." But competition may drive compliance. For television, some visuals are better than no visuals, especially given the high degree of novelty of these visuals.

If the Court were to open itself to television cameras, the television reporters would do their jobs differently. The television networks would have an hour of argument on tape for editing videotape of the proceedings. This type of visual would meet the imperatives of television far more than the artists' depictions of the justices, hence, Court stories would become more frequent fare on television news.

But having visuals of the Court's public proceedings would complicate the editing process for reporters. According to Tim O'Brien, he will have a more difficult time determining how to present a Court story: "My fingernails will go because I will be biting them off wondering how I'm going to get it all into a minute, thirty-five." Reporters would have to balance. The justification for covering stories through traveling to interview the parties involved may become weaker since news executives will suggest that the Court itself provides plenty of visuals.

But one effect, according to Rita Braver, will be a diminution of the reporter's on-camera role. "[If there were cameras in the courtroom], I still have to figure out which quotes of the justices would go into an argument case—except they would be saying them themselves rather than me saying them. You would hear less of me." With soundbytes from the justices, the reporter's interpreter role would be less visible. Reporters would serve as editor of the visuals. Temporarily, other sources— the parties in the case, counsel, and interest group representatives—would be displaced. But over time the novelty of soundbytes of the justices would wear off and they would compete with other sources. Eventually, like other political figures, the justices would be the victims of shrinking soundbytes. The timing of their fate would probably be accelerated if they continued to speak in technical language and failed to speak in the epigrammatic style appealing to television news. That prospect cannot be attractive to the justices. Moving down the path toward greater accommodation to television will ultimately result in a change in a justice's presentation style or a trivialization of the justices' words by news reporters.

Neither coverage of the Congress nor the presidency would be the model. Unlike the Congress, the Court offers one presentation, not multiple ones. In that sense, the Court would retain more control of its visual image. On the other hand, unlike the president, the Court is not adept at manipulating visual images. While the White House is anxious to provide a visual feed for the day, the Court is not. Eventually, the vacuum would invite reporters to continue to seek other visual sources, particularly if they can visually contradict the Court. The image of the justices' soundbytes followed by interest group representatives or parties in the case offering contrast to the justices should be highly appealing to a broadcast news reporter, but not to the justices.

In the short run, the justices' acceptance of cameras may increase broadcast news coverage of the Court's product and displace the attention to the personalities of a case. But, over time the justices' own words will become less visible as their novelty wears off. Hence, the Court will lose its image of distance from the personalities of the cases and from the implications for individuals' lives of its decisions. When visuals of justices are juxtaposed against visuals of individuals harmed by their decisions or against visuals of members of Congress or the president, the association will hardly enhance the justices' desired image of distance from political considerations.

Other Reforms

Another change proposed is the early release of the opinions to reporters on the day of the decision, accompanied with a "lock-up" to prevent leaking. "There is an enormous pressure to get the story first," lamented Tim O'Brien, an advocate of the idea.[31]

But the lock-up idea is not widely shared among the press corps. Less than one-third favored that idea. One explanation is that the proportion of beneficiaries among the press corps is small. The most affected groups would be wire service and broadcast reporters, primarily in major cases where public interest is high. Daily and weekly print media, as well as specialized publications with weekly and monthly deadlines, usually are not involved in this issue since the lock-up idea affects them less.

The press would like to see a more press-friendly Court in other ways as well. Three-fourths of the reporters surveyed said they would like the justices to give more on-the-record interviews. A significant minority also wanted the justices to begin providing post-decision commentary.

In addition, the public information officer, an inside-outsider, has acted to open the Court to the press. The changes have not been earth-shattering—television cameras in the Court building for documentaries and interviews, greater information on the justices' travel and health, participation in on-camera interviews—but they are significant for the tradition-bound Court. "Toni has been a bridge between the cloistered past and what will almost certainly be a more open future for the Court," remarked Carl Stern, former NBC News reporter on the Court beat.[32]

[31]Speech delivered to Washington Council of Lawyers, August 9, 1989.

[32]W. John Moore, "Introducing the Court to a Bit of Openness," *National Journal* (October 7, 1989): 2472.

ABANDONING THE ROBES

But the justices are highly cautious in approaching these changes. They have oscillated between accepting and resisting change in press policy. For example, the potential for a Court where justices give post-decision commentary is extremely slim, while the lock-up idea has not made any headway with the justices. On the other hand, the justices have already given more on-the-record interviews than their predecessors.

The dilemma for some of the justices is to maintain a policy role while preserving their relative anonymity. Some of them, such as Antonin Scalia (who gives speeches to various groups but attempts to exclude television cameras), want to make public appearances without suffering from the exposure of concomitant news coverage.[33]

In an age of financial disclosure forms, public scrutiny of the private lives of policymakers (not only elected but also appointed), and the widespread perception of the Court as a powerful institution, the justices' desires for anonymity may be difficult to maintain. The justices are hewing a line between the demands for change and the instinct of self-preservation. The communications revolution has affected them. But they have approached their relations with the press as individual justices more than as the institution of the Court.

One major difficulty is they are not always acting *en bloc*. Some of the justices have stretched the limits imposed by current judicial norms. "I think they very distinctly do not wish to be personalities," Toni House opined. "I think they know exactly what they're about. Justice Scalia, in particular, has said that he enjoys giving speeches, and he enjoys making himself available, but he doesn't want every single, solitary one of them on C-SPAN because he doesn't want to look like he's running for something. Justice Blackmun makes himself very available to speak to groups, and Justice O'Connor, but they're not particularly interested in every word being recounted."

There are compelling reasons for the individual justices to attempt to remain anonymous and not jeopardize the public's generally favorable perceptions of the justices. The justices distinctly do not want their privacy violated. Some of them can become testy when reporters treat them like presidents or leading presidential candidates. "I am sorry I missed the session today," William O. Douglas, a great defender of the freedom of the press, wrote to Warren Burger in 1975 in the midst of speculation of his pending retirement. "The reason was the press. It ambushed me at the house at 7 A.M. to get more pictures of my wheelchair. If this keeps up, they'll make me wonder about the First Amendment—their big umbrella."[34]

That also explains why William Rehnquist lost his temper at reporters when they suggested the Court keep them informed when justices are hospitalized. Rehnquist, according to Fred Graham, "glared, curled back his lip, and let some of

---

[33]For an example, see "Scalia Bars TV From Ohio Speech," *C-SPAN UPDATE*, November 6, 1989.

[34]Melvin Urofsky, ed., *The Douglas Letters* (Bethesda, Md.: Adler & Adler, 1987), p. 142.

his feelings spill out. "My experience," he said, "has been that where that subject is concerned, you can be a bunch of vultures."[35] The justices' relative obscurity as individuals has allowed them to pursue more normal lives than would be expected for individuals with such power and in an institution so individualized by nature. For example, Harry Blackmun, the author of *Roe v. Wade*, was once able to walk by anti-abortion demonstrators without being recognized.[36] They have cultivated public ignorance of themselves as individuals through the tactics discussed earlier. It is unlikely they will act quickly to destroy their own efforts. They are also sensitive about the process of decision making remaining shrouded. The reaction of Chief Justice Rehnquist to news coverage of the justices' deliberations gleaned from the Thurgood Marshall Papers in May 1993 serves as example. In his letter to James Billington, the Librarian of Congress, Rehnquist cited the "Court's long tradition of confidentiality in its deliberations."[37]

The justices want to perpetuate the images discussed in Chapter One. Toni House: "Nobody understands better than the nine people who wear black robes in this building the limitations of their influence. I'm sure they've all read Hamilton about what their authority is. That's where they have to focus. That's where they want the American people to focus—on their deep commitment to their doing their jobs as justices to the best of their ability and living up to their oath. That's why I don't think you're going to see them in the next 20 years sort of popping up on Good Morning America. I really don't."

But the nine justices have already done more "popping up" in the news media than their predecessors. They have pushed the line set by their predecessors. How far they will push in the future will impact not only themselves, but also the institution they serve.

THE PERMANENCY OF CHANGE

The United States Supreme Court is a tradition-bound institution. But the Court today faces pressures from the public, interest groups, and the press to heed public opinion. The changes affecting the Court in a media age are permanent, due to the contributions of the nomination process and the increasing legitimacy of such efforts, not to mention the perceived success of these lobbying tactics in swaying Court direction.

The Nomination Process

The nomination process has been irrevocably altered. Prior to the Robert Bork nomination, with few exceptions, Supreme Court nominations did not become

---

[35]Fred Graham, *Happy Talk* (New York: W. W. Norton, 1990), p. 133.

[36]Ibid. p. 116.

[37]See Joan Biskupic and Benjamin Weiser, "Chief Justice Castigates Library," *The Washington Post*, May 26, 1993, p. A1.

public battlegrounds between interest groups courting public opinion in order to sway undecided senators. The airwaves and print media were not filled with advertisements urging public mobilization in the judicial selection process. Lengthy televised confirmation hearings and mass demonstrations were rare.

Even in a period of one-party control of government, it is difficult to believe that conservative groups facing unsatisfactory judicial appointments from a Democratic administration will not employ the same tools in the nomination process their liberal counterparts utilized during the Reagan and Bush presidencies. In fact, lacking the ability to control Judiciary Committee proceedings, they may be more inclined to view the public struggle as the only viable option.

The chief obstacle for continuance of a media-oriented nomination battle may be the sense of inevitability of confirmation. However, with the potential of filibuster in the Senate and defections by more conservative Democrats, inevitability of confirmation is unlikely for any but the most nonpartisan of nominees.

Not every nomination in the future is bound to evoke the intense emotions of the Bork and Thomas nominations. But each will involve, to a greater or lesser extent, the media, public opinion, and interest groups in a publicly visible struggle over the confirmation of the nominee.

The Legitimacy of the Mass Role

The Court as the object of intense lobbying is not new. But the public nature of this lobbying—mail campaigns, demonstrations on the Court steps, newspaper and television advertisements—appears to be a dramatic departure from the reliance on amici briefs to communicate group stances and to influence the outcome of the deliberative process. However, the increased resort to these tactics by interest groups has gradually legitimated their role. Protestors on the steps of the Supreme Court building and marches nearby have become accepted events.

The frequency of mass demonstrations adjacent to the Supreme Court building and the interest groups' full-page advertisements in major newspapers, primarily on the issue of abortion, have prompted some debate over the Court's role in society. Critics suggests the Court cannot function as a constitutional arbiter if it is the continual object of lobbying. Edwin M. Yoder, Jr. noted, "Justices who are political enough to be influenced by a demonstration on one day aren't likely, the day after, to ignore a public clamor and affirm an unpopular but valuable liberty."[38] But the issue will continue to live because of the changed perceptions of the Court.

The compelling question in the minds of interest group activists must be: Do these tactics work? The groups who organized in opposition to the Court's overturning of the *Roe* case cannot be faulted for concluding that they succeeded. Not only did the Court not overturn Roe, but three justices, O'Connor, Kennedy, and Souter, who were perceived as ready to dismantle *Roe* to varying extents—

---

[38]"The Court Isn't a Weather Vane," *Washington Post National Weekly Edition*, April 17–23, 1989, p. 28.

reaffirmed its legitimacy while placing limitations on its application. While pro-choice groups did not get all they wanted, it strains credulity to believe the justices were not listening. If such efforts are perceived as potentially successful, their occurrence will be more frequent.

THE COURT IN THE MEDIA AGE

The future of press relations does not hold great promise for maintaining the Court's traditions. If resisted, technological advances will increasingly isolate the Court from its most important base—the mass public. The call for television coverage of the Court has been portrayed by some advocates as not merely a matter of policy, but one of rights. The *New York Times* has editorialized that Americans have "a right to hear and see the arguments, a right the high court denies by keeping out cameras."[39]

The potential is real for a more assertive press corps challenging the Court's traditions. The dilemma for the Court will be to maintain journalistic attention on the Court's agenda. Bob Woodward accuses the press of sidestepping the important issues in Court coverage, and he challenges the press to set its own agenda for Court coverage. "The only two questions really worth asking about the courts are 'Is there justice?' and 'How do they operate as a political institution?' The press doesn't do a very good job of trying to answer either."[40] If reporters pursue those questions, they would spend less time on the final product of the Court and more on cultivating sources who may provide insights on the ongoing process of deliberation. The Court would then have less control over its image.

The Court in the media age will not be the same institution as it has been. Due to its adherence to tradition, the Court will not come willingly, nor wholeheartedly, into the future. In order to avoid isolation, the Court historically has shown adeptness at accommodating its time-honored customs to the requirements of a new age. Of all the Court's time-honored customs, a critical task for the current justices will be to continue that one.

---

[39]"The Court, Still Off Camera," *New York Times*, April 27, 1989, p. A30.

[40]Quoted in David Shaw, *Press Watch* (New York: Macmillan, 1984), p. 120.

A Note
On Methodology

Studies of the U.S. Supreme Court by political scientists have crossed methodological lines. Although the concentration in the past was on historical approaches, more recently quantitative analysis has also been used.[1] Interviewing was the primary method of a recent study of agenda-setting.[2]

In the study of the relationship between the Court and the press, content analysis has been the dominant method.[3] Case studies of press coverage of individual decisions have appeared in the literature.[4] Observations of the Supreme Court press corps at work have also been reported.[5]

[1]For samples of research including quantitative analysis, see John B. Gates, *The Supreme Court and Partisan Realignment: A Macro- and Microlevel Perspective* (Boulder, Colo.: Westview Press, 1992); Thomas R. Marshall, *Public Opinion and the Supreme Court* (Boston: Unwin Hyman, 1989); Larry Berkson, *The Supreme Court and Its Publics* (Lexington, Mass.: Lexington Books, 1978). David W. Rohde and Harold J. Spaeth, *Supreme Court Decisionmaking* (San Francisco: W. H. Freeman, 1976). For a recent quantitative approach to judicial selection, see John Massaro, *Supremely Political: The Role of Ideology and Presidential Management in Unsuccessful Supreme Court Nominations* (Albany, N.Y.: State University of New York Press, 1990).

[2]See H. W. Perry, *Deciding to Decide: Agenda Setting in the United States Supreme Court* (Cambridge, Mass.: Harvard University Press, 1991).

[3]See, for example, David Ericson, "Newspaper Coverage of the Supreme Court," *Journalism Quarterly* 54 (Autumn 1977): 605–607; Michael Solimine, "Newsmagazine Coverage of the Supreme Court," *Journalism Quarterly* 57 (Winter 1980): 661–663; Ethan Katsh, "The Supreme Court Beat: How Television Covers the U.S. Supreme Court," *Judicature* 67 (June–July 1983): 6–12; and Richard Davis, "Lifting the Shroud: News Media Portrayal of the U.S. Supreme Court," *Communications and the Law* 9 (October 1987): 43–58.

[4]See, for example, David Grey, *The Supreme Court and the News Media* (Evanston, Ill.: Northwestern University Press, 1968); and Davis, "Lifting the Shroud," op. cit.

[5]See Grey, *The Supreme Court and the News Media*, op cit.

This research utilizes all of these methods in a unique multimethod approach. The methods employed were observation, interviews, surveys, historical research, and content analysis.

Observation

The Public Information Office provided access to their office and the adjacent pressroom during the 1989 and 1990 terms. I was also allowed to observe from the press section in the courtroom from the same perspective reporters have on the left-hand side of the room. My observation of the Public Information Office and the pressroom occurred over 18 days at frequent intervals between June 1990 and March 1991. From the Public Information Office and the courtroom, I observed the stages of the Court's public activity, including the issuing of orders lists, oral arguments, and decision announcements.

I also observed the press at work by following three reporters through their coverage of Court stories. I followed two print journalists from oral argument and decision announcement in the morning to the filing of their stories in late afternoon. One of them, a network television reporter, I followed to the origin of a story in a southern state and I observed as the reporter interviewed the parties in the case and reported from the scene of the crime that initiated the decision. Subsequently, I communicated with that reporter to follow the preparation of the story and its eventual broadcast at the time of oral argument and again at decision announcement.

Interviewing

I interviewed former and current employees of the Court and reporters in the press corps at the Court. Sixteen reporters and four current and former employees of the Court were interviewed. The designation "employees" included clerks and others close to the justices.

Although most of those interviewed for this research placed no restrictions on subsequent use of the information they provided, some sources, both reporters and Court employees, preferred that their contributions, in full or in part, remain anonymous. Those requests have been honored, necessitating oblique references to sources in some cases, including not identifying the position of the Court employee quoted.

Survey

A survey of the reporters' credentialed with the U.S. Supreme Court Public Information Office was conducted in September 1992. After two solicitations for participation, 18 reporters of 32 (56 percent), completed a survey instrument. A copy of the survey instrument is included in Appendix A.

Historical Research

In addition to secondary sources on the justices' relations with the press and the Court's role as a political institution, the papers of some of the justices were examined at the Manuscript Division of the Library of Congress and at the Manuscript Division of the Sterling Library at Yale University. The former source is the most complete repository for the papers of Supreme Court justices.

Two of the more useful collections at the Library of Congress were the papers of William O. Douglas and Earl Warren. The Douglas collection holds greater currency, including memoranda and recollections of several justices still on the bench nearly 20 years after his retirement.

Content Analysis

Two content analysis studies were conducted. These included three different types of media encompassing a six-year period.

The first study included CBS News and *Time* magazine stories about the Court covering the time period from 1984 to 1989. The study began with September 1, 1984 and ended July 31, 1989. This period covers five terms preceding my observations at the Court.

CBS News stories were drawn from transcripts of CBS Evening News programs located at the CBS Research Library in New York. *Time* stories were culled from the "Nation" and "Law" sections of the magazine's issues during these terms.

The second study concentrated on a single term of the Court and a single medium—the wire copy of the Associated Press. This single medium is the most widely utilized source of information about the U.S. Supreme Court. The Associated Press wire service provides most other news sources—dailies and broadcast stations—throughout the country with copy. Most of the news about the Supreme Court received by newspaper readers comes from AP. Large metropolitan dailies—such as the *New York Times, Washington Post, Los Angeles Times, Chicago Tribune*— have their own reporter at the Court for whom the Court is a major assignment of their beat. But smaller dailies—such as the *Milwaukee Journal, Hartford Courant, Houston Chronicle*—assign people only part-time to the Court. Still other dailies cover the Court with their own staff only when a major decision affects their geographical area.

For the news outlets in the latter two groups, the Associated Press wire service covers the vast majority of the Court's activity. And for even smaller dailies in small metropolitan areas it becomes the exclusive source of information.

The Associated Press wire copy was studied for the 1989 term. Wire copy between September 1, 1989 and July 31, 1990 was included.

For both studies, only those stories primarily about the Supreme Court were included. Also, stories about the judicial selection process were excluded.

Appendix A

The Public Information Office distributes the argument schedule for reporters early in the term. However, the scheduling of actual cases is determined throughout the term.

SUPREME COURT OF THE UNITED STATES
SCHEDULE FOR OCTOBER TERM 1988

1988	M	T	W	
October	3,	4,	5	(Argument)
	H,	11,	12	(Argument)
	17			(No argument)
RECESS—October 18 through October 30				(2 weeks)
October	31,	Nov. 1,	2	(Argument)
	7,	8,	9	(Argument)
	14			(No argument)
RECESS—November 15 through November 27				(2 weeks)
November	28,	29,	30	(Argument)
December	5,	6,	7	(Argument)
	12			(No argument)
RECESS—December 13 through January 8				(4 weeks)

SUPREME COURT OF THE UNITED STATES
SCHEDULE FOR OCTOBER TERM 1988 (cont'd.)

1989	M	T	W	
January	9,	10,	11	(Argument)
	H,	17,	18	(Argument)
	23			(No argument)
	RECESS—January 24 through February 19			(4 weeks)
February	H,	21,	22	(Argument)
	27,	28,	Mar. 1	(Argument)
	6			(No argument)
	RECESS—March 7 through March 19			(2 weeks)
March	20,	21,	22	(Argument)
	27,	28,	29	(Argument)
	Apr. 3			(No argument)
	RECESS—April 4 through April 16			(2 weeks)
April	17,	18,	19	(Argument)
	24,	25,	26	(Argument)
	May 1			(No argument)
	RECESS—May 2 through May 14			(2 weeks)
May	15			(No argument)
	22			(No argument)
	H,	30		(No argument)
June	5			(No argument)
	12			(No argument)
	19			(No argument)
	26			(No argument)

Before an oral argument, reporters receive the following, offering information on the counsel in the case.

WEDNESDAY, OCTOBER 31, 1990

CASES FOR ARGUMENT TODAY

MR. JOHN CHARLES BOGER Chapel Hill, N. C. **MS. MARY BETH WESTMORELAND** Sr. Asst. Atty. Gen. of Georgia Atlanta, Ga.	*No. 89-7024.* (8) **WARREN McCLESKEY,** Petitioner V. **WALTER D. ZANT, SUPERINTENDENT, GEORGIA DIAGNOSTIC & CLASSIFICATION CENTER**	1 hour for argument.
MR. RICHARD A. ALLEN Washington, D.C. **MR. L. JAY BARTEL** Asst. Atty. Gen. of Nebraska Lincoln, Neb.	*No. 89-1555.* (9) **MARK E. DENNIS,** Petitioner V. **MARGARET L. HIGGINS, DIRECTOR, NEBRASKA DEPARTMENT OF MOTOR VEHICLES, ET AL.**	1 hour for argument.

The following is an example of the rare press statement issued from the Public Information Office. Both the letter and Justice Brennan's statement were given to reporters on the day he resigned.

CHAMBERS OF   July 20, 1990
JUSTICE Wm. J. BRENNAN, JR.

MEMORANDUM TO THE NEWS MEDIA

Justice Brennan has today sent the following letter to the President announcing his retirement, effective immediately:

```
The President
The White House
Washington, D.C.

My dear Mr. President:

    The strenuous demands of court work and its
related duties required or expected of a Justice
appear at this time to be incompatible with my
advancing age and medical condition.
    I, therefore, retire effective immediately as an
Associate Justice of the Supreme Court of the United
States.

Respectfully,
```

CHAMBERS OF   July 20, 1990
JUSTICE Wm. J. BRENNAN, JR.

STATEMENT OF JUSTICE BRENNAN

```
My letter to the President explains my reasons for
deciding that I should retire. This was a very
difficult decision after almost 34 years of service
on the Court. It is my hope that the Court during my
years of service has built a legacy of interpreting
the Constitution and federal laws to make them
responsive to the needs of the people whom they were
intended to benefit and protect. This legacy can and
will withstand the test of time.
```

Appendix B

U.S. SUPREME COURT PRESS CORPS SURVEY

First, a few questions about your work. Please check the appropriate response.

How much of your time is spent covering the Supreme Court?

__2__	less than 10 hours per week	__5__	10–20 hours per week
__2__	21–30 hours per week	__5__	31–40 hours per week
__4__	40+ hours per week		

What other beats do you cover in addition to the Supreme Court? (Choose all that apply)

__8__	Justice Department	__6__	lower courts in D.C.
__6__	Congress	__1__	White House
__1__	bureaucracy	__2__	other

Which of the following most closely describes your beat?

__1__	general assignment	__0__	national government
__8__	legal issues	__12__	Supreme Court
__1__	other		

How important are the following as influences in writing your stories? (1– very important, 2 – somewhat important, 3 – not important)

_____ AP   _____ *New York Times*

_____ your editor   _____ colleagues in pressroom

	1	2	3
AP	1	6	9
Editor	11	4	2
New York Times	1	5	10
Colleagues	0	5	12

How often is your copy altered by someone else for the following reasons: (1– often, 2 – occasionally, 3 – seldom, 4 – never)

_____ explain a technical point   _____ conform to the wire version
_____ increase audience interest   _____ enhance factual accuracy
_____ support a political bias   _____ improve political balance

	1	2	3	4
Technical point	2	9	3	4
Increase audience	4	7	2	5
Support Bias	0	0	2	16
Conform to wire	1	0	3	12
Factual accuracy	0	3	9	6
Political balance	0	3	6	9

Please list in descending order of importance up to three news media outlets you use as sources for your news on a daily basis.

_____

_____

_____

	1	2	3
Washington Post	7	8	0
New York Times	9	4	1
Wall Street Journal	0	1	2
Los Angeles Times	0	0	2
AP	2	0	3
Chicago Tribune	0	0	1
Network news	0	0	1
Reuters	0	0	1
NPR	0	0	1

Please list in descending order of greatest usage up to three news media sources you use weekly or monthly.

_____

_____

_____

Legal Times – 3

National Law Journal – 4

CQ Weekly – 1

American Lawyer – 1

Law Week – 1

PREVIEW – 1

What is the frequency of your usage of the following sources for stories? (1 – frequently, 2 – occasionally, 3 – seldom, 4 – never)

_____ interest group spokespersons _____ parties in the case

_____ legal experts _____ counsel

_____ Solicitor General's Office _____ members of Congress

	1	2	3	4
Interest groups	8	7	2	0
Legal experts	11	5	2	0
Solicitor General	0	11	5	1
Parties in case	9	7	1	0
Counsel	10	5	1	0
Members of Congress	0	6	8	3

Please list up to three interest groups you use most often as sources on:

Abortion
NARAL – 12
Right to Life – 7
Americans United for Life – 5
NOW – 2
Planned Parenthood – 3
ACLU – 3
Center for Reproductive Rights – 2

Criminal Rights
ACLU – 8
Washington Legal Foundation – 4
ABA – 2
National Association of District Attorneys – 2
American Association of Criminal Defense Lawyers – 2

First Amendment
ACLU – 8
People for American Way – 3
Reporters Committee for Free Press – 2
Americans United for Separation of Church and State – 2
Washington Legal Foundation – 1

The following question concerns your degree of job satisfaction.

How satisfied are you with the following: (1 – very satisfied, 2 – fairly satisfied, 3 – somewhat dissatisfied, 4 – very dissatisified)

_____ relationship with my editor

_____ relationship with PIO

_____ relationship with pressroom colleagues

_____ control of assignments

	1	**2**	**3**	**4**
with editor	7	5	3	2
with PIO	9	4	3	1
with colleagues	11	6	1	0
control of assign.	9	6	2	1

Here are a couple of questions on your professional activity.

Do you have other *regular* outlets for your reporting on the Court?

___2___ a newspaper column

___1___ appearance on a television or radio program

_____ other

How many times have you served as a panelist in a session at a legal-related professional meeting in your career?

___5___ none ___7___ 1–5 ___1___ 6–10 ___5___ more than 10

What follows are a few questions about your interaction with the justices.

How many of the current justices have you interviewed on-the-record? ———

0–14   1–0   2–3   3–0   4–0   5–9   0

How many of the current justices have spoken with you off-the-record? ———

0–3   1–1   2–4   3–0   4–1   5–2   6–2   7–2   8–1   9–2

How many off-the-record bureau breakfasts or lunches with any of the justices have you participated in?

___13___ none ___4___ 1–5 ___1___ more than five

Do you see one or more of the justices at social occasions away from the Court building?

___0___ frequently ___3___ occasionally ___10___ seldom ___5___ never

On average, how many off-the-record sessions have you had with justices on an *annual basis* since coming on the beat?

___7___ None ___11___ 1–10 _____ 11–20 _____ more than 20

Now some questions about the nature of the Court and potential change.

How important do you think each of the following are in influencing the justices' decision-making process: (1 – very important, 2 – somewhat important, 3 – not important) The factors should not be considered relative to each other.

	1	2	3
_____ justices' personal ideology	12	4	1
_____ justices' personal religious beliefs	2	7	9
_____ justices' socio-economic status	4	9	5
_____ the legal community's potential reaction	1	9	8
_____ Congress and/or White House potential reaction	1	11	7
_____ public opinion polls	0	8	10
_____ interest group-sponsored demonstrations	0	1	17
_____ press coverage of the Court	0	8	10

Should the justices do more of the following? (Check all that apply)

    _14_   give on-the-record interviews

    _3_   hold news conferences

    _7_   participate in public forums and seminars on public policy issues

    _2_   speak out generally on public policy issues

    _7_   provide post-decision explanation and/or commentary

    _1_   express support or opposition towards nominees for the Court

Please indicate how strongly you agree or disagree with the following statements. (1 – strongly agree, 2 – agree, 3 – disagree, 4 – strongly disagree)

_____ A justice's personal life is not news unless it affects his or her job.

_____ The Supreme Court is primarily a political institution.

_____ The Supreme Court should allow its public sessions to be televised.

_____ The Court should hold a lock-up to provide more time to analyze decisions.

	1	2	3	4
personal life not news	4	6	6	2
primarily political	0	8	6	4
televise sessions	11	3	3	0
lock-up	2	3	7	4

Finally, a few background questions:

How many years have you worked full-time in journalism?

   _0_   less than one   _0_ 1–5

   _2_ 6–10   _16_ more than 10

How many years have you been assigned to the Court?

   _2_ less than one   _7_ 1–5

   _1_ 6–10   _8_ more than 10

How many more years do you expect to stay on the Court beat?

   _0_ less than one   _9_ 1–5

   _3_ 6–10   _2_ more than 10

Educational Background (check highest)

        High school   Some college

   _3_ College degree   _10_ Graduate degree (other than law)

   _7_ Law Degree

Undergraduate field of study

   _9_ Journalism

   _5_ Political Science

   _2_ Social Science (other than Political Science)

   _3_ Humanities/Arts

        Science/Technology

        Pre-law

        Business

   _2_ Other _____

        None

Graduate field of Study

   _6_ Journalism

   _2_ Political Science

        Social Science (other than Political Science)

        Humanities/Arts

        Science/Technology

        Business

   _2_ Other _____

        None

Extent of Legal Training

   __4__ None   __5__ One or more college courses

   __2__ 1st year of law school   __7__ Law Degree

Age

   __1__ 20–29   __6__ 30–39

   __8__ 40–49   __3__ 50 and over

Employer

   __3__ wire service   __2__ network television

   __0__ radio   __3__ magazine

   __8__ newspaper   _____ specialized publication

   _____ other _____

Thank you very much. Your cooperation is appreciated.

Appendix C

Reporters at the Court receive the following invitations for press briefings, along with others from various organizations, at the beginning of each term.

THE NATIONAL CHAMBER LITIGATION CENTER

STEPHEN A. BOKAT
Vice President   September 12, 1990

1615 H STREET, N. W.
WASHINGTON, D. C. 20062
(202) 463-5337

Mr. Tony Mauro
USA Today
1000 Wilson Boulevard
Arlington, VA 22209

Dear Mr. Mauro:

　　We're looking forward to seeing you at the National Chamber Litigation Center's third annual Supreme Court Press Briefing. The breakfast briefing will be held Tuesday, September 25 at 8:00 A.M. in the U.S. Chamber of Commerce building, 1615 H St. N.W., Washington, D.C.

Our special guests will be Timothy B. Dyk and Carter G. Phillips.

Mr. Dyk and Mr. Phillips of the Washington, D.C., law firms of Jones, Day, Reavis & Pogue and Sidley & Austin, respectively, have represented a wide array of business organizations before the Court, and share an impressive record of successful Supreme Court litigation. Both served as Supreme Court clerks. Their curricula vitae are attached for your review.

Their commentary, followed by a question-and-answer period, will offer fresh analyses and insight into the 1990 business docket.

The session begins with a buffet breakfast, followed by the briefing which concludes at 9:30 A.M. Staff of the National Chamber Litigation Center, the Chamber's public policy law firm, also will be on hand to provide additional information and copies of briefs.

This breakfast will surely be worthy of your time. Please call Sophia Werning of the Chamber's Media Relations staff at (202) 463-5682 by Friday, September 21, to let her know if you can join us.

I look forward to meeting you.

Sincerely,

Stephen A. Bokat

Enclosures

FOR IMMEDIATE RELEASE   **August 3, 1990**

WLF LEGAL STUDIES DIVISION TO HOLD MEDIA BRIEFING
ON SUPREME COURT'S UPCOMING TERM

The Legal Studies Division of the Washington Legal Foundation (WLF) will be holding a press briefing Tuesday, September 11, 1990 at 9:00 A.M. at the National Press Building, Main Lounge...The briefing will be a comprehensive review of the Supreme Court's 1990-91 term's upcoming cases, especially those affecting business. The impact of Justice William Brennan's retirement and the nomination of Judge David H. Souter will also be assessed.

Featured speakers will include Richard Willard, Joseph diGenova, and Gary Born.

Mr. Willard is Chairman of WLF's Legal Policy Advisory Board, partner with the Washington, D.C., firm of Steptoe & Johnson, former Assistant Attorney General in charge of the Civil Division, and former law clerk to Justice Harry Blackmun and Justice Anthony Kennedy.

Mr. diGenova is a member of WLF's Legal Policy Advisory Board, a partner with Bishop, Cook, Purcell & Reynolds, former U.S. Attorney for the District of Columbia, and a former Administrative Assistant to U.S. Senator Charles McC. Mathias.

Mr. Born is a partner with Wilmer, Cutler & Pickering, former law professor at the University of Arizona College of Law, and former law clerk to then Associate Justice William Rehnquist.

WLF has filed briefs on behalf of the Foundation, Members of Congress, victims of crime, and others in a number of cases in such areas as affirmative action, the death penalty, commercial speech, drug testing, RICO, and separation of powers. The briefing will cover cases in which WLF has filed or will file briefs with the Supreme Court.

WLF is a national public interest law and policy center dedicated to promoting the free-enterprise system. WLF promotes this policy through precedent-setting litigation and through public policy research and publications (Legal Studies Division).

For further information, please contact Alan Slobodin, President and General Counsel, Legal Studies Division, Washington Legal Foundation, 1705 N Street, N.W., Washington, D.C. 20036, (202) 857-0240.

Interest groups attempt to shape the tone of press coverage through press releases.
The first one below was issued following the Court's acceptance of a case for review.
The second was issued at the time of oral argument.

NATIONAL WOMEN'S LAW CENTER

FOR IMMEDIATE RELEASE   Contact: Laura Epstein
March 26, 1990   (202)328-5160

COURT WEIGHS WOMEN'S EMPLOYMENT OPTIONS IN *JOHNSON CONTROLS* CASE

WASHINGTON—The Supreme Court is poised to hear a case which will have significant consequences for American women according to the National Women's Law Center.

"This case will leave an indelible mark on women's future employment patterns and opportunities," said Center attorney Ellen Vargyas.

The Court today agreed to hear *UAW v. Johnson Controls,* a case which challenges so-called fetal protection employment policies which exclude all women from certain jobs unless they can show proof of sterility.

"Should the Court uphold the decision of the 7th Circuit approving such a policy, all women, regardless of whether they intend to have children or not, will be shut out of many high-paying jobs," said Vargyas.

"On the other hand, the Court could put an immediate end to clearly discriminatory employment practices by ruling the Johnson Controls policy illegal under Title VII of the Civil Rights Act of 1964," Vargyas said.

The Johnson Controls policy affects jobs which may put employees' reproductive health at risk.

"Unsafe work environments harm the reproductive health of men as well as women," Vargyas said. "The solution to a dirty workplace is to clean them up, not to discriminate against women."

1616 P Street Suite 100 Washington D.C. 20036 (202) 328-5160

Public Information
Planned Parenthood of New York City

FOR IMMEDIATE RELEASE   CONTACT: Judy Epstein
OCTOBER 30, 1990   Associate Director, Media Relations
                                          (212) 777-2002

TITLE X "ABORTION GAG RULE" HEARD BY THE U.S. SUPREME COURT

Today the U.S. Supreme Court heard a landmark case for reproductive rights, *Rust v. Sullivan.* It is the first abortion-related case heard by the Court since Justice David Souter joined it.

The suit, brought by Planned Parenthood of New York City (PPNYC) along with other New York service providers and the City and State of New York, challenged the Administration's 1987 regulations which sought to strip federal funding from family planning clinics that mention abortion when counseling patients or that have an abortion facility on site.

"This case is about suppressing information between a patient and her doctor and interfering in that relationship," said Diana Gurieva, President of PPNYC. "The regulations are unethical and set up two kinds of health care. Quality care if you're wealthy, second-rate care if you're poor."

PPNYC's South Bronx clinic serves 6,000 patients annually and is in the poorest Congressional district in the country. The clinic receives almost $500,000 through Title X funding, about 27% of its budget. The Title X program, first created by Congress in 1970 and strongly supported by then Congressman George Bush, was designed to provide poor women and teens with subsidized contraception and gynecological care—and in the event of an unintended pregnancy, counseling on all options available to them. It was never intended, nor, has it ever been used, to finance abortion services. In 1987, the Reagan Administration proposed new regulations (subsequently endorsed by the Bush Administration) which sought to "gag" health professionals from discussing or making referrals for abortion, even if their clients requested information. They also stipulated that only facilities providing prenatal care could be used as referrals.

"Ethically and professionally, I could not abide by these regulations," said Dr. Irving Rust, medical director of PPNYC's Bronx clinic. (He is the Rust of *Rust v. Sullivan.*) "My clients rely on me to provide full information to them. I could not breach their trust by short-changing them."

The South Bronx is 95% black, Hispanic, and poor. "It is a community where people are struggling to survive," Dr. Rust said, "despite the problems of crime, health, drugs, illiteracy, high unemployment, and AIDS. And there are few resources. To take away access to information about medical care legally available is just to add to the burden of people already overburdened."

In addition, as Ms. Gurieva pointed out, "the economic costs of the regulations are punitive. If PPNYC were to physically separate its federally funded family planning services from its separately funded abortion services as the regulations demand, it would have to spend at least $1 million to create a new and separate abortion facility, which would not be feasible. Separating the services would also destroy the capacity to provide continuity of care to patients at risk of repeat pregnancy and trying to use contraception effectively."

"We are hopeful that the justices listened to Professor Tribe's arguments today, and will not sentence America's doctors to silence and their patients to ignorance," said Ms. Gurieva. "What is at stake here is the health and well being of millions of poor women and teens across the country."

Should PPNYC lose the case, it will not comply with the regulations and will give up the Title X funding. It will consider every possible recourse to make up the deficit and keep the facility open.

Planned Parenthood Federation of America, Inc.
810 Seventh Avenue New York, New York 10019 (212) 541-7800
2010 Massachusetts Ave. NW Washington, D.C. 20036 (202) 785-3351

When reporters are seeking interest group representative reaction to decisions, interest groups send the following advisories to alert reporters to the presence of their representatives at the Court or at a press conference on a certain day contingent upon the decision's release.

June 25, 1990
PPFA Contacts: (In Washington):
Hampton Shaddock (202) 387-6556
(In New York):
Roberta Synal (212) 603-4660

MEDIA ADVISORY RE: SUPREME COURT ABORTION DECISIONS

If the U. S. Supreme Court announces decisions in *Hodgson v. Minnesota* and *Akron Center for Reproductive Health v. Ohio* on Monday, June 25, Planned Parenthood Federation of America Director of Litigation Roger Evans will be available for comment in front of the Court immediately after the ruling.

AMERICAN CIVIL LIBERTIES UNION
REPRODUCTIVE FREEDOM
PROJECT

Planned Parenthood
Federation of America, Inc.

June 25, 1990
PPFA Contacts: (In Washington):
Hampton Shaddock (202) 387-6556
(In New York):
Roberta Synal (212) 603-4660

ACLU Contacts: (In New York):
Colleen O'Connor or
Lisa Beattie (212) 944-9800

MEDIA ADVISORY RE: SUPREME COURT ABORTION DECISIONS

If the U. S. Supreme Court announces decisions in *Hodgson v. Minnesota* and *Akron Center for Reproductive Health v. Ohio* on Monday, June 25, Planned Parenthood Federation of America (PPFA) and the ACLU will hold a press conference at 1:00 P.M. in the ACLU office, 122 Maryland Avenue, N. E., across from the Supreme Court.

PPFA President Faye Wattleton and ACLU Reproductive Freedom Project Director Janet Benshoof will speak on the decisions and their impact.

The following news releases were issued immediately after a decision to provide reporters with easy reaction quotes for a decision story.

Legal Defense and Education Fund

99 HUDSON STREET—NEW YORK, NY 10013 * (212) 925-6635 *
FAX: (212) 226-1066

FOR IMMEDIATE RELEASE   contact: Alison Wetherfield
March 20, 1991   (212) 925-6635

HIGH COURT DECISION ON FEMALE EXCLUSION POLICIES IN
EMPLOYMENT HAILED BY WOMEN'S LEGAL RIGHTS GROUP

NEW YORK—Lawyers at NOW Legal Defense & Education Fund (NOW LDEF) today hailed the Supreme Court's decision in *International Union UAW v. Johnson Controls, Inc.* as a victory for all employees, male and female. The Court unanimously struck down as sex discrimination a battery manufacturer's policy which effectively excluded all fertile women of child bearing age from industrial jobs, allegedly out of concern for the future offspring of such women who might be affected by airborne lead in the workplace.

"Lead in the workplace is a problem for all employees, male and female, because it can damage sperm and eggs as well as fetuses. Excluding all women from jobs where they may come into contact with lead does not solve the problem and is simply sex discrimination. Employers must clean up the workplace for the benefit of all workers," said Alison Wetherfield, legal director at NOW LDEF.

"Five justices of the nine on the court, including new justice David Souter, agreed that exclusion of all women from ages 15 to 55 from employment in the name of fetal protection is always illegal. Four others—the Court's ultra conservative justices—Rehnquist, White, Scalia, and Kennedy—agreed that this policy is illegal but thought some variations might be legal. Justice Souter was therefore an important swing vote in securing the rights of women in employment," Wetherfield added.

The decision prevents as many as 20 million jobs from becoming sex-segregated and shut off to women. "Fetal protection policies, which prevent women from working and earning the wages needed to buy the adequate nutrition and health care that all women need for healthy pregnancies and babies, make no sense—women everywhere can breath a sigh of relief that they are now illegal," concluded Wetherfield.

JOHNSON CONTROLS

NEWS RELEASE

Johnson Controls, Inc.

5757 North Green Bay Avenue, Post Office Box 591, Milwaukee, WI 53201

Johnson Controls, Inc., headquartered in Milwaukee, Wisconsin, is a leader in facility management and control systems, automotive seating, batteries and plastics. Founded in 1885, it operates in 350 locations worldwide. Johnson Controls securities (JCI) are listed on the NYSE.

JOHNSON CONTROLS TO FOLLOW HIGH COURT DECISION

MILWAUKEE, March 20/PRNewswire/—Johnson Controls, Inc. (NYSE: JCI) said it was disappointed by today's U.S. Supreme Court ruling which invalidated the company's fetal protection policy barring fertile women from some battery manufacturing jobs.

Denise Zutz, director of corporate communication, said that the company had used a voluntary policy, under which women could elect to transfer to jobs less hazardous to a fetus, between 1975 and 1982, before the mandatory policy was implemented. She said that the company would consider reinstituting a similar voluntary program.

The company said that it would continue its comprehensive educational and medical monitoring programs for all employees as well as its investments in engineering controls to reduce lead exposure. Johnson Controls said that together these programs are expected to sustain the company's record of continuously improving health and safety conditions.

The company added that the economic impact of the ruling on Johnson Controls is not expected to be material.

-0-   3/20/91

/CONTACT: Denise M. Zutz of Johnson Controls, Inc. 414-228-3155/
(JCI)

At times even members of Congress send news releases to Supreme Court reporters in the wake of a decision of interest to them.

Congressman

DON EDWARDS

San Jose — Milpitas — Fremont — Newark — Union City

NEWS RELEASE

FOR IMMEDIATE RELEASE: JUNE 25, 1990   Contact: Catherine LeRoy
2307 Rayburn House Office Building   (202) 226-7680
Washington, DC 20515   90-26

CONGRESSIONAL PRO-CHOICE LEADER CRITICIZES COURT DECISIONS ON ABORTION

Rep. Don Edwards (D-CA), Chairman of the House Judiciary Subcommittee on Civil and Constitutional Rights, issued the following statement on the Court's decisions in the parental notification cases:

"The Court's unfortunate decision in the Ohio parental notification case highlights the necessity for enactment of the Freedom of Choice Act which would codify *Roe v. Wade*. The decision today only adds to the anarchy that already exists in state legislatures on this issue.

"Although I am relieved that the Court struck down the Minnesota decision, the narrow, 5-4 majority means that teenagers' privacy rights are still at risk.

"Moreover, the Court's decision to uphold the Ohio statute is very troubling. While the statute permits a teenager to go to court when she cannot notify her parents, the judicial procedure is seriously flawed. It does not preserve confidentiality, nor does it provide an expeditious process.

"These two flaws alone will guarantee an increase in the number of teenagers who will try to self-abort, delay the procedure unnecessarily, or unwillingly carry an unwanted pregnancy to term. All of these are dangerous and unnecessary alternatives.

"Congress must move ahead quickly to take this issue away from the state legislatures, so that the right of women to make their own decisions on this most personal of issues will no longer be at the mercy of 50 state legislatures and a wavering Supreme Court."

Index

ABC News, 44

Abortion issue, 26, 81, 136, 137–43, 145. *See also Planned Parenthood of Southeastern Pennsylvania v. Casey; Roe v. Wade; Webster v. Reproductive Health Services*

Abraham, Henry J., 24, 33*n*, 34*n*

Abrams, Floyd, 89

Allen, Robert S., 13*n*, 14*n*, 31*n*, 32*n*, 34*n*

Aloofness, message of, 14–15

America and the Courts program (C-SPAN), 65

American Civil Liberties Union (ACLU), 72, 87, 139

American Lawyer magazine, 67, 74

American United for Life, 87

Americans United for Separation of Church and State, 87

Amici curiae (friend of the court) briefs, 147

Anonymity, justices' desire for, 156. *See also* Privacy of justices

Apple, R.W., Jr., 17*n*, 147*n*

Appointments on bench, new, 136

Aristocracy, justices as intellectuals, 14

Armstrong, Scott, 14, 32*n*, 41*n*, 44, 54*n*, 115, 122*n*, 123*n*

Associated Press, 38, 79, 92, 93, 132, 133, 134, 136, 138, 140, 142, 162

Association of American Law Schools, 43

Attitudes toward the Court:
changing, 146–48
reporters', 126–30

Attorneys as sources, 86

Audience, remembering one's, 83–84

Audio tape, reporters' access to, 77

Aukofer, Frank, 71, 73

Baas, Larry R., 24*n*

Background sessions with reporters, 41–42, 119–22
reporters' attitudes toward, 128–29

Baker v. Carr, 7

Bakke case, 123

Ball, Howard, 33*n*

Baltimore Sun, 42, 48, 54, 64, 132, 140, 141, 142, 143

Barbash, Fred, 114

Barnette case, 33

Barnum, David G., 18

Baum, Lawrence, 11*n*, 18*n*, 19*n*

Berkowitz, Dan, 22*n*

Berkson, Larry, 2, 10*n*, 11*n*, 16*n*, 160*n*

Bernstein, Carl, 101

Berry, Mary Frances, 6*n*, 40*n*

Bickel, Alexander, 3, 4, 25

Billington, James, 157

Biskupic, Joan, 108*n*, 157*n*

Black, Hugo, 33, 39, 40, 43–44, 110, 111
Blackmun, Harry, 18, 20, 26, 27, 52, 53, 106, 109, 110, 112, 121, 122, 134, 138, 141, 156, 157
Blake, Judith, 20
Blaustein, Albert P., 34n
Bokat, Stephen, 72, 85, 89
Bork, Robert, 27, 64, 101, 109, 153–54, 157, 158
Bowsher v. Synar, 24, 123
Braver, Rita, 65, 71, 75, 76, 77, 84, 86, 95, 98, 112, 151, 153, 154
Brennan, William, 19, 25, 27, 52, 55, 80, 106, 108–9, 110, 112, 118, 120, 121, 134, 150
Brethren, The (Woodward and Armstrong), 14, 23, 37
Briefings, invitations for press, 175–77
Briefs on cases before the Court, 49
preparation of stories from, 73
Brigham, John, 4n, 13n
Broadcast journalists, 71
preparation of stories by, 74–75
Brown v. Board of Education, 5, 15
Bureau gathering, 121
Burger, Warren, 3, 7, 15, 18, 23, 37, 44, 52, 54, 58, 61, 68, 115, 122, 125, 134, 135, 149, 153, 156
Burnham, David, 40n
Burton, Harold H., 6, 17, 39–40, 43
Bush, George, 27, 148
Bush administration, 138

Cable News Network (CNN), 81
Caldiera, Gregory, 2, 12, 25n
Calley, William, 7
Cameras in the courtroom, 57, 149–55, 159
Carelli, Richard, 66, 68, 70, 79, 84, 91, 103, 104, 106–7, 111, 115, 116, 118, 121, 126, 128, 138, 139
Carmody, Dierdre, 150n
Carswell, G. Harrold, 14
Carter, Jimmy, 54
Caseload for the Court, size of, 117
Casey case, 3, 21, 26, 27, 77, 81, 117, 132
Casper, Jonathan, 18n
CBS News, 42, 133, 134, 162
CBS/*New York Times* survey, 11
Ceol, Dawn Weyrich, 80, 84, 116
"Cert." petitions, 49
Chamber of Commerce, 72

Changes affecting the Court, permanency of, 157–59
Chase, Salmon P., 6
Chicago Tribune, 121
Chief justices, annual meeting between regulars and, 125–26
Childs, Marquis W., 41n
Christian Science Monitor, 42, 119, 121
Cibes, William J., Jr., 6n, 109n
Clark, Tom, 113
Clerks, preventing leaks from, 122–25
Clinton, Bill, 27
Cohen v. Cowles, 95
Collings, Tony, 73, 81, 93
Communication:
channeling attention to opinions, 114–17
for deference, 8–16
salience of, 10–12
Compliance, transforming deference toward Court into widespread, 10
Concurring opinions, 105, 108, 115–16, 135
Conference list, 49–50
Confirmation hearings, 27, 153–54
Congressional Press Gallery, 36
Congressional Quarterly's Guide to the U.S. Supreme Court, 74
Connally, Tom, 40
Consensual journalism, 90–91
Constraints on manipulation of information, 8–9
Content analysis, 160, 162
Cooper, Phillip J., 33n
Court-packing plan proposed by Roosevelt, 31–33
Courtroom:
cameras in, 57, 149–55, 159
message conveyed by, 13
Courtroom Television Network (Court TV), 150
Coyle, Marcia, 10n, 108n, 147n
Cramer, Jerome, 48, 65, 71, 73, 84, 87, 90, 93, 95, 118
Cranberg, Gilbert, 40n
Cravens, Rene, 89
Cruzan case, 97
C-SPAN, 65, 150, 151
"Cult of the judge," 13
Cynicism of reporters, 126–27

Dahl, Robert, 9
Dalton, Donald H., 36n

Davis, John, 36n
Davis, Richard, 21n, 114n, 160n
Daynes, Byron, 24n
Decision, news releases issued after, 182–84
Decision day:
  announcement of, 37
  ritual of, 45–47
Decision-making process of justices, 115, 116
Decision story, writing, 77–99
  elite, role of the, 92
  following the formula, 83
  information sharing, 90–91
  interpreting the opinion, 84–85
  reading and culling for, 82
  remembering the audience, 83–84
  time factor in, 81–82
  using sources, 85–90
  wires, influence of, 92–94, 97
  working with editors and producers, 94–99
Deference reinforcer, the press as, 19–20
Deference toward the Court, 4
  communicating for, 8–16
  explanations for, 129–30
Dellinger, Walter, 89, 139
Dennis, Everette, 23n
Denniston, Lyle, 6, 42, 48, 49, 55, 56, 58, 60, 61, 65, 68, 69, 72, 84, 86, 90–91, 95, 97, 107, 120, 121, 125, 126–27, 128, 132, 139–43, 153
Dershowitz, Alan M., 108n
Dewar, Helen, 123n
Dignity of the Court, message conveying, 12–13
Dione, E.J., Jr., 26n
Disincentives for violating reporting norms on the Court, 129
Disputes among justices, 33–34, 108–9
Disputes between other political institutions, Court's role in, 24
Dissenting opinion, 105, 108, 115–16
Distance, image of, 6, 155
Docket, portraying the, 135–36
Docket Sheet, The, 50
Douglas, William O., 5, 6, 7, 14, 30, 35, 38, 39, 40–41, 43–44, 54, 57, 112, 119, 122, 148, 156, 162
Dred Scott case, 30, 109
Dukakis, Michael, 27
Dukes, James O., 21n
Dyk, Timothy, 72

Eastland, James, 31
Editorial alterations, 96–97
Editorial control, allowing justices some, 119
Editors:
  choosing which decision stories to write, 79–80
  influence of wire services on, 94
  working with, 94–99
Electronic distribution system (Project Hermes), 57, 85, 149
Elite in the press corps, 64–65, 79, 92, 94
Elsasser, Glen, 93, 94, 121
Engel v. Vitale, 11
Entman, Robert, 20
Epstein, Aaron, 109n
Epstein, Edward J., 22n
Ericson, David, 21, 160n
Ethics, judicial, 8, 108
Evans, Rowland, 42
Expertise, image of, 4, 5, 13
Extrajudicial activities of justices, 34, 35

Facts section of opinion, 82
Fairman, Charles, 30n
Feedback mechanism, press as poor, 20
Fein, Bruce, 88–89
Fitzwater, Marlin, 54
Flag-burning case, 72–73, 115, 132
Flynt, Larry, 78
Formulaic writing style of Court press corps, 83
Fortas, Abe, 6, 18, 30, 31, 34–35
Fowler, Joseph S., 22n
Frankfurter, Felix, 6, 7, 14, 15, 18, 38, 39, 42, 130
Franklin, Charles H., 24n
Freedman, Max, 42
Friendly, Alfred, 37
Friendly, Fred, 9
Funston, Richard, 18n

Gamarekian, Barbara, 108n
Gannett v. DePasquale, 11
Gans, Herbert, 22n
Gates, John B., 160n
Gauge, the press as, 17–19
Geller, Kenneth, 90
Gilstrap, Max K., 42n, 119n
Ginsburg, Douglas, 64
Gobitis case, 33
Goldberg, Arthur, 34

Graham, Fred, 37*n*, 42, 43, 112, 119, 156, 157*n*
Gramm-Rudman Budget Balancing Act, 123, 124
Greenhalgh, William, 72
Greenhouse, Linda, 20, 55, 65, 66, 68, 70, 77, 80, 83, 85, 86, 87, 91, 97, 98, 100, 104, 119*n*, 124, 128, 130, 142
Grey, David L., 23*n*, 36*n*, 160*n*

Hamilton, Alexander, 1
Harmon, Mark D., 22*n*
Harper's magazine, 41
Harris, Richard, 14*n*
Hartford Courant, 50, 66, 71, 116, 118
Hayden, Jay G., 14*n*, 34*n*
Headnotes, 38, 82
Hentoff, Nat, 118
Hess, Stephen, 65–66, 68, 74, 94
Historical research, 162
Hodson, Thomas S., 75*n*
Homogeneity in coverage of Court, 143
Horowitz, Donald L., 2*n*, 24*n*
House, Toni, 46–48, 51, 52, 54, 56–61, 78, 108, 117, 120, 124, 149, 153, 156, 157
Hruska, Roman, 14
Hughes, Charles Evans, 6, 32, 39
Human interest vs. technicality, 142

Imagemaking by the Court, 3–8
    distance, image of, 6, 155
    immunity, image of, 7–8
    independence, image of, 6
    nonpolitical image, change in, 146–47
    paradox in, 9
    personal image, justices' interest in their, 106
    public information officer as protector of image, 53–54
    shaping image via the press, 40–44
    tarnished image, 31–35
    unanimity, image of, 4–5
Immunity, image of, 7–8
Imperatives, the press vs. the Court, 21–23
Inaccuracy of news stories, 23
Independence, image of, 6
Information sharing, 90–91
In-house televising of oral arguments, 154
Institutionalization of press relations. *See under* Press corps, the

Institutional objectives of Supreme Court, 1–3
INS v. Chadha, 24
Interest groups, 7
    choosing what stories to cover and, 72
    influence of, 26, 100–101
    media advisories from, 180–81
    preparation of stories and, 73
    press releases from, 76, 89, 139, 178–80
    pressure on Court from, 146–47
    public nature of lobbying by, 158–59
    as sources, 86–88, 89, 90
Interpretation of the opinion, 84–85
Interviews with justices, 40–41, 51, 107, 108–9, 118–19
    background sessions, 41–42, 119–22, 128–29
Invisible dance. *See* Justices; News, Supreme Court as

Jackson, Robert, 33, 39, 40
Jay, John, 29
Johnson, Lyndon, 18, 34
Johnson, Richard M., 4*n*, 13
Jones, G.C., Jr., 148*n*
Judicial code of ethics, 8, 108
Judicial Conference of the United States (1990), 150
Judis, John, 118
Justices:
    decision-making process of, 115, 116
    extrajudicial activities of, 34, 35
    interviews with, 40–41, 51, 107, 108–9, 118–19
    background sessions, 41–42, 119–22, 128–29
    invisible dance with reporters, 113–30
    channeling attention to opinions, 114–17
    closing off other access points, 122–25
    dominance of justices in, 113–14, 126–30
    emphasizing minor points, 125–26
    offering backgrounders, 119–22, 128–29
    selective public interaction with press, 118–19
    motives in press relations of, 104–5
    objectives of, 104–10
    personal conflicts on the Court between, 33–34, 108–9

as personalities, minimizing, 134–35
political backgrounds of, 110–11
privacy of, 104–5, 146, 152, 156
references to individual, in stories, 134–35
reporting activities of, 50
surveillance of the press by, 38–40
tactics of, choosing, 110–13

Kalman, Laura, 34n
Kamen, Al, 55, 123n
Katsh, Ethan, 8, 21n, 22n, 160n
Kennedy, Anthony, 27, 50, 51, 64, 118, 134, 141, 150, 151, 153, 158
Knight-Ridder, 93
Kosaki, Liane C., 24n
Kraft, Joe, 42
Ku Klux Klan, 33
Kurland, Philip B., 1n

Ladd, Everett Carl, 11n
Language:
  of the Court, 13, 15–16
  journalistic, 20
    editorial negotiations over, 97
    remembering the audience and, 83–84
Larson, Stephanie Greco, 21n
Leads, 83
Leaks to the press, 44, 124
  preventing, 122–25, 155
  reporters' approach to, 128
Legal experts as sources, 86
Legal publications, 73–74
Legal Times, 67, 74
Legal training for reporters, 42–43
Legal training of reporters, 42–43, 66–69, 130
Legitimacy of mass role, 158–59
Legitimacy of the Court:
  perception of, 4
  reinforced by courtroom, 13
Lewis, Anthony, 42
Life magazine, 34
Lobbying, public nature of, 158–59. *See also* Interest groups
"Lock-up" to prevent leaks, 155
Los Angeles Times, 121

McCulloch v. Maryland, 109
McCune, Wesley, 32n

McGurn, Barrett, 54, 56, 57, 61
McLean, John, 6
MacNeil-Lehrer News Hour, 65
Majesty of the Court, message conveying, 12–13
Manipulation of information, constraints on, 8–9
Mansfield, Mike, 3
Manwaring, David R., 19n
Marcus, Ruth, 55, 80n, 91, 140
Marshall, John, 5, 29
Marshall, Thomas R., 18n, 160n
Marshall, Thurgood, 25, 51, 53, 99, 109, 127, 134, 141, 148, 153–54
Mason, Alpheus Thomas, 31n, 32n, 33n, 41n
Massaro, John, 160n
Mass role, legitimacy of, 158–59
Mauro, Tony, 51, 60, 67, 72, 95, 98, 100-101, 103, 111n, 113, 123, 129
Media, justices' attention to popular, 111–12. *See also* Press corps, the; Television coverage:
Media age, the Court in, 145–59
  accommodations of Court, 148–55
    cameras in courtroom, 149–55
    other reforms, 155
    Project Hermes, 57, 85, 149
  changing attitudes toward Court and, 146–48
  permanence of changes affecting, 157–59
Meese, Edwin, 27, 109–10
Mersky, Roy M., 34n
Message of the Court to the public:
  managing, via the press, 23–28
  nature of, 12–16
Methodology, 160–62
Metropolitan Broadcasting Co. v. FCC, 80
Miller, Arthur, 89
Miller, Samuel, 30
Mills, Dean, 54n
Milwaukee Journal, 71
Minersville School District v. Gobitis, 33
Miranda decision, 41
Miscommunication, 11
Misquotation problem, 76–77
Moore, W. John, 147n, 155n
Moyers, Bill, 149
Murphy, Bruce A., 6n, 30n, 35n
Murphy, Frank, 113
Murphy, Walter F., 10, 11, 25
Murrow, Edward R., 119

National Chamber Litigation Center, 72
National Law Journal, 74
National Law Journal/Lexis survey
    (1990), 10, 108, 147
National newsmagazines, 71
National Observer, 119
National Organization for Women Legal
    Defense Fund, 72
National Right to Life Committee
    (NARAL), 87, 139
New Deal legislation, 32
Newland, Chester A., 11*n*, 23*n*
Newmeyer, R. Kent, 29*n*
News, Supreme Court as, 132–44
    case study of news story, 137–43
        homogeneity or variety in, 143
        oral argument, covering, 137–39
        sources, use of, 142
        stories, 140–42
        technicality vs. human interest in, 142
    following rhythm of Court's activities,
        133–34
    minimizing justices as personalities,
        134–35
    portraying the docket, 135–36
News conferences, 119
News coverage. *See* Press corps, the
News releases issued after decision, 182–84
Newsweek, 41
Newsworthiness, 72–73, 91
New Yorker, The, 118
New York Times, 40, 42, 43, 63, 68, 71, 84,
    93, 104, 118, 119, 124, 130, 140,
    141, 142, 143, 159
New York Times Magazine, 118
Nixon, Richard, 35, 41
Nixon, United States v., 3, 5, 7, 15, 24
Nominations to the Court, 109, 157–58

Objectives:
    of justices, 104–10
    of reporters, 103–4
O'Brien, David, 4*n*, 5*n*, 105
O'Brien, Tim, 65, 67, 68, 71, 74, 76, 77, 79,
    81, 82, 97, 98–99, 107, 112, 116,
    117, 120, 124, 128, 130, 153, 154,
    155
Observation, method of, 161
O'Callaghan, Jerome, 21*n*
O'Connor, Sandra Day, 10, 26, 53, 59, 105,
    107–8, 110, 112, 121, 134, 143,
    147, 156, 158

Off-the-record (background sessions) inter-
    views, 41–42, 119–22, 128–29
Opinions:
    channeling attention to, 114–17
    concurring, 105, 108, 115–16, 135
    dissenting, 105, 108, 115–16
    interpretation of the, 84–85
    mention of justices in press upon issuance
        of, 135
    number released, 79
    process of writing, 115–16
    reading and culling from, 82
    release of, 36
    spacing of announcement of, 116–17
Oral arguments:
    covering, 75–77, 137–39
    in-house televising of, 154
    schedule of, 49, 117, 163–65
Oral argument story, 133
Orders list, 49, 70–71, 133, 135
Organizational imperatives, 22–23
Outsider status of public information offi-
    cer, 54–61

"Pack journalism," 90-91
Paletz, David, 20
Parties to the case as sources, 86
PBS, 118
Pearson, Drew, 13*n*, 14*n*, 31, 32*n*, 34*n*, 39–
    40, 41, 43
People for the American Way, 87
Perceptions of the Court, 3–4. *See also* Im-
    agemaking by the Court
Perry, H.W., Jr., 19*n*, 160*n*
Persian Gulf War, 64
Personalities, minimizing justices as, 134–
    35
Personnel transition on the Court, 25
Petitions for writ of certiorari ("cert." peti-
    tions), 49
Pine, Rachel, 139, 142
Pittsburgh Post-Gazette, 33
Planned Parenthood, 87, 143
Planned Parenthood of New York, 137, 138
*Planned Parenthood of Southeastern Penn-
    sylvania v. Casey*, 3, 21, 26, 27, 77,
    81, 117, 132
Pledge of Allegiance, issue of, 136
Policy-making role of Supreme Court, 2
Political institution(s):
    attitudinal changes among the press to-
        ward, 126–27

Supreme Court as, 1–2, 146–48
Political pressure on the Court:
    image of immunity to, 7–8
    from interest groups, 146–47
Posner, Richard, 105
Powell, Jody, 54
Powell, Lewis, 7–8, 52, 104, 111–12, 120,
    134
Predictability, allure of Court's, 129. *See also*
    Public Information Office (PIO)
Presidential election campaigns, 27, 110
Press briefings, invitations for, 175–77
Press corps, the, 63–69
    character traits of, 66
    conflict between factions in, 103–4
    the elite among, 64–65, 79, 92, 94
    institutionalizing relations with, 29–44
        accommodation of the press, 35–38
        Court's tarnished image and, 31–35
        shaping Court's image via press, 40–44
        surveying press coverage, 38–40
    invisible dance with justices, 113–30
        channeling attention to opinions, 114–
            17
        closing off other access points, 122–25
        dominance of justices in, 113–14, 126–
            30
        emphasizing minor points, 125–26
        offering backgrounders, 119–22, 128–
            29
        selective public interaction with press,
            118–19
    leaks to, 44, 122–25, 128, 155
    as linking mechanism between the Court
        and the public, 16–28
        as deference reinforcer, 19–20
        as gauge, 17–19
        managing the message via the press,
            23–28
        press vs. court imperatives and, 21–23
        problems with, 20–21
    quantity and quality of news coverage, 21
    regulars vs. nonregulars in, 63–64
    specialist role, 65–69
    survey of, 161, 167–74
    work routine of, 70–77
        choosing what to cover, 70–72
        covering oral arguments, 75–77
        determining newsworthiness, 72–73
        preparing stories, 73–75
    writing decision story, 77–99
        elite, role of the, 92
        following the formula, 83

information sharing, 90–91
interpreting the opinion, 84–85
reading and culling for, 82
remembering the audience, 83–84
time factor in, 81–82
using sources, 85–90
wires, influence of, 92–94
working with editors and producers,
    94–99
Pressroom, 69–70
PREVIEW, 73–74
Privacy of justices, 104–5, 146, 152, 156
Process guidance from public information
    officer, 58–60
Producers, working with, 94–99
Project Hermes, 57, 85, 149
Protectiveness toward the Court, reporters',
    127–29
Public, the Court and, 1–28
    communicating for deference, 8–16
    imagemaking and, 3–8
        distance, image of, 6, 155
        immunity, image of, 7–8
        independence, image of, 6
        unanimity, image of, 4–5
    institutional objectives of Court and, 1–3
    press as linking mechanism between, 16–
        28
        as deference reinforcer, 19–20
        as gauge, 17–19
        managing the message via the press,
            23–28
        press vs. court imperatives and, 21–23
        problems with, 20–21
    public's lack of knowledge or faulty in-
        formation, 11–12
    trends in support for the Court, 25
Public Information Office (PIO):
    author's observation of, 161
    decision day ritual and, 45–47
    establishment of, 30, 35–36
    evenhandedness in dissemination of
        news from, 129
    as mechanical channel, 47–50
        as documentary source, 48–50
        as "no information" office, 48
        reporting justices' activities, 50
    press statement issued from, 165–66
    as protector of image, 53–54
Public information officer:
    outsider status of, 54–61
        as dispenser of process guidance, 58–
            60

Public information officer: (*cont'd.*)
   as friend of press corps, 60–61
   as press policy advisor, 56–58
   reforms to open Court to the press and,
      155
   screening function of, 50–53
   See also House, Toni
Public opinion, power of, 17–19
Public television programming, 118
Pundits, 89

Randolph, Eleanor, 150*n*
Reeves, Richard, 42
Regional publications, 71
Rehnquist, William, 10, 13, 17, 19, 20, 25,
      51, 52, 57, 59, 78–79, 92, 106, 110,
      118, 119, 121, 122, 125, 128, 134,
      150, 151, 156–57
Reporters:
   attitudes toward the Court, 126–30
   objectives of, 103–4
   tension between editorial role and expert
      status of, 98–99
   See also Press corps, the
Resignations:
   announcements of, 52–53
   rumor squelching about, 59
Reske, Henry, 55, 82, 86, 93–94, 107, 120,
      122–25
Reuters, 93
"Reverential attitude," abandonment of,
      126–27
Rhythm of Court's activities, following,
      133–34
Riley, George, 34*n*, 41*n*
Rituals of the Court, 13
Rivers, William L., 42*n*
Rodell, Fred, 32*n*
Roe v. Wade, 7, 18, 20, 26, 27, 70, 122–23,
      136, 138, 157
Rohde, David W., 160*n*
Roosevelt, Franklin, 18, 31, 32, 39
Roosevelt, Theodore, 36
Rosenberg case, 43
Roshco, Bernard, 22*n*
Rothfeld, Charles, 89*n*
Rumors, squelching, 59
Rust, Irving, 139
Rust v. Sullivan, 21, 75, 81, 96
   coverage of oral argument in, 137–43
Rutledge, John, 29
Rutledge, Wiley, 40

Savage, David, 86
Scalia, Antonin, 25, 26, 51, 52, 108, 110,
      111, 112, 115–16, 117, 118, 120–
      22, 131, 134, 135, 137–38, 141,
      152–53, 156
Schedule of oral arguments, 49, 117, 163–65
Schmidhauser, John R., 14*n*
Schrader, H.H., 148*n*
Screening mechanism, public information
      officer as, 50–53
Segregation decisions, 15
Selective public interaction with the press,
      118–19
Self-censorship of reporters, 121
Seniority of the press, 129–30
Severeid, Eric, 40, 43, 110
Shaw, David, 11*n*, 81*n*, 146*n*, 159*n*
Sherill, Martha, 123*n*
Sherman, Rorie, 66*n*
Showalter, Stuart, 22*n*
Slotnick, Elliot E., 21*n*, 23*n*, 116*n*
Social policy, Court's expanding responsi-
      bility in realm of, 24
Solomine, Michael, 114*n*, 160*n*
Soundbytes from justices, 154
Sources, using, 85–90, 142
Souter, David H., 10, 27, 75, 96, 108, 109,
      110, 138, 139, 140, 141, 143, 152,
      158
Spaeth, Harold J., 160*n*
Specialist in press corps, 65–69
Spivack, Miranda, 50, 66, 67, 68, 71, 76, 90,
      97, 98, 116, 118, 130
St. Louis *Post-Dispatch*, 33
Starr, Kenneth W., 72, 138
Stern, Carl, 118, 155
Stevens, John Paul, 52, 107, 109, 110, 120,
      121, 134, 143, 149, 150–51
Stewart, Potter, 5, 41–42, 64, 106
Stone, Harlan, 13, 31, 33, 39, 41, 148
Stories:
   number of, throughout term, 133
   references to individual justices in, 134–
      35
Story, Joseph, 29
Sununu, John, 148
Supreme Court:
   constituencies of, 2
   institutional objectives of, 1–3
   internal disputes in, 33–34, 108–9
   justices' comments on role of, 109–10
   as news. *See* News, Supreme Court as
   as political institution, 1–2, 146–48

Supreme Court building, construction of new, 35
Surveillance of the press by justices, 38–40
Survey of U.S. Supreme Court press corps, 161, 167–74
Sutherland, George, 40
Swisher, Carl B., 30*n*
Syllabus, 82

Tactics of justices, choosing, 110–13
Taft, William Howard, 6, 35
Tanenhaus, Joseph, 10, 11, 25
Taney, Roger, 29–30
Tatalovich, Raymond, 24*n*
Taylor, Stuart A., Jr., 27*n*, 67, 106, 109*n*, 110*n*, 111, 112, 118, 121, 123
Technicality vs. human interest, 142
Television coverage:
    argument stories, 75–76
    inside courtroom, 43, 57, 149–55, 159
    justices' attention to, 112
Texas v. Johnson, 91, 136
"This Honorable Court" (documentary), 58, 118
Thomas, Clarence, 10, 27, 51, 108, 110, 146, 158
Thomas, Dan, 24*n*
Thornberry, Homer, 34
Thurgood Marshall Papers, 157
Time factor in writing decision story, 81–82
Time magazine, 42, 44, 87, 123, 133, 134, 162
Timing of decisions, 116–17
Title X, 142
Totenberg, Nina, 52, 65, 119
Training of journalists:
    legal, 42–43, 66–69, 130
    shaping, 42–43
Transcripts, reporters' access to, 77
Tribe, Laurence, 89, 138, 139, 141, 143
Trofsky, Melvin I., 122*n*
Tropin, Mitchell J., 23*n*, 52*n*, 68*n*, 114*n*
Truman, Harry, 18, 34
Tunstall, Jeremy, 22*n*
Turnover of personnel in Court, 25
"20-second rule," 122

Unanimity, image of, 4–5
United Press International (UPI), 69, 93
U.S. Law Week, 74
United States v. Nixon, 3, 5, 7, 15, 24
Urofsky, Melvin I., 112*n*

USA Today, 60, 63, 107, 153

Vicini, Jim, 81, 83
Victim impact statements, constitutionality of, 74–75, 98–99
Village Voice, 118
Vinson, Fred, 6, 18
Vinson, John Kenneth, 146*n*

"Wages and hours session," 125–26
Wall Street Journal, 63, 68, 71, 97, 118
Warren, Earl, 5, 6, 9, 10, 15–17, 37–43, 57, 60, 119, 162
Wasby, Stephen L., 24*n*, 27*n*
Washington Legal Foundation, 87
Washington Post, 39, 40, 42, 64, 112, 122, 140, 141, 142, 147
Washington Star, 60
Washington Times, 64, 116
Watergate crisis, 25
Weaver, John D., 40*n*
Webster, Daniel, 29
Webster v. Reproductive Health Services, 11, 21, 26, 77, 81, 109, 115–16, 117, 123, 132
Weiser, Benjamin, 157*n*
Weissberg, Robert, 24*n*
Wermiel, Stephen, 52, 55, 67, 68, 79, 91, 94, 97–98, 106, 111*n*
West Virginia State Board of Education v. Barnette, 33
Wheeler, Burton, 32
White, Byron, 20, 68, 107, 121, 134, 150
White House Press Room, 35
Whittington, Bert, 38, 56, 57, 60
Wire services, 82, 136
    influence of, 92–94, 97
    See also Associated Press; United Press International (UPI)
Witt, Elder, 36*n*, 123*n*
Wolfson, Lewis, 114
Wood, Lewis, 36*n*
Woodward, Robert, 14, 32*n*, 41*n*, 44, 54*n*, 101, 115, 122*n*, 123*n*, 146, 159
Woolsey, Mark H., 37*n*

Yard, Molly, 146–47
Yoder, Edwin M., Jr., 158

Zelnick, C. Robert, 119*n*